ASCENT
CENTER FOR TECHNICAL KNOWLEDGE

AutoCAD® Civil 3D® 2017 (SP1.1) Grading

Student Guide
1ˢᵗ Edition

AUTODESK.
Authorized Publisher

ASCENT - Center for Technical Knowledge®
AutoCAD® Civil 3D® 2017 (SP1.1)
Grading
1st Edition

Prepared and produced by:

ASCENT Center for Technical Knowledge
630 Peter Jefferson Parkway, Suite 175
Charlottesville, VA 22911

866-527-2368
www.ASCENTed.com

Lead Contributor: Michelle Rasmussen

ASCENT - Center for Technical Knowledge is a division of Rand Worldwide, Inc., providing custom developed knowledge products and services for leading engineering software applications. ASCENT is focused on specializing in the creation of education programs that incorporate the best of classroom learning and technology-based training offerings.

We welcome any comments you may have regarding this student guide, or any of our products. To contact us please email: feedback@ASCENTed.com.

AS-C3D1711-GRD1IM-SG   //   IS-C3D1711-GRD1IM-SG

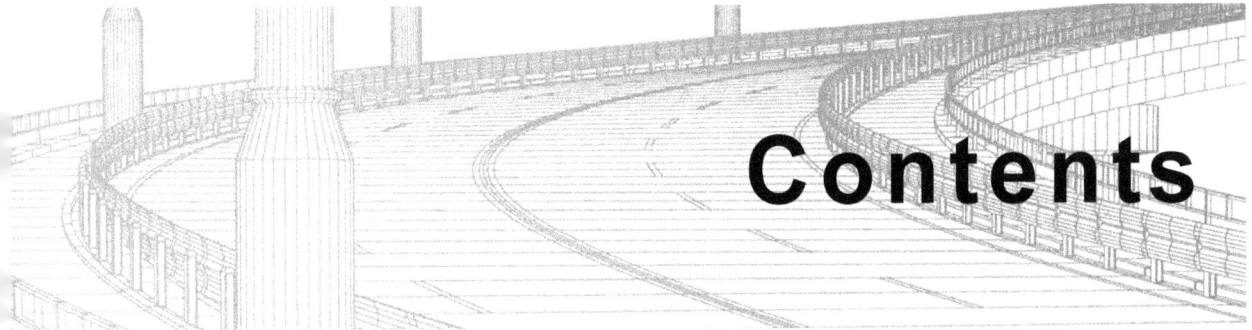

Contents

Preface

The AutoCAD® Civil 3D® 2017 (SP1.1) software supports a wide range of civil engineering tasks and creates intelligent relationships between objects. The *AutoCAD® Civil 3D® 2017 (SP1.1): Grading* student guide is recommended for users that are required to create site grading plans using the AutoCAD Civil 3D software. This student guide is also ideal for managers that require a basic overview and understanding of this aspect of the AutoCAD Civil 3D software.

Users use feature lines and grading tools to create a commercial site containing a parking lot, building pad, pond, and simple sewage lagoon. An existing road has been included in the survey and a survey team collected the existing conditions. Users also work on a residential site to grade a small subdivision for proper grading of each lot.

Topics Covered

- Introduction to Grading

- Parcel Grading

- Grading using Feature Lines

- Grading using Grading Objects and Grading Groups

- Grading using Corridors

- Combining Surfaces

- Visualization

Note on Software Setup

This student guide assumes a standard installation of the software using the default preferences during installation. Lectures and practices use the standard software templates and default options for the Content Libraries.

Students and Educators can Access Free Autodesk Software and Resources

Autodesk challenges you to get started with free educational licenses for professional software and creativity apps used by millions of architects, engineers, designers, and hobbyists today. Bring Autodesk software into your classroom, studio, or workshop to learn, teach, and explore real-world design challenges the way professionals do.

Get started today - register at the Autodesk Education Community and download one of the many Autodesk software applications available.

Visit www.autodesk.com/joinedu/

Note: Free products are subject to the terms and conditions of the end-user license and services agreement that accompanies the software. The software is for personal use for education purposes and is not intended for classroom or lab use.

Lead Contributor: Michelle Rasmussen

Specializing in the civil engineering industry, Michelle authors student guides and provides instruction, support, and implementation on all Autodesk infrastructure solutions, in addition to general AutoCAD.

Michelle began her career in the Air Force working in the Civil Engineering unit as a surveyor, designer, and construction manager. She has also worked for municipalities and consulting engineering firms as an engineering/GIS technician. Michelle holds a Bachelor's of Science degree from the University of Utah along with a Master's of Business Administration from Kaplan University.

Michelle is an Autodesk Certified Instructor (ACI) as well as an Autodesk Certified Evaluator, teaching and evaluating other Autodesk Instructors for the ACI program. In addition, she holds the Autodesk Certified Professional certification for Civil 3D and is trained in Instructional Design.

As a skilled communicator, Michelle effectively leads classes, webcasts and consults with clients to achieve their business objectives.

Michelle Rasmussen has been the Lead Contributor for *AutoCAD Civil 3D: Grading* since its initial release in 2011.

In this Guide

The following images highlight some of the features that can be found in this Student Guide.

Practice Files

To download the practice files for this student guide, use the following steps

1. Type the URL shown below into the address bar of your Internet browser. The URL must be typed **exactly as shown**. If you are using an ASCENT ebook you can click on the link to download the file

   Address bar
   `http://www.ASCENTed.com/getfile?id=xxxxxxxx`
   File Edit View Favorites Tools Help

2. Press <Enter> to download the .ZIP file that contains the Practice Files

3. Once the download is complete, unzip the file to a local folder. The unzipped file contains an .EXE file

4. Double-click on the .EXE file and follow the instructions to automatically install the Practice Files on the C:\ drive of your computer.

   Do not change the location in which the Practice Files folder is installed. Doing so can cause errors when completing the practices in this student guide

`http://www.ASCENTed.com/getfile?id=xxxxxxxx`

Stay Informed!
Interested in receiving information about upcoming promotional offers, educational events, invitations to complimentary webcasts, and discounts? If so, please visit www.ASCENTed.com/updates/

Help us improve our product by completing the following survey:
www.ASCENTed.com/feedback
You can also contact us at: feedback@ASCENTed.com

FTP link for practice files

Practice Files

The Practice Files page tells you how to download and install the practice files that are provided with this student guide.

Chapter

1

Getting Started

In this chapter you learn how to start the AutoCAD® software, become familiar with the basic layout of the AutoCAD screen, how to access commands, use your pointing device, and understand the AutoCAD Cartesian workspace. You also learn how to open an existing drawing, view a drawing by zooming and panning and save your work in the AutoCAD software.

Learning Objectives in this Chapter

- Launch the AutoCAD software and complete a basic initial setup of the drawing environment.
- Identify the basic layout and features of AutoCAD interface including the Ribbon, Drawing Window, and Application Menu.
- Locate commands and launch them using the Ribbon, shortcut menus, Application Menu, and Quick Access Toolbar.
- Locate points in the AutoCAD Cartesian workspace
- Open and close existing drawings, and navigate to file locations
- Move around a drawing using the mouse, the **Zoom** and **Pan** commands, and the Navigation Bar.
- Save drawings in various formats and set the automatic save options using the **Save** commands.

Learning Objectives for the chapter

Chapters

Each chapter begins with a brief introduction and a list of the chapter's Learning Objectives.

Side notes

Side notes are hints or additional information for the current topic.

Instructional Content

Each chapter is split into a series of sections of instructional content on specific topics. These lectures include the descriptions, step-by-step procedures, figures, hints, and information you need to achieve the chapter's Learning Objectives.

Practice Objectives

Practices

Practices enable you to use the software to perform a hands-on review of a topic.

Some practices require you to use prepared practice files, which can be downloaded from the link found on the Practice Files page.

Chapter Review Questions

Chapter review questions, located at the end of each chapter, enable you to review the key concepts and learning objectives of the chapter.

Command Summary

The Command Summary is located at the end of each chapter. It contains a list of the software commands that are used throughout the chapter, and provides information on where the command is found in the software.

Icons in this Student Guide

The following icons are used to help you quickly and easily find helpful information.

New in 2017	Indicates items that are new in the AutoCAD Civil 3D 2017 (SP1.1) software.
Enhanced in 2017	Indicates items that have been enhanced in the AutoCAD Civil 3D 2017 (SP1.1) software.

Practice Files

To download the practice files for this student guide, use the following steps:

1. Type the URL shown below into the address bar of your Internet browser. The URL must be typed **exactly as shown**. If you are using an ASCENT ebook, you can click on the link to download the file.

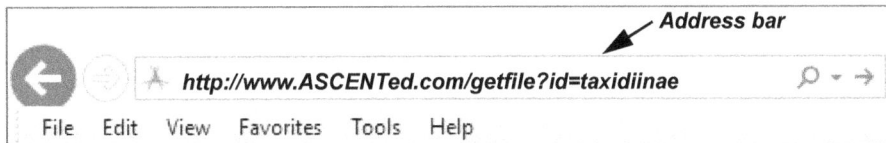

Address bar

http://www.ASCENTed.com/getfile?id=taxidiinae

File   Edit   View   Favorites   Tools   Help

2. Press <Enter> to download the .ZIP file that contains the Practice Files.

3. Once the download is complete, unzip the file to a local folder. The unzipped file contains an .EXE file.

4. Double-click on the .EXE file and follow the instructions to automatically install the Practice Files on the C:\ drive of your computer.

   Do not change the location in which the Practice Files folder is installed. Doing so can cause errors when completing the practices in this student guide.

http://www.ASCENTed.com/getfile?id=taxidiinae

Stay Informed!

Interested in receiving information about upcoming promotional offers, educational events, invitations to complimentary webcasts, and discounts? If so, please visit:

www.ASCENTed.com/updates/

Help us improve our product by completing the following survey:

www.ASCENTed.com/feedback

You can also contact us at: *feedback@ASCENTed.com*

Introduction to Grading

During the grading process, it is important for a designer to be able to visualize how the ground is affected when it is reshaped. Designers need to understand where the water runs so that they can make any necessary changes. In this chapter, you learn how to create styles that make it easier to visualize a ground surface and understand its impact on flowing water.

Learning Objectives in this Chapter

- State the purpose of grading and reshaping the earth's surface.
- List the tools in the AutoCAD Civil 3D software that can be used for grading and the items that are affected by their changes.
- Identify the required settings to set up a new grading project.
- Set up feature line styles.
- Set up a grading group style for easy viewing of grading objects.
- Create grading criteria sets for multiple types of grading tasks.
- Create surface styles that make the effects of your grading easier to see and adjust.
- Create sites for managing common topology, such as parcels, alignments, grading groups, and feature lines.

1.1 Overview

Grading is used in construction to create the proper slope conditions for drainage, transportation, landscaping, and so much more. Its purpose is to provide stability for the site by minimizing soil erosion and sedimentation. When reshaping the ground surface, engineers and designers strive to prevent drainage problems, such as standing water on roads, flooding of homes and businesses, and having the ground wash away with storms, as shown in Figure 1–1. A properly graded project establishes drainage areas, directs drainage patterns, and affects runoff velocities.

Figure 1–1

Before creating a grading plan, the existing conditions of a site must be gathered. Land surveys, soil investigations, and storm data should all be studied before starting to consider where to create cut or fill areas. Another consideration is the newly created hard surfaces that create additional runoff.

Parts of the Grading Object

Grading objects contain several components. A basic grading object contains a footprint or base line, projection lines, daylight or target lines, and faces. Each of the parts are shown in Figure 1–2.

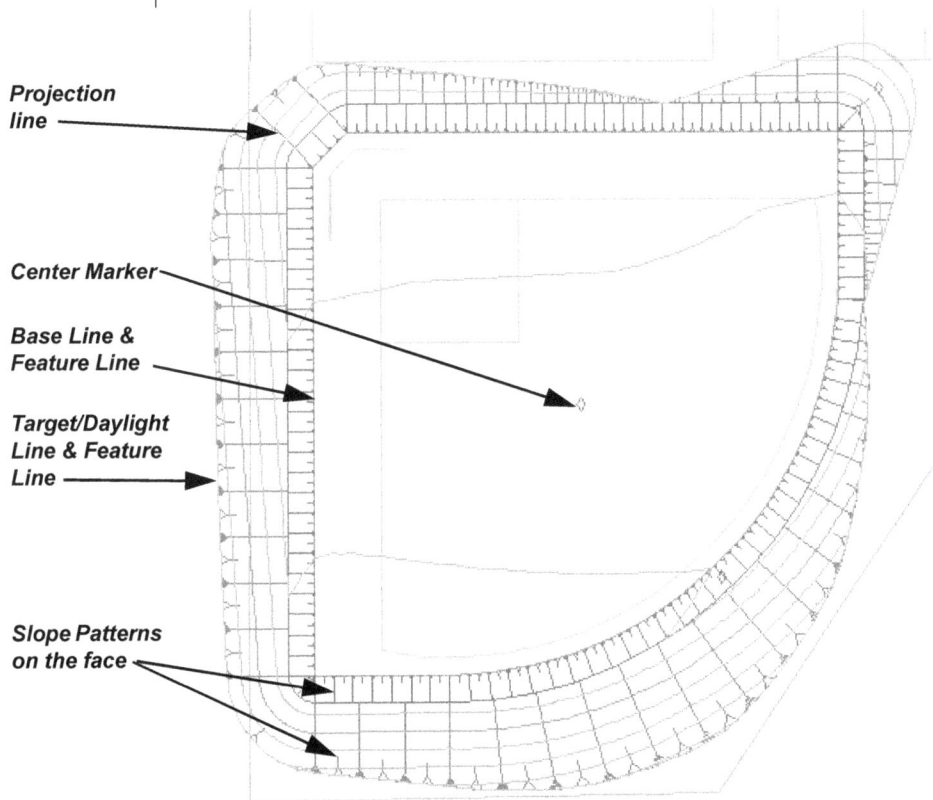

Projection
line

Center Marker

Base Line &
Feature Line

Target/Daylight
Line & Feature
Line

Slope Patterns
on the face

Figure 1–2

- **Base Lines** act as the footprint for the grading object. They can be a parcel line or any open or closed feature line. Feature lines can represent ridge or swale lines, building footprints, parking lots, and a number of other design features.

- A **Target Line** is the end result of a grading object. It can be defined by a distance, elevation (relative or absolute), or surface. If a surface is used as the target, the result is a daylight line. In all cases, the target line will be a feature line that can then be used as the base line for another grading object.

- A **Face** is the slope area created by the application of a grading criteria. Depending on the grading object's specified style, slope patterns might be displayed on each face according to the type of grading solution. The slope pattern for a distance grading object might look different than the slope pattern on a cut or fill slope, as shown in Figure 1–2.

- **Projection Lines** define the face edges within a region of a grading object and are used for the facets along curves and break points on the base line and target line.

- The **Center Marker** is a diamond that marks a graded face's center and is used for display and selection purposes. When you edit each grading object, select the center marker that displays the *Grading* contextual tab in the Ribbon.

- A **Grading Group** is a collection of grading objects that is used to organize gradings and make surface creation and volume calculations easier. By setting a volume base surface in the grading group properties (as shown in Figure 1–3), grading volume tools can be used to calculate a quick volume between the new grading surface and the existing ground surface.

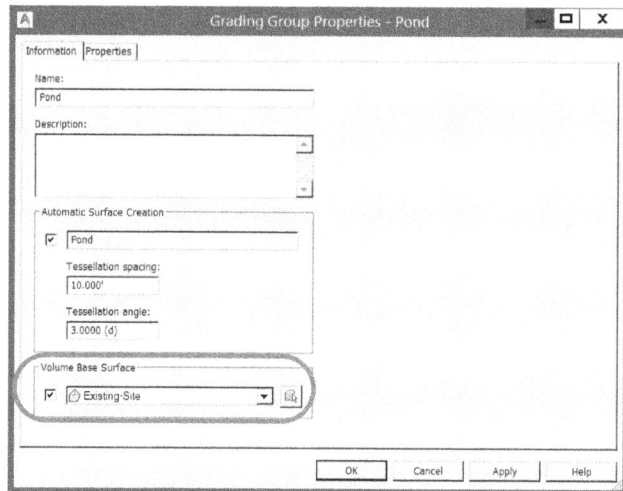

Figure 1–3

Grading Workflow

Setting Up Gradings

In the preliminary phase of a project, you can save a lot of time and effort if your drawing is set up beforehand with the settings and styles needed to convey design intent effectively. Then save it as a template.

1. **Establish Grading Settings:** This is where you will define units of measurement to be used throughout the project for gradings.
2. **Create Grading Styles:** Styles determine how feature lines, surfaces, and grading groups display in the drawing and on the printed sheet.

3. **Define Grading Criteria:** Predefining the methods and projections for grading saves time and ensures that the proper standards are followed.

Designing and Creating Gradings

The process used to create gradings might vary from one project to another. The list of tasks below is intended to be a high-level overview.

1. **Create Feature Lines:** Parcel lines can be used to create feature lines or convert existing linework into feature lines. Nearly every grading project contains at least one feature line.
2. **Create Grading Groups:** The interaction between feature lines can be controlled along with grading projections using grading groups.
3. **Create the Grading:** By creating multiple grading objects, you can determine the slope of the ground from the base line to the target line.
4. **Modify the Grading as Required:** Editing commands can be used to make easy adjustments to grading objects and feature lines as the design changes.

Outputting Grading Information

It is very important to be able to convey the grading design to others. During the design phase, community leaders and the public might need to be able to visualize the finished project. Creating renderings for the public makes visualizing the project easier for them. However, contractors are more familiar with reading contour data with cut and fill slopes labeled or shaded to indicate how much dirt needs to be moved from one area to another. They might also need cut and fill reports to help them order the correct volume of material for the site.

1. **Select the Grading Group Surface Creation:** Once the grading group satisfies your grading specifications, you need to create contours for it. This is only accomplished by creating a surface.
2. **Edit Grading Styles:** Viewing the surface in various ways assists in finding problems and communicating design intent.
3. **Plot and Publish the Drawings:** Drawings can be plotted onto paper or published electronically to send to interested parties more efficiently.
4. **Produce Reports:** Reports complement drawings to communicate design intent and volumes to interested parties.

1.2 Tools in AutoCAD Civil 3D

The AutoCAD® Civil 3D® software is a powerful application for civil engineering design. Although it runs in the familiar AutoCAD® environment, the software is based on a dynamic engineering model that contains all of the core geometry and integrates all of the data. When you make a change to the design, the AutoCAD Civil 3D software automatically updates the related objects, views, annotations, tables, etc.

The objects used for grading in the AutoCAD Civil 3D software establish intelligent relationships. The following table lists items that can be used for grading and shows these relationships and how a change made to one object is reflected in others.

When you edit these objects...	These objects are updated...
Points	Surfaces
Surfaces	Grading Groups, Profiles, Pipe Networks, and Corridors
Parcels	Grading Groups and Corridors
Alignments	Grading Groups, Corridors, Profiles, Parcels, Sections, and Pipe Networks
Profiles	Grading Groups, Corridors, Parcels, Sections, and Pipe Networks
Grading Groups	Surfaces and Corridors
Subassembly	Assembly, Corridors, and Surfaces
Assembly	Corridors and Surfaces
Feature Lines	Grading Groups, Corridors, and Surfaces
Sample Lines	Sections and Corridors

1.3 Settings and Defaults

The AutoCAD Civil 3D software has default drawing settings that control all of the basic commands for the drawing, unless there is a specific override at the feature or command level. In the Drawing Settings dialog box, **Ambient Settings** can be set to control the units for area and volume. For example, by changing the unit value, the software knows that you want the volume measurements to be in cubic yards rather than cubic meters, as shown in Figure 1–4.

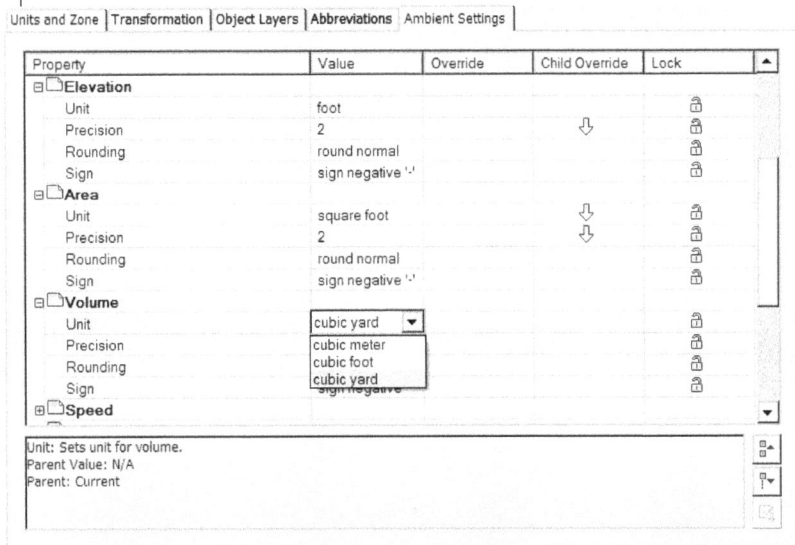

Figure 1–4

The *Object Layers* tab in the Drawing Settings dialog box enables you to specify layers for objects. By default, layers are named in accordance with the national CAD Standards if one of the Autodesk supplied templates is used. The object's name can be added at the beginning or ending of the layer by selecting the prefix or suffix modifier and placing an asterisk (*) in the *Value* column, as shown in Figure 1–5.

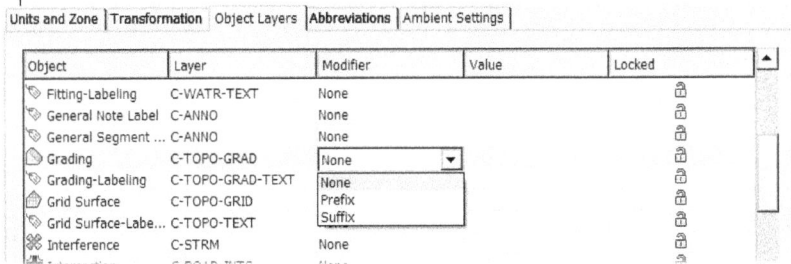

Figure 1–5

Command settings enable you to set default styles for specific commands. This helps you save time by automatically setting the correct style for feature lines, grading styles, and cut and fill slopes, as shown in Figure 1–6.

Property	Value	Override	Child Override	Lock
⊞ General				
⊞ Degree of Curvature				
⊞ Labeling				
⊟ Grading Creation				
Transition Region Length	10.00'			🔓
⊞ Time				
⊟ Default Styles				
Feature Line Style	Basic Feature ...	☐		🔓
Grading Style	Residential Gr...	☐		🔓
Cut Style	Cut Slope Displ...	☐		🔓
Fill Style	Fill Slope Displ...	☐		🔓
⊟ Default Name Format				
Feature Line Name Template	Feature <[Next ...	☐		🔓
Grading Group Name Template	Grading Group ...	☐		🔓
⊞ Unitless				
⊞ Distance				
⊞ Dimension				
⊞ Coordinate				
⊞ Grid Coordinate				

Figure 1–6

Practice 1a

Settings and Defaults

Practice Objective

- Identify the required settings to set up a new grading project.

Estimated time for completion: 5 minutes

In this practice, you will create a template based on National CAD Standards to include the correct settings and defaults for the types of grading done in the project.

1. Open the AutoCAD Civil 3D software. In the Application Menu, select **New** to start a new drawing using **_AutoCAD Civil 3D (Imperial) NCS.dwt**, which comes with the software, as shown in Figure 1–7. Click **Open**.

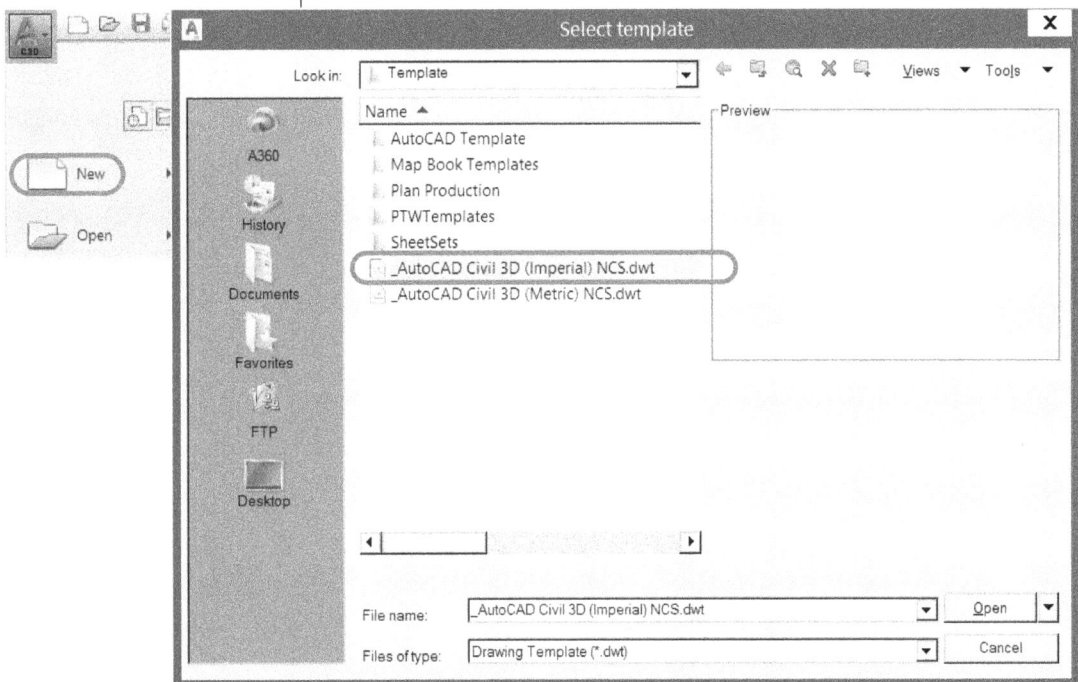

Figure 1–7

2. In the Toolspace, in the *Settings* tab, right-click on the drawing name and select **Edit Drawing Settings**.

3. In the *Object Layers* tab, set the *Tin Surface Modifier* to a **Suffix**, and type **-*** (dash, asterisk) in the *Value* field, as shown in Figure 1–8.

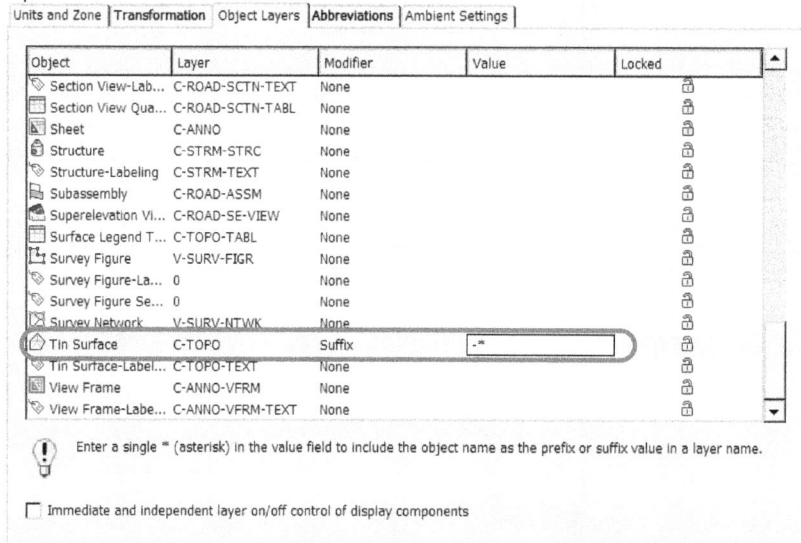

| Units and Zone | Transformation | Object Layers | Abbreviations | Ambient Settings |

Object	Layer	Modifier	Value	Locked
Section View-Lab...	C-ROAD-SCTN-TEXT	None		🔓
Section View Qua...	C-ROAD-SCTN-TABL	None		🔓
Sheet	C-ANNO	None		🔓
Structure	C-STRM-STRC	None		🔓
Structure-Labeling	C-STRM-TEXT	None		🔓
Subassembly	C-ROAD-ASSM	None		🔓
Superelevation Vi...	C-ROAD-SE-VIEW	None		🔓
Surface Legend T...	C-TOPO-TABL	None		🔓
Survey Figure	V-SURV-FIGR	None		🔓
Survey Figure-La...	0	None		🔓
Survey Figure Se...	0	None		🔓
Survey Network	V-SURV-NTWK	None		🔓
Tin Surface	C-TOPO	Suffix	-*	🔓
Tin Surface-Label...	C-TOPO-TEXT	None		🔓
View Frame	C-ANNO-VFRM	None		🔓
View Frame-Labe...	C-ANNO-VFRM-TEXT	None		🔓

💡 Enter a single * (asterisk) in the value field to include the object name as the prefix or suffix value in a layer name.

☐ Immediate and independent layer on/off control of display components

Figure 1–8

4. In the *Ambient Settings* tab, verify that *Volume* is set to **Cubic yard**, *Grade* is set to **percent**, and *Slope* is set to **run:rise**, as shown in Figure 1–9.

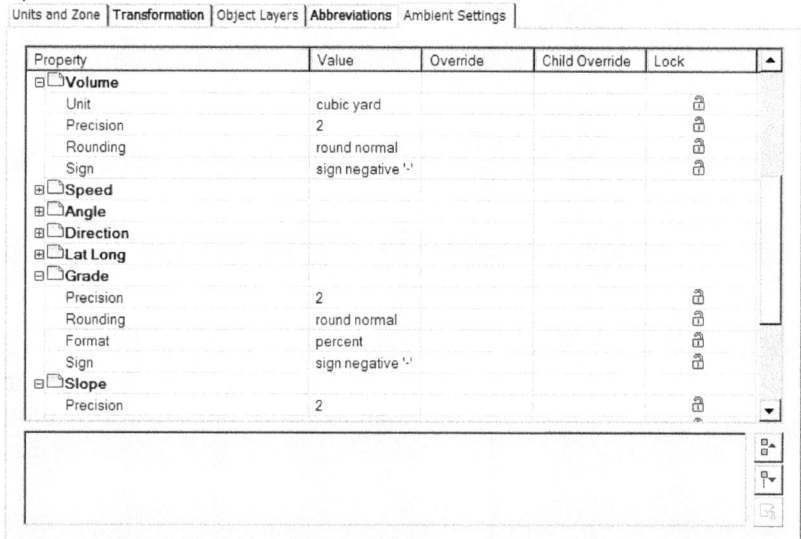

| Units and Zone | Transformation | Object Layers | Abbreviations | Ambient Settings |

Property	Value	Override	Child Override	Lock
⊟ Volume				
Unit	cubic yard			🔓
Precision	2			🔓
Rounding	round normal			🔓
Sign	sign negative '-'			🔓
⊞ Speed				
⊞ Angle				
⊞ Direction				
⊞ Lat Long				
⊟ Grade				
Precision	2			🔓
Rounding	round normal			🔓
Format	percent			🔓
Sign	sign negative '-'			🔓
⊟ Slope				
Precision	2			🔓

Figure 1–9

5. Click **OK** to close the dialog box.

6. In the *Settings* tab, do the following:
   - Expand **Grading>Commands**
   - Right-click on CreateFeatureLines
   - Select **Edit Command Settings**

7. In the Edit Command Settings dialog box, do the following, as shown in Figure 1–10:
   - Select the Plus symbol next to *Feature Line Creation* to expand it.
   - Select **True** for the values of the **Feature Line Name** and **Use Feature Line Style**.
   - Expand Default Styles and set the *Feature Line Style* to **Basic**.
   - Click **OK**.

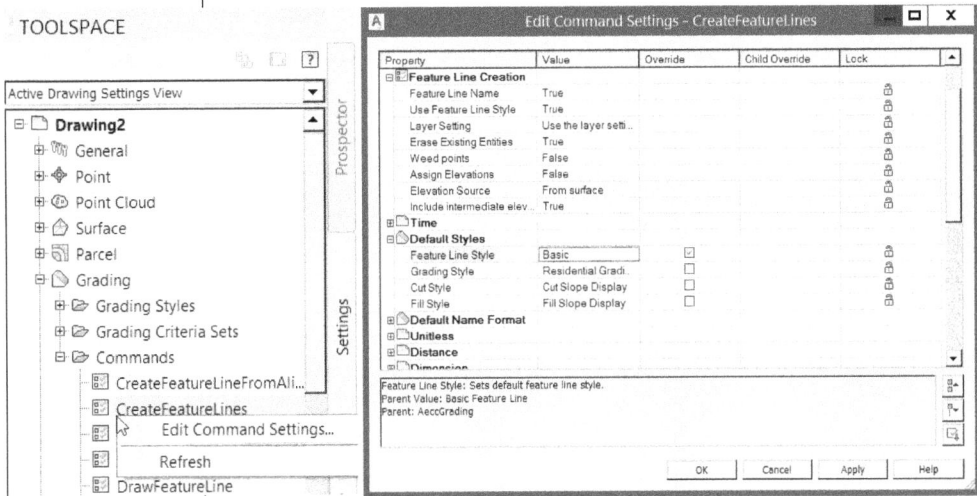

Figure 1–10

8. Save the drawing as **Styles.dwg** in the *C:\Civil3D-Grading* folder.

1.4 Feature Line Styles

Styles assist you in creating the design documentation required for construction documents so that you can focus on the design rather than drafting standards.

Feature lines are complex, linear 3D objects that define a string of known or proposed elevations. Feature lines can be used as breaklines in surfaces or as grading object baselines and are created during the corridor creation process. Corridor feature lines can be extracted for use in grading groups. When a drawing is created using one of the standard AutoCAD Civil 3D templates, it contains a large number of feature line styles, as shown in Figure 1–11.

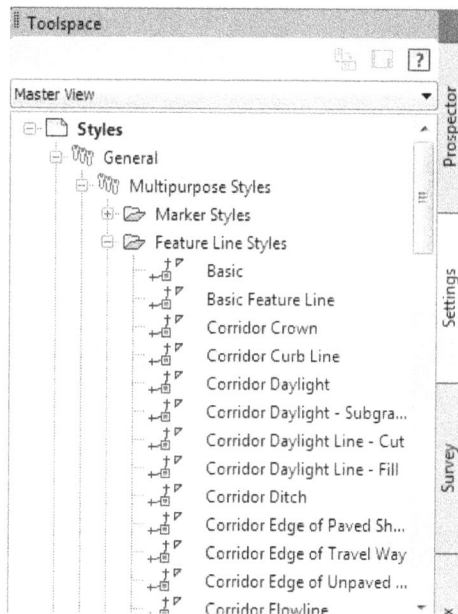

Figure 1–11

Additional feature line styles can easily be created. In the Settings tab, expand **General>Multipurpose Styles**, right-click on Feature Line Styles and select **New**. The Feature Line Styles dialog box opens as shown in Figure 1–12.

The *Information* tab assigns a name and description. It also indicates who created the style and when it was last modified.

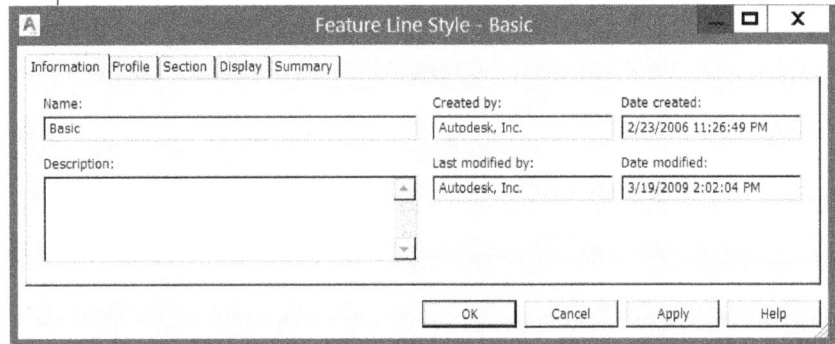

Figure 1–12

The *Profile* tab sets the marker symbol that displays at the end points and internal vertices of the feature line in the profile view, as shown in Figure 1–13. The markers are set to not display when the **_No Markers** style is selected.

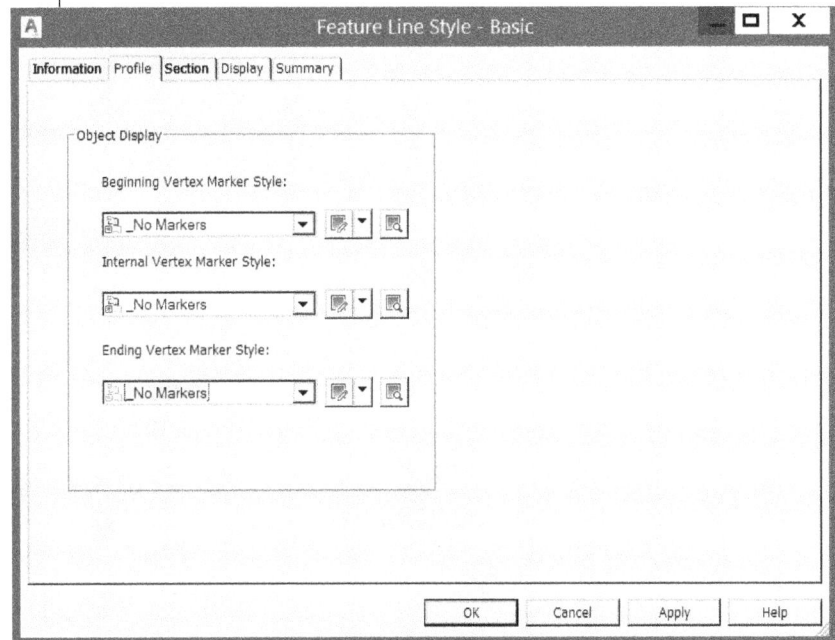

Figure 1–13

The *Sections* tab sets the marker symbol that displays in the section view, as shown in Figure 1–14. The markers are set to not display when the **_No Markers** style is selected.

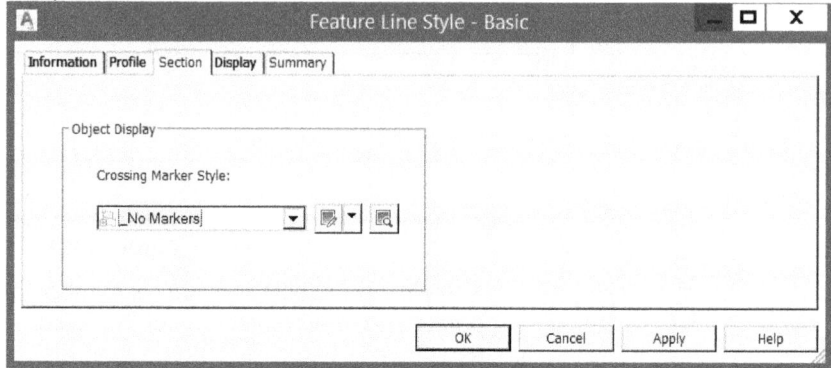

Figure 1–14

The *Display* tab is where you set the layer, color, linetype, visibility, etc., of the feature line in the various views, as shown in Figure 1–15. If the layer is set to layer 0 (zero), the drawing settings determine the layer on which the feature line is located. If it is set to any other layer in the Feature Line Style dialog box, it overrides the drawing settings.

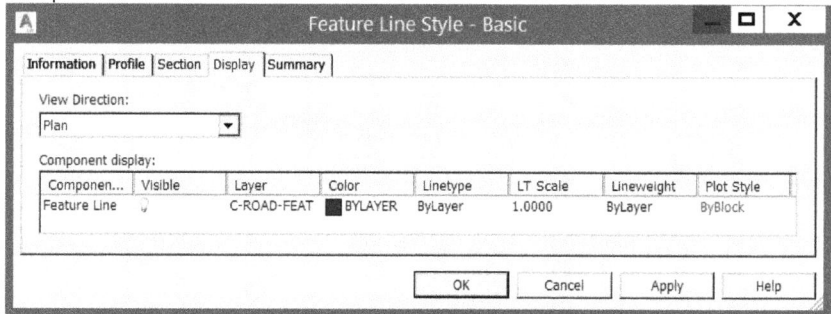

Figure 1–15

The *Summary* tab displays the settings that are set on all of the other tabs and is useful for quickly referencing what is happening in a specific style.

1.5 Grading Group Styles

The grading group style determines what is displayed in the drawing. You can set the layers for the various grading components to a no print layer in the *Display* tab of the Grading Style dialog box (as shown in Figure 1–16). This enables you to create grading groups, which enable the grading objects to be displayed while you are working and not when the drawing is printed. Therefore, only the contours and labels are displayed on the printed sheet.

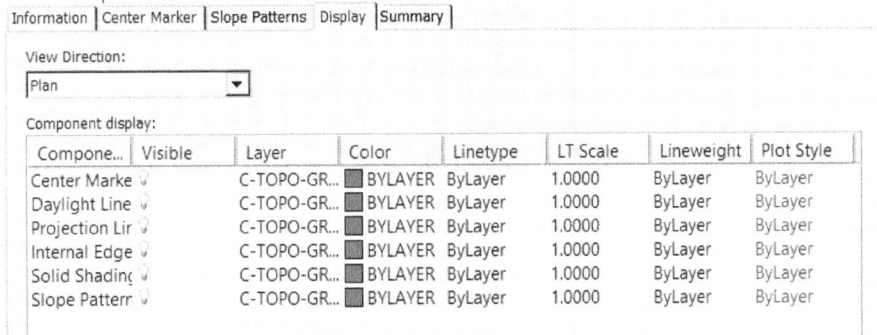

Compone...	Visible	Layer	Color	Linetype	LT Scale	Lineweight	Plot Style
Center Marke	⌄	C-TOPO-GR...	BYLAYER	ByLayer	1.0000	ByLayer	ByLayer
Daylight Line	⌄	C-TOPO-GR...	BYLAYER	ByLayer	1.0000	ByLayer	ByLayer
Projection Lir	⌄	C-TOPO-GR...	BYLAYER	ByLayer	1.0000	ByLayer	ByLayer
Internal Edge	⌄	C-TOPO-GR...	BYLAYER	ByLayer	1.0000	ByLayer	ByLayer
Solid Shadinç	⌄	C-TOPO-GR...	BYLAYER	ByLayer	1.0000	ByLayer	ByLayer
Slope Patterr	⌄	C-TOPO-GR...	BYLAYER	ByLayer	1.0000	ByLayer	ByLayer

Figure 1–16

The *Center Marker* tab determines the size of the center mark (diamond at the center of the grading face). The center mark size can be:

*   A percentage of the screen, as shown in Figure 1–17.

*   A fixed size (using feet or meters) according to the drawing units.

*   Based on the drawing scale so that it prints a specific size.

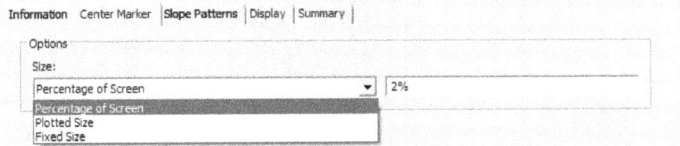

Figure 1–17

The *Slope Pattern* tab determines the patterns used to mark the grading slopes. If you select the option to display a slope pattern, an additional style needs to be created to define the number of components to use and the length of each of those components. To access this style, select the **Edit Current Selection** option as shown in Figure 1–18. Alternatively, you can go to the *Settings* tab and expand **General>Multipurpose Styles>Slope Pattern Styles**. This enables a symbol to be placed at the beginning of the slope. The symbol can be a block, triangle (opened or closed), or tapered lines (with or without a gap). You can also have multiple components for the slope pattern with different symbols and line lengths for each.

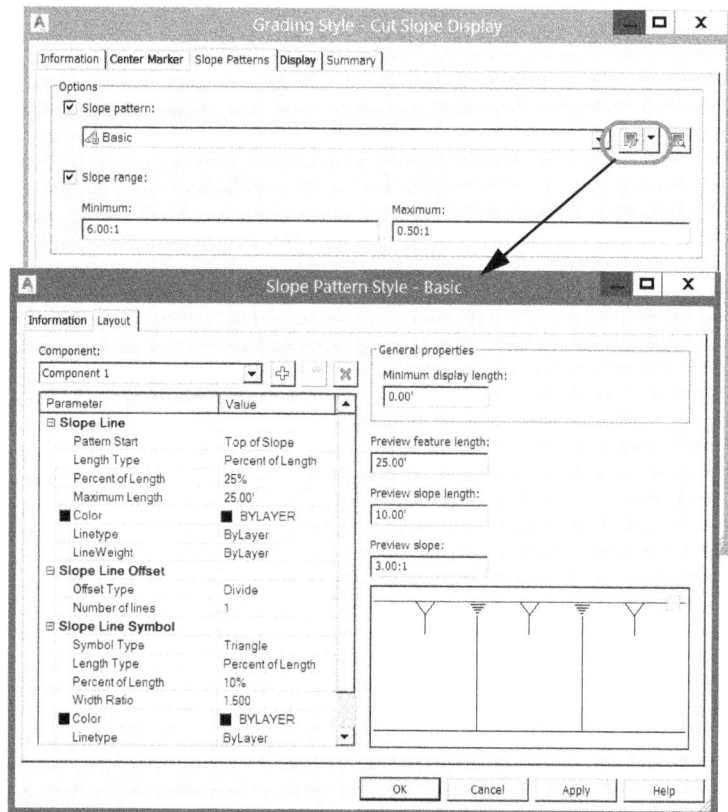

Figure 1–18

In the *Slope Pattern* tab, the slope ranges can also be turned on. This enables you to apply the slope patterns to a limited range of slope values that you specify.

In the *Display* tab, you can set the layer, color, linetype, visibility, etc., of the various components in the plan or model views, as shown in Figure 1–19. If the layer is set to layer **0** (zero), the drawing settings determine the layer on which the grading group components are placed. If it is set to any other layer in the Grading Style dialog box, it overrides the drawing settings.

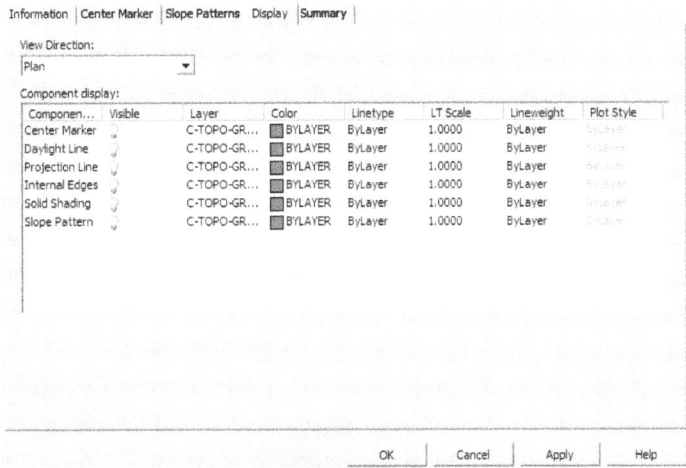

Figure 1–19

The *Summary* tab is a quick way of determining which center marker and slope pattern styles were set on previous pages, as shown in Figure 1–20.

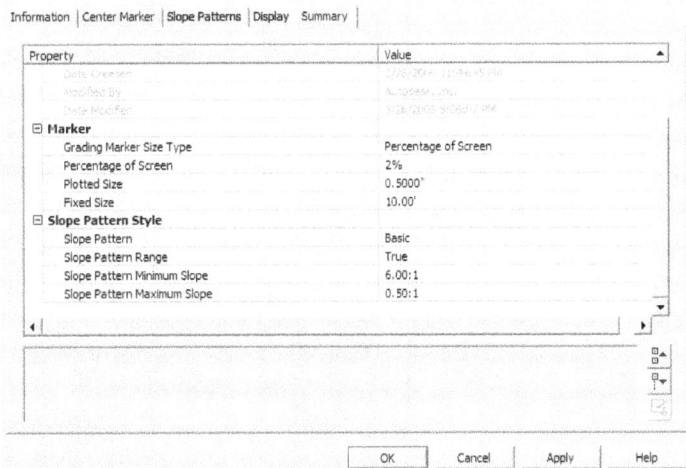

Figure 1–20

1.6 Grading Criteria Sets

Grading criteria is applied to a base line or footprint to create grading projections. Different types of projects require different grading criteria. A pond grading might require a 2:1 slope up to a specific elevation on the interior while the exterior of the pond might require a maximum of a 3:1 slope that daylights to a surface. Each of these criteria can be set in an AutoCAD Civil 3D template to speed up and control the grading process during design. Design criteria can be locked in the criteria to ensure that predefined design specifications are used every time. This also permits faster completion of grading projects by reducing the redundant typing of grading parameters. Once each type of grading criteria has been created, they can be included in a Grading Criteria Set so that they are in one location, making them easier to use (as shown in Figure 1–21).

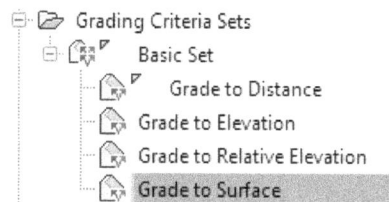

Figure 1–21

There are four different types of grading criteria:

1. Grade to a distance.
2. Grade to an elevation.
3. Grade to a relative elevation.
4. Grade to a surface.

Grade to Distance

When you need to keep a specific grade or slope for a specified horizontal distance, you use the Grade to Distance criteria, as shown in Figure 1–22. For example, a building pad for a house might require that the ground slope away from the house at a 2% grade for a specified distance to ensure that standing water is directed away from the foundation. Use this criteria to set the target at a specific distance and then lock that distance so that it cannot be changed.

Information   Criteria

Parameter	Value	Lock
⊟ **Grading Method**		
Target	Distance	
Distance	1.00'	🔓
Projection	Slope	
⊟ **Slope Projection**		
Format	Slope	🔓
Slope	2.00:1	🔓
⊟ **Conflict Resolution**		
Interior Corner Overlap	Use Average Slope	🔓

Figure 1–22

Grade to Elevation

When you need to keep a specific grade or slope to a specified elevation, you need to use the Grade to Elevation criteria (as shown in Figure 1–23) to set the target to be a specific elevation. You can then decide which slope or grade to use for the fill slopes separate from the cut slopes. This is most useful in pond grading since the top of the pond needs to be level.

Information   Criteria

Parameter	Value	Lock
⊟ **Grading Method**		
Target	Elevation	
Elevation	0.00'	🔓
Projection	Cut/Fill Slope	
⊟ **Cut Slope Projection (up)**		
Format	Slope	🔓
Slope	2.00:1	🔓
⊟ **Fill Slope Projection (down)**		
Format	Slope	🔓
Slope	2.00:1	🔓
⊟ **Conflict Resolution**		
Interior Corner Overlap	Use Average Slope	🔓

Figure 1–23

Grade to Relative Elevation

Sometimes it is necessary to project a grade up or down a specific vertical distance. This strategy requires using the Grade to Relative Elevation criteria, as shown in Figure 1–24, which enables you to set the target to a specific vertical distance and the slope or grade for that relative elevation. You can then lock the relative elevation so that it cannot be changed.

Information   Criteria

Parameter	Value	Lock
⊟ **Grading Method**		
Target	Relative Elevation	
Relative Elevation	1.00'	🔓
Projection	Slope	
⊟ **Slope Projection**		
Format	Slope	🔓
Slope	2.00:1	🔓
⊟ **Conflict Resolution**		
Interior Corner Overlap	Use Average Slope	🔓

Figure 1–24

Grade to Surface

When you need to keep a specific slope until the projection finds daylight, you need to use the Grade to Surface criteria, as shown in Figure 1–25. It enables you to set the target to be a specific surface name. You can then decide which slope or grade to use for the separate fill and cut slope solutions. This criteria is typically used last to finish the grading solution.

Information   Criteria

Parameter	Value	Lock
⊟ **Grading Method**		
Target	Surface	
Projection	Cut/Fill Slope	
Search Order	Cut first	🔓
⊟ **Cut Slope Projection (up)**		
Format	Slope	🔓
Slope	2.00:1	🔓
⊟ **Fill Slope Projection (down)**		
Format	Slope	🔓
Slope	2.00:1	🔓
⊟ **Conflict Resolution**		
Interior Corner Overlap	Use Average Slope	🔓

Figure 1–25

- When locking grading criteria parameters, note that once they are locked, they cannot be changed (not even during the editing process). If you change the design parameters, you might need to redefine the grading group rather than just edit it as you would if the grading criteria was not locked.

Practice 1b

Grading Styles

Practice Objective

- Create feature line styles, grading group styles, and a grading criteria set to be used in the project.

Estimated time for completion: 10 minutes

In this practice, you will add to the template to include the correct styles and grading criteria.

Task 1 - Create feature line styles.

1. Continue working in the drawing from the previous practice or open **INTRO-B1-Styles.dwg** from the *C:\Civil3D-Grading\ Intro* folder.

2. In the *Settings* tab, expand the General tree, expand Multipurpose Styles, right-click on Feature Line Styles and select **New**, as shown in Figure 1–26.

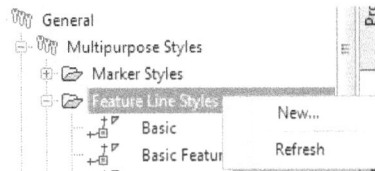

Figure 1–26

3. In the *Information* tab, for the *Name*, type **Parking Lot**. For the *Description*, type **Parking lot foot print**.

4. In the *Profile* tab, set each of the *Vertex Marker Styles* to **_No Markers**, as shown in Figure 1–27.

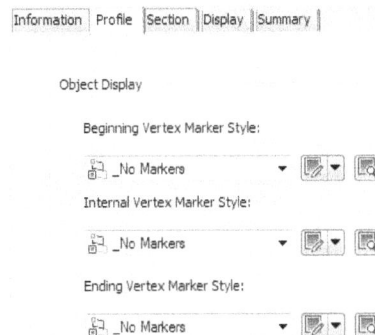

Figure 1–27

5. In the *Section* tab, set the *Crossing Marker Style* to **_No Markers**, as shown in Figure 1–28.

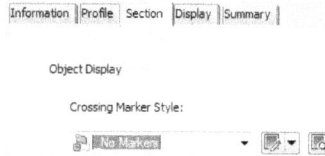

Figure 1–28

6. In the *Display* tab, select the Layer to the right of the Feature Line component. In the Layer Selection dialog box, click the **New** button as shown in Figure 1–29.

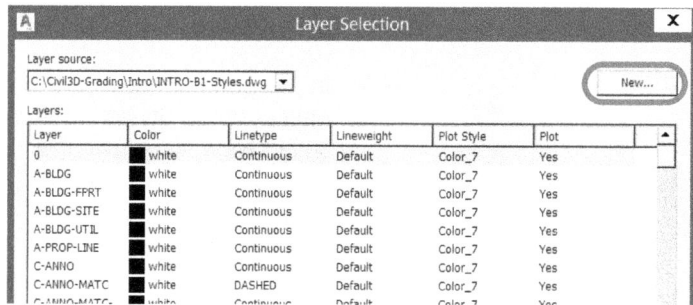

Figure 1–29

7. For the *Layer name*, type **C-GRAD-PARKING** and set the *Color* to **40**, as shown in Figure 1–30. Click **OK** three times to close all of the dialog boxes.

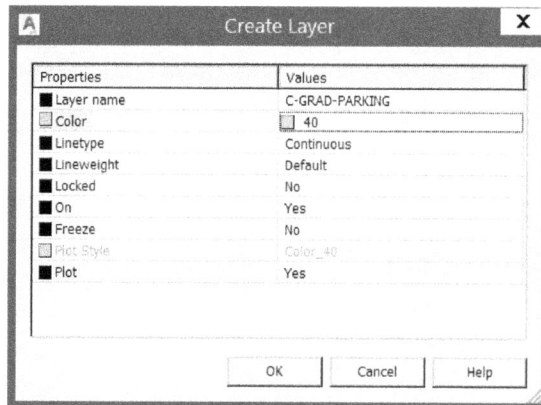

Figure 1–30

8. Repeat Steps 2-7 to create additional feature lines for the design objects listed in the following table. Keep the same settings unless otherwise noted.

Feature Line Style Name	Layer Name	Color
Building Pad	C-GRAD-BLDG	Blue (5)
Pond	C-GRAD-POND	Yellow (2)
Lagoon	C-GRAD-LAGOON	Green (3)

9. Save the drawing.

Task 2 - Create grading group styles.

1. Continue working in the drawing from the previous task or open **INTRO-B2-Styles.dwg** from the *C:\Civil3D-Grading\ Intro* folder.

2. In the Toolspace, in the *Settings* tab, expand **General> Multipurpose Styles**, right-click on Slope Pattern Styles and select **New**, as shown in Figure 1–31.

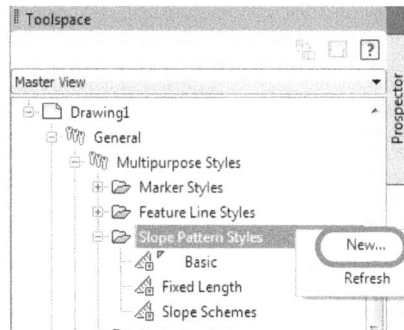

Figure 1–31

3. In the *Information* tab, type **Easy Viewing** for the name.

4. In the *Layout* tab, for Component 1, in the *Slope Line Symbol* area, set the following:
   - *Symbol Type* to **Triangle**
   - *Percent of Length* to **10%**.

5. Set the *Component* to **Component 2**, as shown in Figure 1–32.

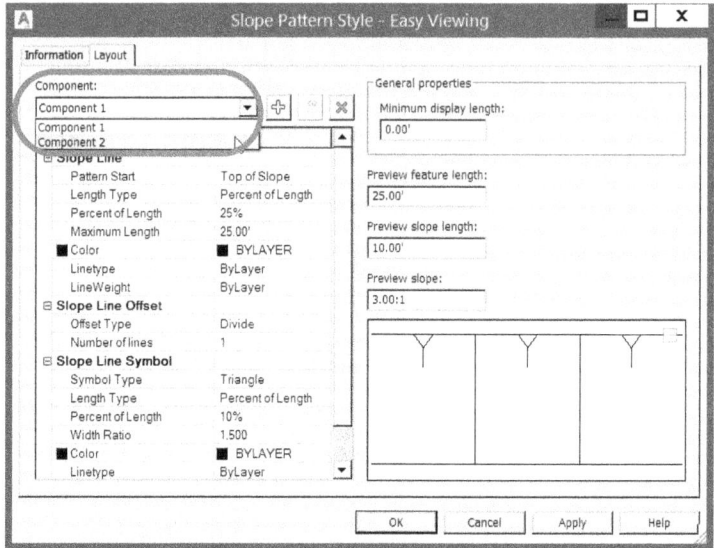

Figure 1–32

6. For Component 2, in the *Slope Line* area, set the *Percent of Length* to **75%** as shown in Figure 1–33.

This will ensure that the slope lines are not mistaken for projection lines.

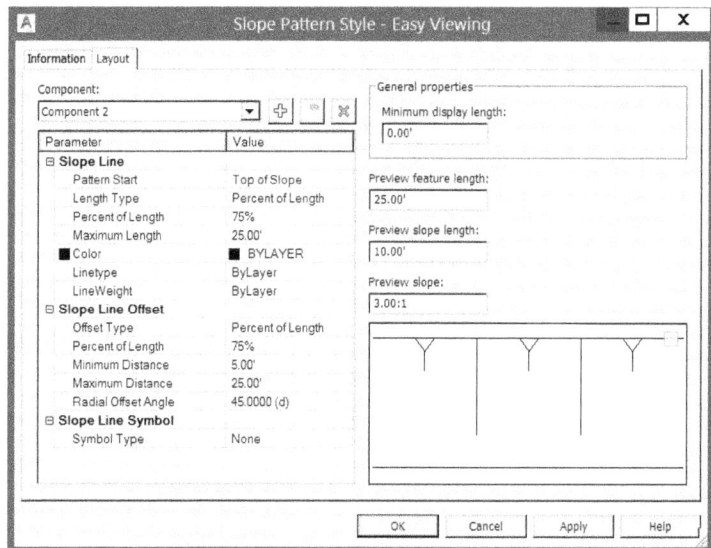

Figure 1–33

7. Click **OK**.

8. In the *Settings* tab, expand Grading, right-click on Grading Styles and select **New**, as shown in Figure 1–34.

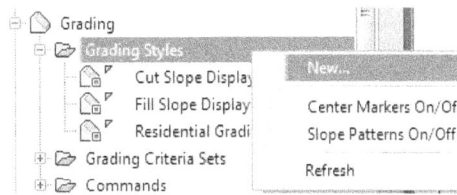

Figure 1–34

9. In the *Information* tab, type **Pond Grading Display**.

10. On the *Center Marker* tab, type **5** for the *Percentage of Screen* size.

11. In the *Slope Patterns* tab, select the **Slope pattern** option and set the *Style* to **Easy Viewing**, as shown in Figure 1–35.

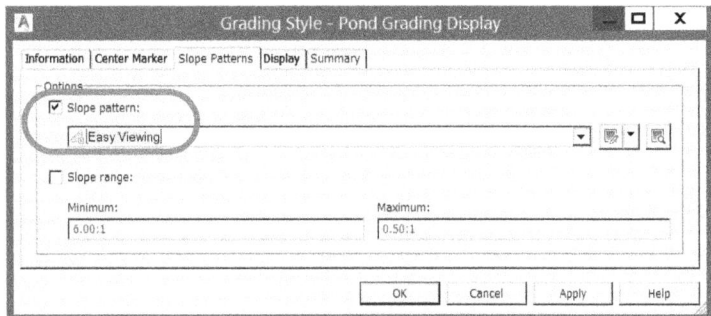

Figure 1–35

12. In the *Display* tab, select all of the components using <Shift>, and then select a **0** (zero) in the *Layer* column. In the Layer Selection dialog box, click the **New** button. For the *Layer name*, type **C-GRAD-NoPlot** and set *Plot* to **No**, as shown in Figure 1–36.

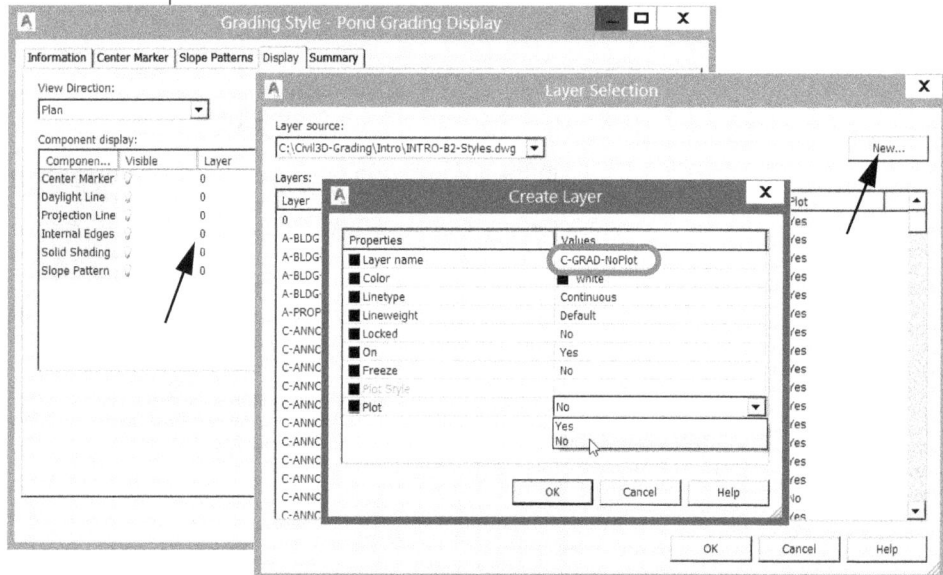

Figure 1–36

13. Click **OK** three times to close all of the dialog boxes.

14. Save the drawing.

Task 3 - Create grading criteria sets.

---

1. Continue working in the drawing from the previous task or open **INTRO-B3-Styles.dwg** from the *C:\Civil3D-Grading\ Intro* folder.

2. In the *Settings* tab, expand **Grading>Grading Criteria Set>Basic Set**.

   • Note that it includes the criteria for each type of projection that can be created in the AutoCAD Civil 3D software. When this set is used, the designer can select which slope/grades to use and the distance to which to grade. For Pond grading, you will want more control of the slopes to ensure that the correct specifications are used.

3. Right-click on Grading Criteria Sets and select **New**, as shown in Figure 1–37.

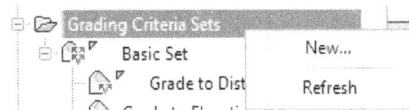

Figure 1–37

4. For the *Name*, type **Pond Grading**. Click **OK**.

5. In the *Settings* tab, right-click on the Pond Grading criteria that you just created and select **New**, as shown in Figure 1–38.

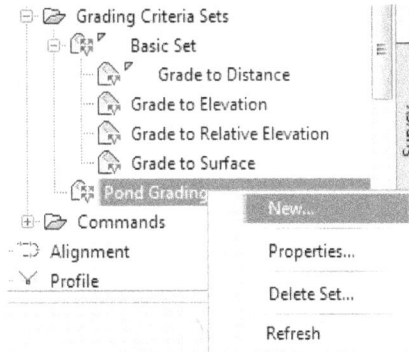

Figure 1–38

6. In the *Information* tab, for the *Name*, type **Interior**.

Note: You might have to save the drawing for the new criteria to be displayed.

7. In the *Criteria* tab, do the following, as shown in Figure 1–39:
   - Set *Target* to **Elevation**.
   - For *Elevation*, type **160**.
   - Set the *Format* of both the Cut Slope and Fill Slope projections to **Slope**.
   - For both the Cut Slope and Fill Slope, set *Slope* to **3**.
   - Select each **Lock** icon to lock each parameter and ensure that it cannot be changed when used in a grading.
   - Click **OK**.

Figure 1–39

8. Repeat Steps 5 to 7 to create the following grading criteria. Keep the same settings unless otherwise noted in the following table and shown in Figure 1–40.

Grading Criteria Name	Grading Method	Slop Projection	Lock
Rim	Distance, 6', Slope	Grade, 2%	Yes
Outer Slope to Surface	Surface, Cut/Fill Slope, Cut first	Slope, 3:1 cut, 3:1 fill	Yes

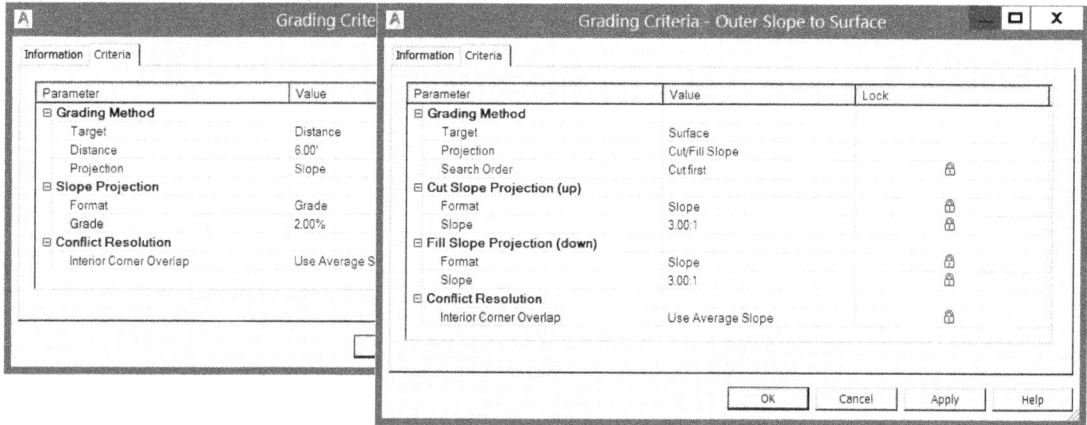

Figure 1–40

9. Save the drawing.

1.7 Surface Styles

Visualizing the grading results is best done using a predefined surface style. Components, such as watershed boundaries, slope arrows, and slope directions, can be turned on in a surface style to visually indicate which way the ground is sloping and draining, as shown in Figure 1–41.

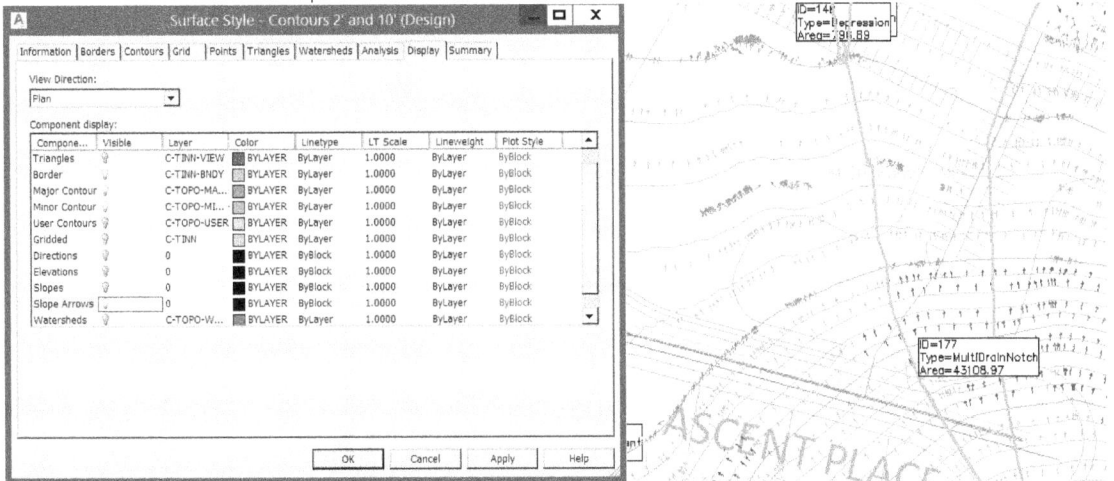

Figure 1–41

As with any styles, the *Display* tab determines which components are visible and how they display by setting their layer, color, linetype, etc., as shown in Figure 1–41.

The Surface Styles dialog box has additional tabs that also control the display of various surface components. For example, in the *Watersheds* tab the color, linetype, hatch pattern, etc. can be set for each watershed area type, as shown in Figure 1–42.

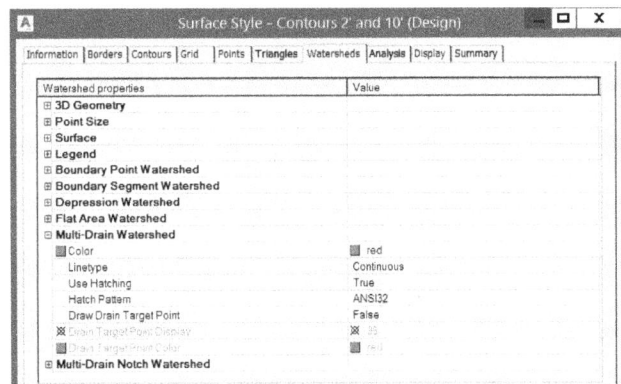

Figure 1–42

In the *Analysis* tab, the color scheme and method of division for the surface analysis ranges can be set, as shown in Figure 1–43. If the same number of ranges in for the slope analysis are constantly used, it can be set here. However, only equal interval, quantile, or standard deviation for the groups can be used. To set specific ranges, use the *Analysis* tab in the Surface Properties dialog box.

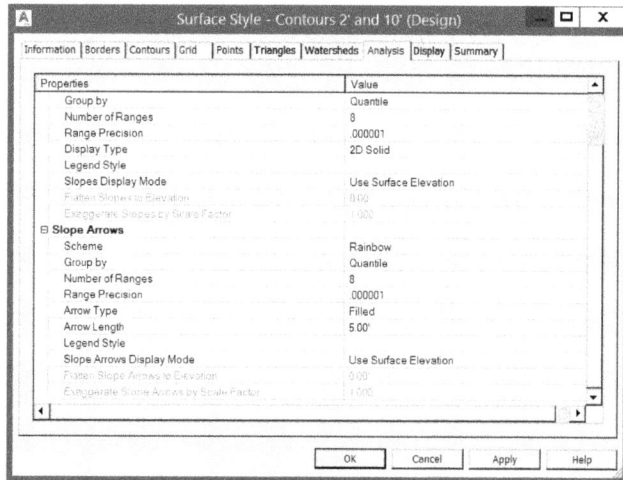

Figure 1–43

In the *Contours* tab, the contour interval, smoothing factor, and color scheme for ranges can be set. By default, only one range is defined, but more ranges can also be defined. With more contour ranges, the contours can be divided into groups similar to the *Analysis* tab, as shown in Figure 1–44.

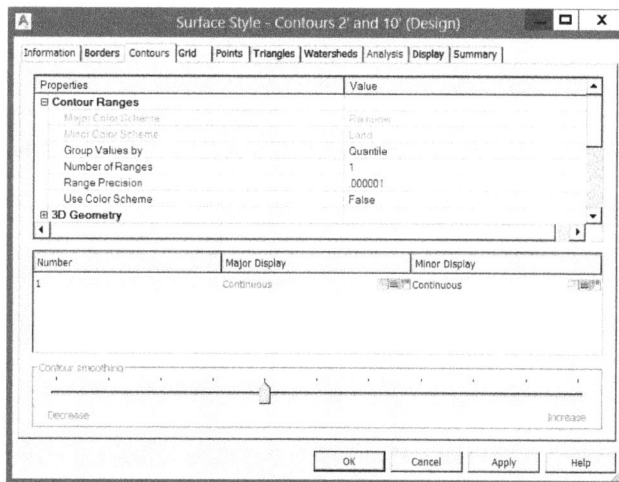

Figure 1–44

1.8 Sites Overview

In the AutoCAD Civil 3D software, sites are used as a collection point for common topologies that share relationships with each other. When an alignment and a parcel reside in the same site, they interact with each other. An alignment that resides in the same site as a parcel subdivides the parcel. Grading groups and feature lines also reside in sites and interact with each other when they share the same site. Each drawing can have multiple sites for various purposes, as shown in Figure 1–45.

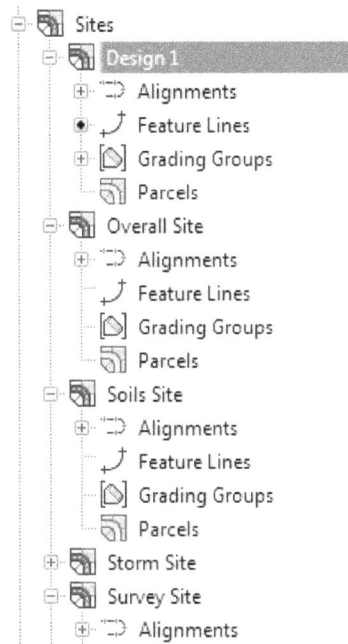

Figure 1–45

Sites for Design Options

It is recommended that you always start your project with an overall site in which you place all of the existing parcel linework. Then before adding alignments, feature lines, and grading groups to your design, you can create another site, label it **Design option 1**, and copy the parcels with which you are going to be working into that site, as shown in Figure 1–46.

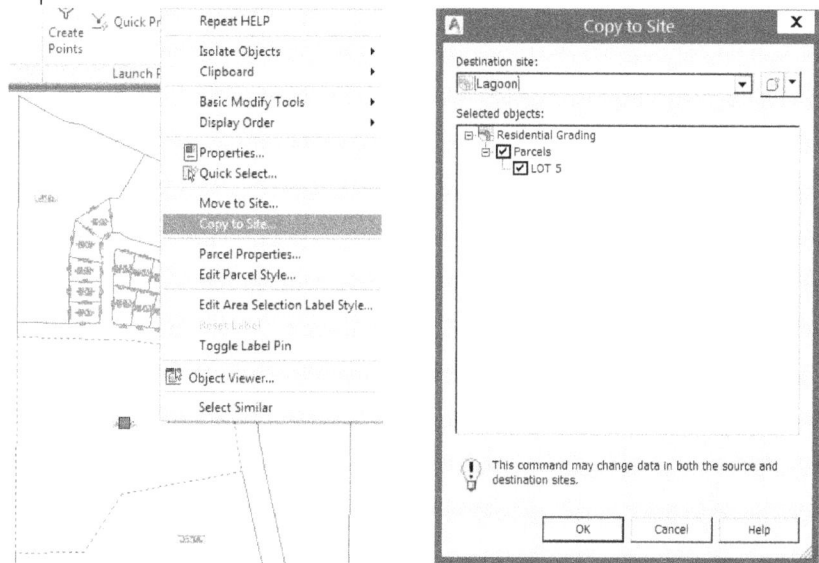

Figure 1–46

This enables you to provide more options to your clients without having many file versions in multiple drawings on a server. Once a client decides which design option to pursue, the other sites can easily be deleted, removing all of the design components within it at the same time, as shown in Figure 1–47.

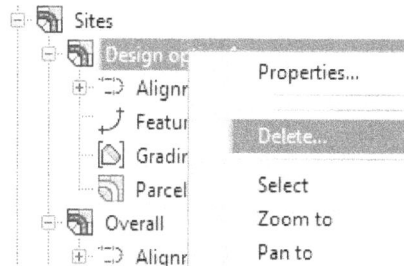

Figure 1–47

Creating Sites

To create a new site, select the *Prospector* tab in the Toolspace, right-click on Sites and select **New**. In the *Information* tab, type a name that is relevant to the entire team. In the *3D Geometry* tab, set the *Site Display Mode*, as shown in Figure 1–48.

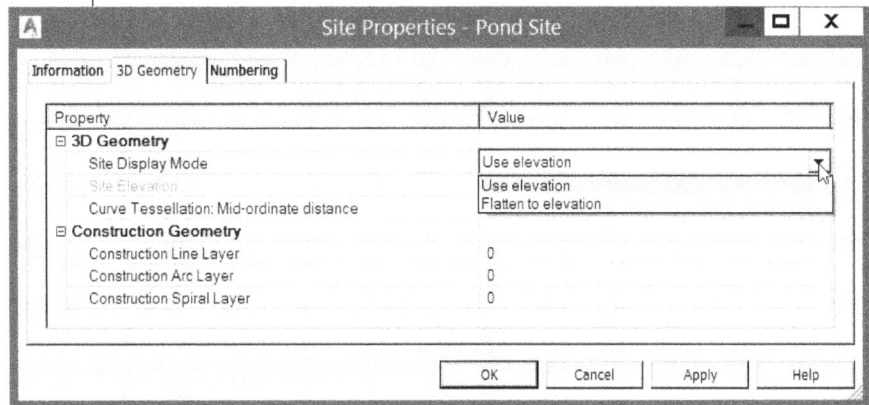

Figure 1–48

- It is recommended that you leave the default option as **Use elevation** so that the site's linework displays at its actual elevations, making it easier to view design intent from any direction in the object viewer.

- The optional **Flatten to elevation** option causes all of the site's linework to become 2D and to be located at the elevation that you set.

- In the *3D Geometry* tab, you can also set the layers on which the construction geometry is to be located.

The *Numbering* tab enables you to set the Automatic number for parcels and the counting interval to use for the next number, as shown in Figure 1–49.

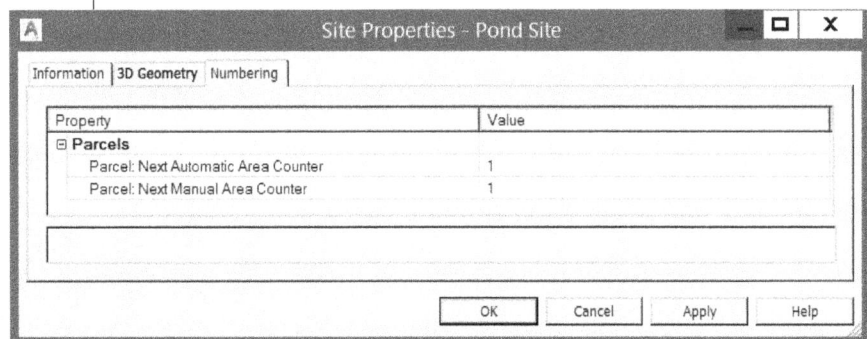

Figure 1–49

- Note: If you do not take the time to create the project site(s) before starting to create feature lines, parcels, or grading groups, a default site is created automatically, called **Site 1**. By default, alignments are placed in the alignments tree rather than in a specific site.

Practice 1c

Estimated time for completion: 10 minutes

Prepare for the Project

Practice Objective

- Create a surface style and sites in preparation for the grading project.

In this practice, you will add a surface style to the template to make it easier to display the site grading. You will also create some sites to give multiple design options to the client. Finally, you will save the drawing as a template to be used on multiple projects.

Task 1 - Create a surface style.

1. Continue working in the drawing from the previous practice or open **INTRO-C1-Styles.dwg** from the *C:\Civil3D-Grading\ Intro* folder.

2. In the *Settings* tab, expand **Surfaces>Surface Styles**. Right-click on Contours 2' and 10' (Design) and select **Copy**, as shown in Figure 1–50.

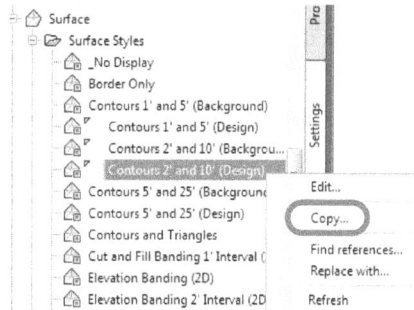

Figure 1–50

3. In the *Information* tab, type **Temporary Grading View**.

4. In the *Display* tab, turn on the layers **Slope Arrows** and **Watersheds**, as shown in Figure 1–51.

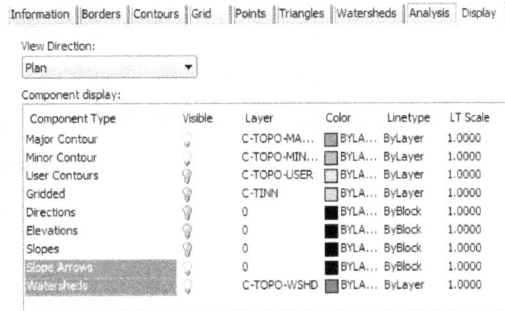

Figure 1–51

5. In the *Watersheds* tab, expand 3D Geometry. Verify that *Watershed Display Mode* is set to **Use Surface Elevation**, as shown in Figure 1–52.

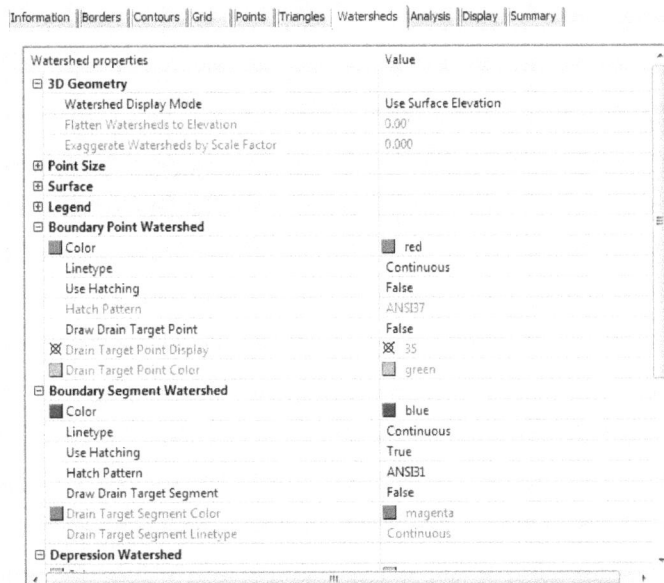

Figure 1–52

6. Click **OK** to close the dialog box.

7. Save the drawing.

Task 2 - Create sites.

1. Continue working in the drawing from the previous practice or open **INTRO-C2-Styles.dwg** from the *C:\Civil3D-Grading\ Intro* folder.

2. In the *Prospector* tab, right-click on Sites and select **New**.

3. In the *Information* tab, for the *Name*, type **Multi-Family**. For the description, type **Parcels, building pads, and parking lots for multi-family property**.

4. Click **OK** to close the dialog box and accept the defaults on the other tabs.

5. Repeat Steps 2 to 4 to create the following sites. Keep the same settings unless otherwise noted in the following table.

Site Name	Description
Pond Site	Storm water retention pond
Lagoon	Lagoon and wetland grading
Residential Grading	Single family lot grading

6. Save the drawing as **Grading Template.dwt** in the *C:\Civil 3D-Grading* folder.

Chapter Review Questions

1. What geometric shape is the Center Mark of a grading object?

   a. Diamond

   b. Circle

   c. Triangle

   d. Rectangle

2. Figure 1–53 shows each of the parts of a grading object. Match the numbers with their corresponding names.

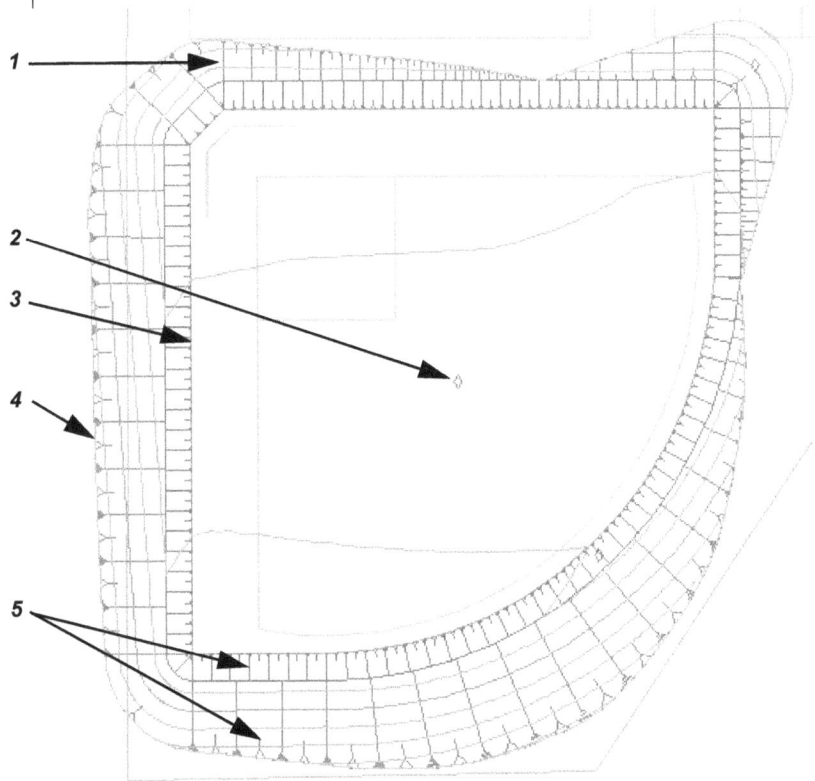

Figure 1–53

   a. Slope Pattern

   b. Center Mark

   c. Target Line

   d. Projection Line

   e. Base Line

3. When you edit a grading group, which of the following objects are updated?

   a. Feature Lines, Alignments, and Surfaces.

   b. Points, Surfaces, and Corridors.

   c. Surfaces and Corridors.

   d. Assemblies, Profiles, and Feature Lines.

4. How can you have the software automatically use one style when creating a feature line from objects and a different style when creating a feature line from scratch?

   a. Set it in Drawing Settings, in the *Ambient Settings* tab.

   b. Set it in Command Settings.

   c. Set it in Drawing Settings, in the *Object Layers* tab.

   d. Set it in the grading group style.

5. If you create a grading criteria with locked parameters, you can still change the parameters during the editing process.

   a. True

   b. False

6. What are sites used for? (Select all that apply.)

   a. To group the collection of common topology that share relationships with each other.

   b. To provide different design options within the same project.

   c. To house the sample sections for a grading design.

   d. To set the settings and styles to use for grading projects.

Parcel Grading

Site properties enable you to assign elevations to lot lines or treat them as 2D representations of parcels. The advantage of assigning elevations to parcel lines is that it helps to speed up the building of a grading model and to finish the ground surface. In this chapter, you create a residential grading plan in which the front of the lots take on elevations in reference to the corridor model. The back of the lots take on the existing ground surface elevations and designed elevations to accommodate walk out basements. Finally, retaining walls and other feature lines are added to indicate where the building footprint causes a drastic change in grade.

Learning Objectives in this Chapter

- Set parcel line elevations using the feature line Edit Elevation tools.
- Create wall breaklines representing large grade breaks to add definition to the site.
- Edit surfaces to make them more accurate.
- Create split points where parcel lines cross feature lines or share elevation points.

2.1 Setting Parcel Line Elevations

You can create and edit parcel lines in the AutoCAD® Civil® 3D software. If site properties are set correctly, parcels can be assigned elevations. Once parcel lines have been assigned elevations, they can be added to a surface as breaklines to grade a site. The tools that are used to edit feature lines can also be used to assign elevations to parcel lines.

There are two places that enable you to edit parcel, feature line, or survey figure elevations. The first is in the *Parcel Segment* contextual tab>Edit Elevations panel and the second is in the *Parcel Segment* contextual tab>Edit Elevations panel in the Edit Elevations vista.

Site Properties

Before you can edit parcel line elevations, you need to ensure that the site they are in is set up to use the elevations you assign. In the *Prospector* tab, expand the Sites tree, right-click on the site in which the parcels reside and select **Properties**, as shown in Figure 2–1.

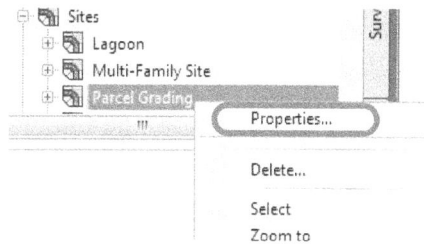

Figure 2–1

In the Site Properties dialog box, go to the *3D Geometry* tab. Change the *Site Display Mode* to **Use elevation**, as shown in Figure 2–2.

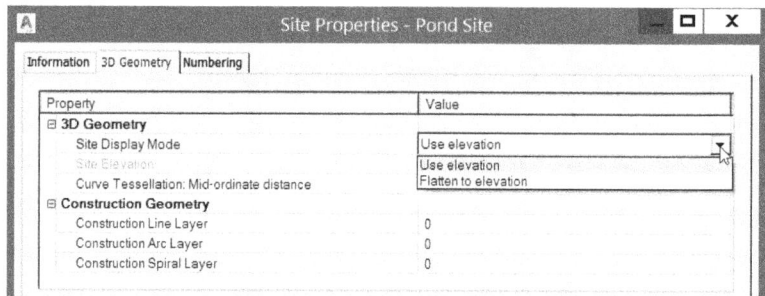

Figure 2–2

Move/Copy Parcels to Another Site

Next you need to ensure that all of the parcels are in the site in which you plan to work. To put them in the correct site you can move them or make a copy of them.

Move Parcels to Another Site

To move parcels to another site, select the parcel segment(s). In the *Parcel Segments* contextual tab>Modify panel, click

(Move to Site), as shown in Figure 2–3.

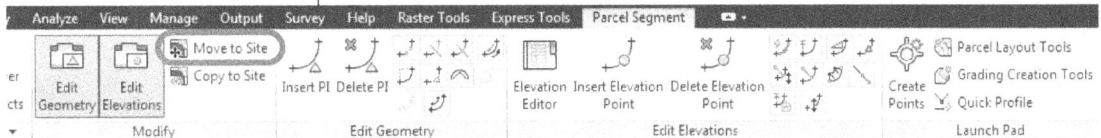

Figure 2–3

When parcels move to a new site, their style changes to the default parcel style for the drawing. A new parcel is also created in the original site that takes on the overall outline of all of the parcels moved, as shown in Figure 2–4.

Figure 2–4

If your intention is not to create an overall parcel in place of the parcels you move to a new site, you can select the area label when selecting parcels. This moves the selected parcels along with any surrounding parcels without changing their styles.

Copy Parcels to Another Site

To copy parcels to another site, select the parcel segment(s) or their area labels. In the *Parcel Segments* contextual tab>Modify panel, click ⬚ (Copy to Site), as shown in Figure 2–5.

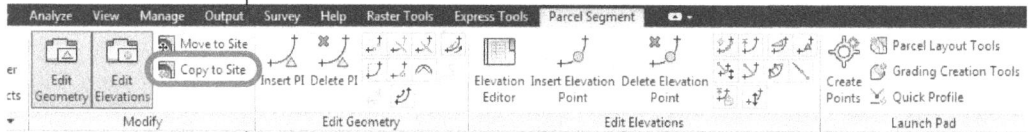

Figure 2–5

Note that copying the parcels and placing them in a new site causes them to lose any interaction they have with other objects, such as feature lines, alignments, or grading groups. It is recommended that you create a style that turns off the display of parcel segments. You can then set the parcels in the site that you are not working with to that style to ensure that you are working with the correct site's parcels as you add elevations and make other edits.

Edit Elevations Panel

Select a parcel segment. In the *Parcel Segment* contextual tab> Modify panel, click ⬚ (Edit Elevations) to display the Edit Elevations panel. The tools in the Edit Elevations panel are as follows:

Icon	Command	Description
	Elevation Editor	Opens the Elevation Editor vista in which you can edit each vertex elevation of feature lines, survey figures, and parcel lines.
	Insert Elevation Point	Adds an elevation control to the feature line. Elevation points provide an elevation control without creating a whole new vertex. These points are Z-controls without X- or Y-components.
	Delete Elevation Point	Permits vertical grade breaks to be removed anywhere other than horizontal vertices.
	Quick Elevation Edit	Displays elevation values at vertices and elevation points along a feature line or parcel line. Selecting one of these points enables you to edit it in the Command Line.
	Edit Elevations	Edits elevations at vertices along a feature line, parcel line, or 3D polyline as you step through each vertex in the Command Line.

	Set Grade/Slope Between Points	Sets the grade or slope between two points on a feature line, parcel line, or 3D polyline. The elevations of the points between the two selected points are interpolated to maintain the grade/slope/elevation/elevation difference entered.
	Insert High/Low Elevation Point	Inserts a high or low break point where two grades intersect on a feature line, survey figure, parcel line, or 3D polyline.
	Raise/Lower by Reference	Raises or lowers a feature line, survey figure, parcel line, or 3D polyline a specified grade or slope from a selected COGO point or surface elevation.
	Set Elevation by Reference	Sets a single vertex elevation on a feature line, survey figure, parcel line, or 3D polyline a specified grade or slope from a selected COGO point or surface elevation.
	Adjacent Elevations by Reference	Sets elevations of one feature line, survey figure, parcel line, or 3D polyline based on a grade/slope/elevation/elevation difference from points on another feature running alongside the first feature.
	Grade Extension by Reference	Extends the grade of one feature line, survey figure, parcel line, or 3D polyline across a gap to set the elevations of another feature and maintain the same slope.
	Elevations from Surface	Takes the elevations of all of the vertices from the surface if no vertices are selected. If a vertex is selected, it takes the surface elevation for just that vertex.
	Raise/Lower	Raises or lowers all of the feature line vertices by the elevation entered.

Edit Elevations Panel

The second location where parcel line elevations can be assigned is in the Elevation Editor vista. To access these tools, select a parcel segment. This displays the *Parcel Segment* tab in the Ribbon, as shown in Figure 2–6.

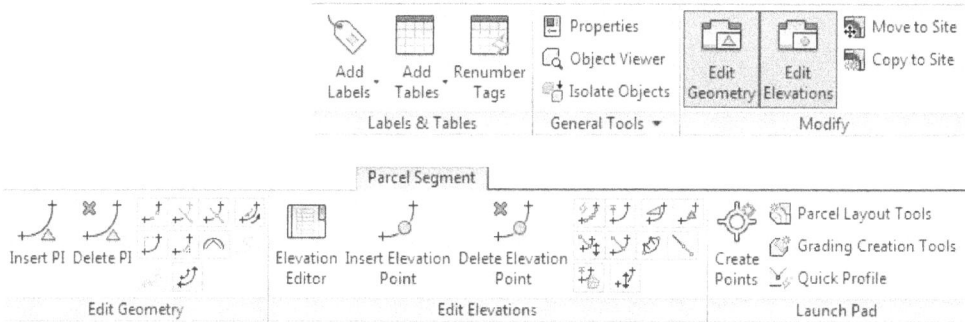

Figure 2–6

In the Modify panel, select **Edit Elevations** to display the Edit Elevations panel, as shown in Figure 2–7.

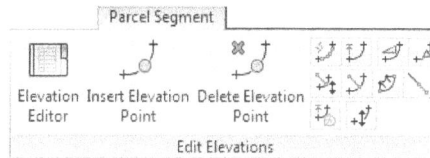

Figure 2–7

In the Edit Elevations panel, select the **Elevation Editor** to open the Elevation Editor panorama, as shown in Figure 2–8.

Station	Elevation	Length	Grade Ahead	Gra
0+00.00	175.59'	6.63'	-4.51%	
0+06.63	175.29'	7.27'	4.23%	
0+13.90	175.60'	6.63'	4.30%	
0+20.53	175.88'	27.11'	4.23%	
0+47.64	177.03'	6.63'	-4.30%	
0+54.27	176.74'	15.39'	4.23%	
0+69.67	177.39'	86.01'	-5.71%	
1+55.68	172.48'	15.39'	-0.91%	
1+71.07	172.34'	6.63'	-8.07%	
1+77.70	171.81'	27.11'	-1.02%	
2+04.81	171.53'	6.63'	4.26%	
2+11.44	171.81'	7.27'	-2.54%	
2+18.71	171.63'	6.63'	-3.95%	
2+25.34	171.37'	27.11'	-2.36%	
2+52.45	170.73'	6.63'	3.18%	
2+59.08	170.94'	7.27'	-2.54%	
2+66.36	170.75'	6.63'	-3.18%	
2+72.99	170.54'	27.11'	-2.54%	
3+00.09	169.85'	6.63'	3.18%	
3+06.73	170.07'	7.27'	-0.66%	
3+14.00	170.02'	6.63'	-5.25%	
3+20.63	169.67'	27.11'	-1.91%	

Figure 2–8

The Elevation Editor contains the properties of the vertices of the selected feature lines or lot lines. The properties for each vertex include a station, elevation, length, grade ahead, and grade back. To make changes to a station's elevation, select the row in which it is located. Selecting one or more rows in the panorama causes a green triangle to display in the drawing indicating which vertex (or vertices) you are working with, as shown in Figure 2–9.

- Stations displaying a ▲ triangular symbol to the left of their station can be edited horizontally and vertically.

- Stations displaying a ◉ circular symbol to the left of their station are elevation points and can only be edited vertically.

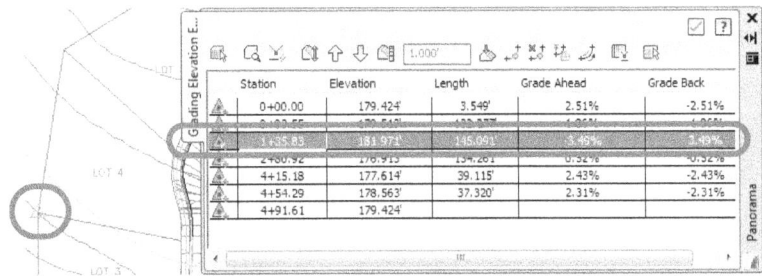

Figure 2–9

Once the required vertices have been selected, you can use the tools at the top of the panorama to change the elevation of each vertex or the slope between vertices. The function of each tool is as follows:

Icon	Command	Description
	Select Feature Line	Selects the feature line, parcel line, or survey figure.
	Zoom To	Zooms to the selected vertex or vertices.
	Quick Profile	Creates a profile view of the selected feature line.
	Raise/Lower	Enables you to type an elevation value in the input field to raise or lower selected vertices to the specified elevation.
	Raise Incrementally	Raises the vertex or vertices selected by the increment set in the input field.
	Lower Incrementally	Lowers the vertex or vertices selected by the increment set in the input field.

	Set Increment	Enables you to type a distance value in the input field to raise or lower selected vertices by a specified increment.
	Input Field	Type a distance or elevation to raise or lower selected vertices.
	Flatten Grade or Elevations	Flattens selected vertices to a constant elevation or sets a constant grade.
	Insert Elevation Point	Enables you to add additional vertical grade breaks without having to add additional horizontal vertices.
	Delete Elevation Point	Permits vertical grade breaks to be removed anywhere other than horizontal vertices.
	Elevations from Surface	Takes the vertex or vertices elevations from the specified surface.
	Reverse the Direction	Changes the direction from which the feature line is stationed.
	Show Grade Breaks Only	Reduces the number of vertices displayed in the table by only displaying feature line stations where the grade changes.
	Unselect All Rows	Removes all rows from the current selection.

How To: Use Elevations from Surface

1. In the *Modify* tab>Design panel, click ⬡ (Parcel) to open the *Parcel* contextual tab.

2. In the *Parcel* contextual tab>Modify panel, click ⬡ (Edit Elevations) to open the Edit Elevations panel.

3. In the Parcel contextual tab>Edit Elevations panel, click

   ⬡ (Elevations from Surface) to assign surface elevations to the vertices of the parcels.

4. In the Set Elevations from Surface dialog box, select the surface from which to set the pull elevations.

5. Determine whether intermediate grade break points are required. If not, do not select the **Insert intermediate grade break points** option, as shown in Figure 2–10. Click **OK** to close the dialog box.

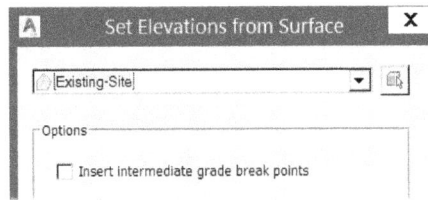

Figure 2–10

6. In the drawing, select the parcel segments that need to be changed.

How To: Use Edit Elevations

1. In the *Modify* tab>Design panel, click ⬚ (Parcel) to display the *Parcel* contextual tab.

2. In the *Parcel* contextual tab>Modify panel, click ⬚ (Edit Elevations) to open the Edit Elevations panel.

3. In the *Parcel* tab>Edit Elevations panel, click ⬚ (Edit Elevations).

4. In the drawing, the current vertex is highlighted with a green triangle, as shown in Figure 2–11. In the Command Line, you have the following options: **Elevation**, **Previous**, **Grade**, **SLope**, **SUrface**, **Insert**, or **eXit**.

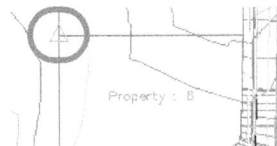

Figure 2–11

5. If the option is set to **Elevation** (the default until a different option is selected), the current elevation displays in brackets <188.000>. In the Command Line, you can press <Enter> to accept the elevation and go to the next vertex, type an elevation to override the current elevation, or type the capital letter(s) for the required option. The expected results for the selected options are as follows.

Type	Option	Description
E	**Elevation**	Sets the elevation to a typed in value.
P	**Previous**	Changes the selected vertex to the vertex just before the current one.
G	**Grade**	Sets the slope out to the percent typed in the Command Line.

SL	Slope	Sets the slope out to the rise/run ratio typed in the Command Line. (Note that you type the rise and the run is a default value of 1.)
SU	Surface	Sets the elevation at the selected surface value for that location.
I	Insert	Inserts a new vertex between the current and next vertex along the feature line, survey figure, or parcel.
X	Exit	Ends the command

How To: Use Set Elevation by Reference

1. In the *Modify* tab>Design panel, click (Parcel) to open the *Parcel* contextual tab.

2. In the *Parcel* contextual tab>Modify panel, click (Edit Elevations) to open the Edit Elevations panel.

3. In the *Parcel* tab>Edit Elevations panel, click (Set Elevations by Reference).

4. In the drawing, pick a point to reference (from a surface, feature line, another parcel, survey figure, or corridor model).

5. In the drawing, select the parcel segment, feature line, or survey figure to edit.

6. In the drawing, specify the vertex or elevation point to adjust by clicking near it.

7. In the Command Line, enter a grade or select one of the other two options for setting the elevation. You can type **S** to set the slope or **D** to set a difference in elevation.

8. Press <Esc> to end the command.

Setting elevations by reference does not create a link to the referenced point. If the referenced point changes, the parcel lines, feature line, or survey figures need to be updated manually.

Practice 2a

Estimated time for completion: 10 minutes

Set Parcel Line Elevations

Practice Objective

• Assign elevations to parcel lines using the Edit Elevation tools.

In this practice you will review the site and prepare the drawing. You will then set the parcel elevations to a surface, set parcel elevations by design, and set parcel elevations by reference.

Task 1 - Review the site and prepare the drawing.

1. Open **PARCELS-A1-Grading.dwg** from the *C:\Civil3D -Grading\Parcels* folder.

2. In the *Prospector* tab, expand **Sites>Residential Grading> Parcels**. Note which parcels reside in this site, as shown in Figure 2–12.

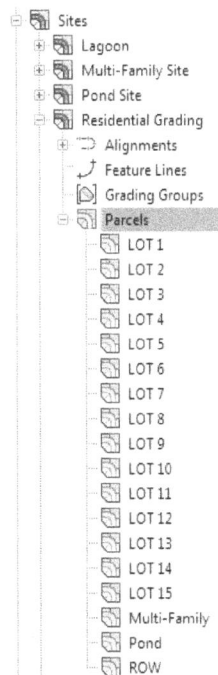

Sites
  Lagoon
  Multi-Family Site
  Pond Site
  Residential Grading
    Alignments
    Feature Lines
    Grading Groups
    Parcels
      LOT 1
      LOT 2
      LOT 3
      LOT 4
      LOT 5
      LOT 6
      LOT 7
      LOT 8
      LOT 9
      LOT 10
      LOT 11
      LOT 12
      LOT 13
      LOT 14
      LOT 15
      Multi-Family
      Pond
      ROW

Figure 2–12

3. In the *View* tab>Views panel, select **Site** to view the entire site.

4. In the *Prospector* tab, select the **Pond**, **Multi-family**, and **ROW** parcels. Right-click and select **Select**, as shown in Figure 2–13.

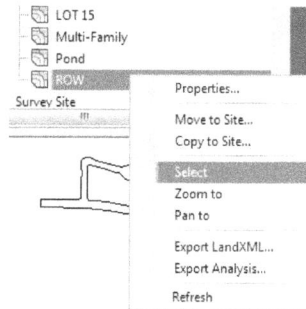

Figure 2–13

5. In the *Parcels* contextual tab>expanded General Tools panel, click (Send to Back), as shown in Figure 2–14. Press <Esc> to release the selection.

Figure 2–14

Task 2 - Set parcel elevations to a surface.

---

1. Continue working in the drawing from the previous task or open **PARCELS-A2-Grading.dwg** from the *C:\Civil3D-Grading\Parcels* folder.

2. In the *View* tab>Views panel, select **Single Family Lots** to zoom in on the residential area to be graded.

3. In the drawing, select **Lot 1** by selecting its area label.

4. In the *Parcel* contextual tab>Modify panel, click (Edit Elevations) to open the Edit Elevations panel.

5. In the *Parcel* contextual tab>Edit Elevations panel, click (Elevations from Surface) to assign surface elevations to the vertices of the parcels.

6. In the Set Elevations from Surface dialog box, select **Existing Ground** for the surface. Do not select the **Insert intermediate grade break points** option, as shown in Figure 2–15. Click **OK** to close the dialog box.

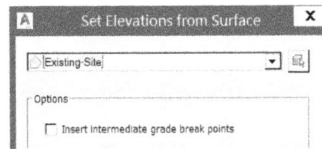

Figure 2–15

7. In the Command Line, you are prompted to select objects. Type **M** and press <Enter> to permit crossing window selections. Select all 15 single family lot segments, the Multi-Family parcel segments, and the Pond parcel segments (17 Total), as shown in Figure 2–16. Press <Enter> to end the selection and exit the command.

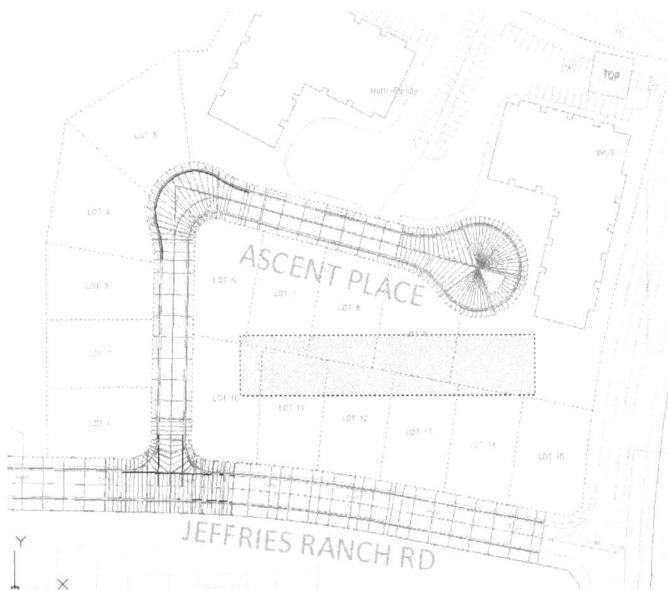

Figure 2–16

8. Verify that elevations were assigned by opening the Elevation Editor and selecting some different parcel segments. In the *Parcel* contextual tab>Edit Elevations panel, click

(Elevation Editor) to open the Elevation Editor vista.

9. When prompted to select objects, select the parcel segments of one of the parcels. Verify that elevations are assigned to each vertex. Check other parcels by clicking 🔲 (Select Feature) to select them without closing the Elevation Editor vista, as shown in Figure 2–17.

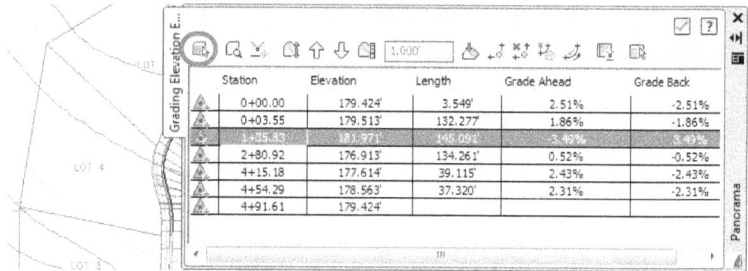

Figure 2–17

10. In the Edit Elevations vista, click ☑ to close the vista.

11. Save the drawing.

Task 3 - Set parcel elevations by design.

The lots on the west side of Ascent Pl have been assigned elevations to ensure that the pond grading elevations to their west coordinate with each other.

1. Continue working in the drawing from the previous task or open **PARCELS-A3-Grading.dwg** from the C:\Civil3D-Grading\Parcels folder.

2. In the *View* tab>Views panel, select **Storm Pond** to zoom in on the pond area.

3. In the drawing, select the parcel segments representing the pond boundary. In the *Parcels* contextual tab> expand the General Tools panel and click 🔲 (Bring to Front), as shown in Figure 2–18.

Figure 2–18

4. In the drawing, select the pond's parcel segments again if you released the selection.

5. In the *Parcel* tab>Edit Elevations panel, click ⨎ (Edit Elevations). Press <Enter> until the green triangle displays at the northern-most vertex of Lot 5, as shown in Figure 2–19.

Figure 2–19

6. Type **180.5** and press <Enter> for the elevation. The green triangle should move to the next vertex when you press <Enter> to assign the remaining elevations, as shown in Figure 2–20. Press <Esc> twice when done to release the pond segments.

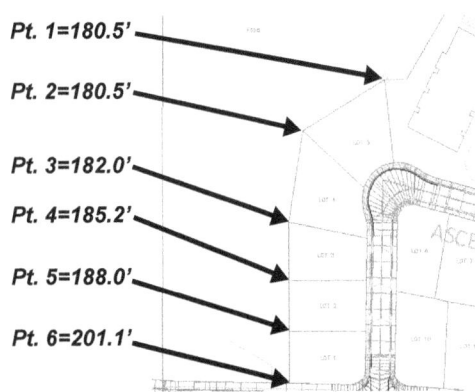

Pt. 1=180.5'
Pt. 2=180.5'
Pt. 3=182.0'
Pt. 4=185.2'
Pt. 5=188.0'
Pt. 6=201.1'

Figure 2–20

7. Lots 1-5, in the Residential Grading site, share these vertices. Therefore, their elevations also update. Verify this by opening the Elevation Editor vista and selecting the parcel segments of one of the parcels. In the *Parcel* contextual tab>Edit Elevations panel, click ▧ (Elevation Editor) to open the Elevation Editor vista.

8. Save the drawing.

Task 4 - Set parcel elevations by reference.

Setting elevations by reference does not create a link. If the corridor design changes, the parcel lines need to be updated manually.

In this task, you will assign elevations to the front of the lots according to the corridor elevations. At vertices that do not fall directly on the corridor model, use a -2% grade if it falls outside the corridor and a 2% grade if it falls inside the corridor model.

1. Continue working in the drawing from the previous task or open **PARCELS-A4-Grading.dwg** from the *C:\Civil3D-Grading\Parcels* folder.

2. In the *View* tab>Views panel, select **Lot1** to zoom in on the area to be graded.

3. In the drawing, select the Corridor models (**Intersection**, **Ascent Pl**, and **Jeffries Ranch Rd**). In the *Corridors* contextual tab>expanded General Tools panel, click

   (Bring to Front). Press <Esc> to end the selection.

4. In the drawing, select the **Lot 1** parcel segments. In the *Parcel* tab>Edit Elevations panel, click (Set Elevations by Reference).

5. In the drawing, select the endpoint of the corridor section line directly north of the first parcel corner for the reference point, as shown in Figure 2–21.

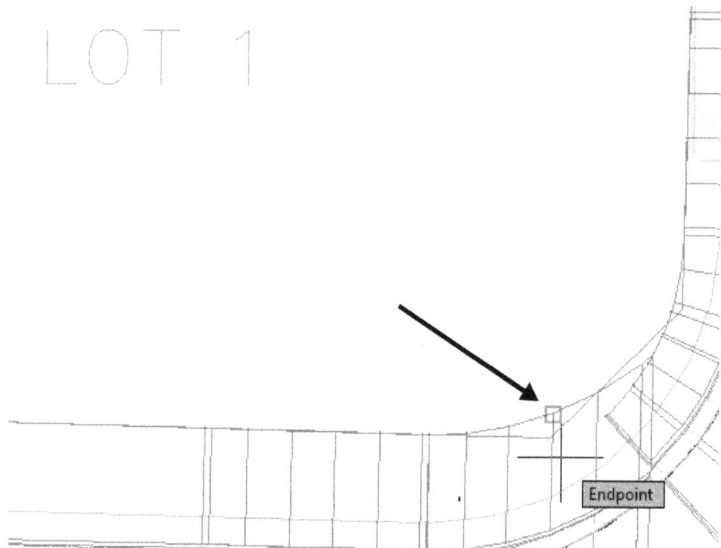

Figure 2–21

6. In the drawing, select the parcel vertex near the corridor section line that you selected for the reference point, as shown in Figure 2–22.

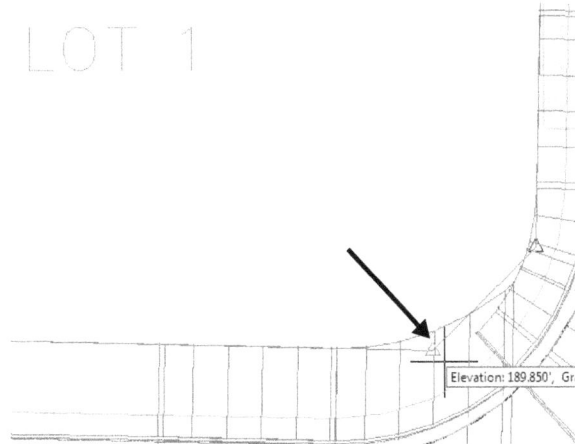

Elevation: 189.850', Gra

Figure 2–22

7. At the Command Line, verify that it is prompting you for the grade. If not, type **G** and press <Enter>. Since the parcel line is up slope from the end of the corridor, type **2** to maintain the corridor grade of 2%. Press <Esc> to end the command.

8. Repeat Steps 5 to 8 to set the elevation for the next vertex running counter-clockwise along the Lot 1 perimeter, as shown in Figure 2–23.

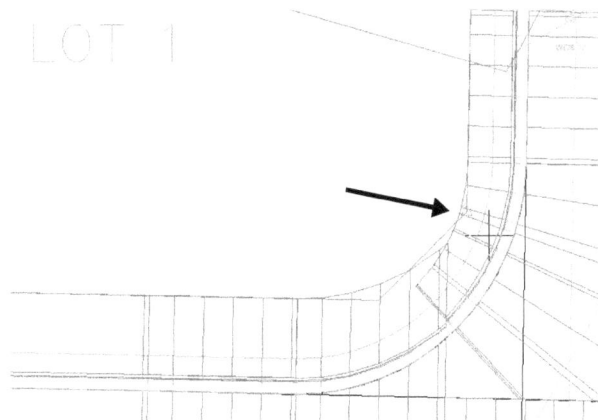

Figure 2–23

9. In the *Parcel* tab>Edit Elevations panel, click ⤴ (Set Elevations by Reference).

10. Using the nearest Osnap, select a point on the corridor near the reference point, as shown in Figure 2–24. This point should be perpendicular from the parcel corner to the corridor.

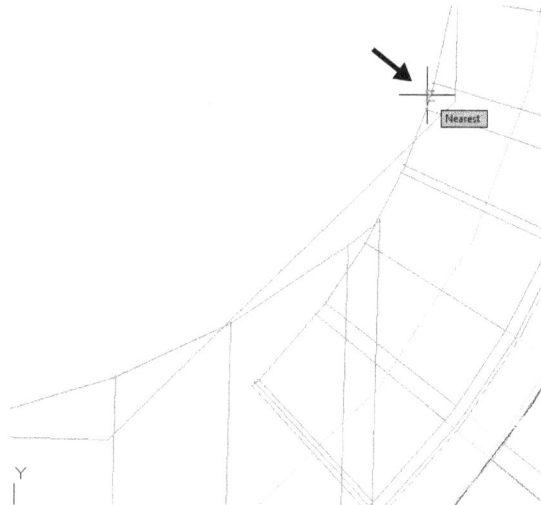

Figure 2–24

11. In the drawing, select the parcel corner near the reference point for the vertex to change, as shown in Figure 2–25.

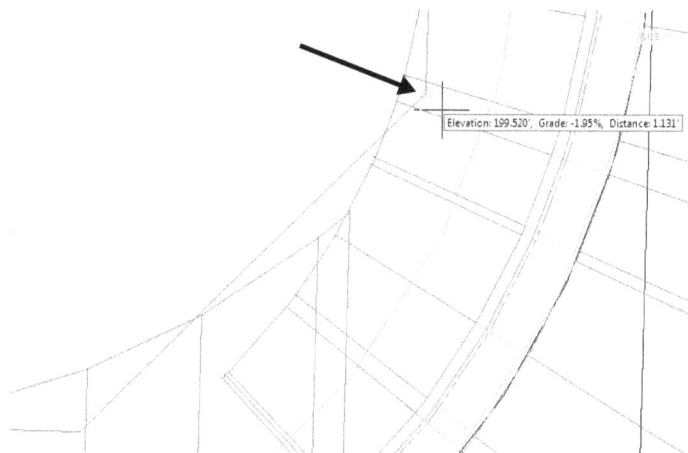

Figure 2–25

12. Since the parcel line falls inside the corridor being referenced, type **2** and press <Enter> to indicate a positive 2% grade change in elevation. Press <Esc> to end the command.

13. In the drawing, select the **Lot 1** parcel segments again. In the *Parcel* tab>Edit Elevations panel, click ⤴ (Set Elevations by Reference).

14. In the drawing, select the nearest point on the corridor feature line at the north-east parcel corner for the reference point, as shown in Figure 2–26.

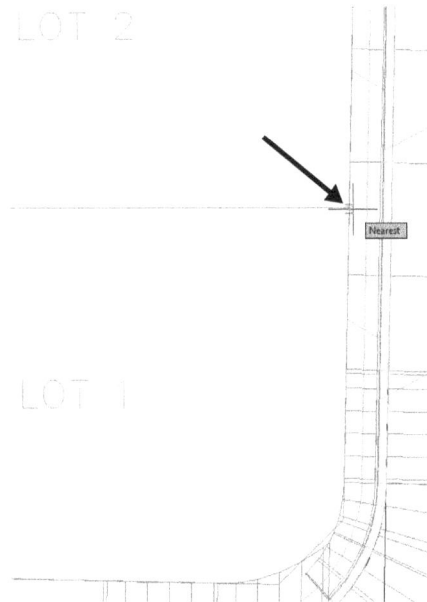

Figure 2–26

15. In the drawing, select the parcel corner near the reference point for the vertex to change, as shown in Figure 2–27.

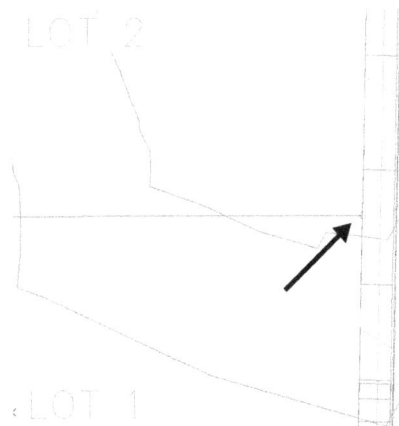

Figure 2–27

16. Since the parcel line falls directly on the corridor being referenced, type **0** to indicate that there is no change in elevation. Press <Esc> to end the command.

17. Repeat this process for all of the lot corners adjacent to or touching the corridor model, including the Multi-Family parcel.

   • At vertices that do not fall directly on the corridor model, ensure you pick points that are perpendicular to the corridor model and then use a -2% grade if it falls outside of the corridor and a 2% grade if it falls inside the corridor model.

18. Save the drawing.

2.2 Retaining Walls

Adding elevations to parcel segments helps define the finished grade. However, it does not do anything until you add them to a surface. This section covers adding breaklines to a surface since you add parcel segments to surfaces as breaklines.

Breaklines created by Proximity leave the original polylines in the drawing even though they are defined as a Standard breakline. This Standard definition can be inserted into the drawing and manipulated. The original line can be deleted.

A breakline created as a Standard breakline is linked to the original line in the drawing. If this line is deleted, the breakline definition is also deleted. The different breakline definitions are as follows:

Breakline Type	Description
Standard	Creates a breakline that is defined by selecting 3D lines, feature lines, parcel segments, survey figures, and 3D polylines.
Proximity	Creates a breakline that is defined by drawing or selecting a feature line, parcel segment, survey figure, or polyline within the extents of the surface boundary. The location and elevation of each vertex is determined by the nearest surface point.
Wall	A wall breakline is stored as a standard breakline but is defined differently. You provide an offset side, elevation difference at each vertex or along the entire breakline.
Non-destructive	Creates a breakline that is defined using grading feature lines and open or closed AutoCAD® objects. A non-destructive breakline does not affect the original surface.

How To: Add parcel segments to a surface

1. To create a surface, in the *Home* tab>Create Ground Data panel, expand the Surfaces drop-down list and click

    (Create Surface).
2. In the Create Surface dialog box, type a name and description, and select a style. Click **OK** to close the dialog box.

3. In the *Prospector* tab, expand Surfaces>[Surface you are working with]>Definition. Right-click on Breaklines and select **Add**, as shown in Figure 2–28.

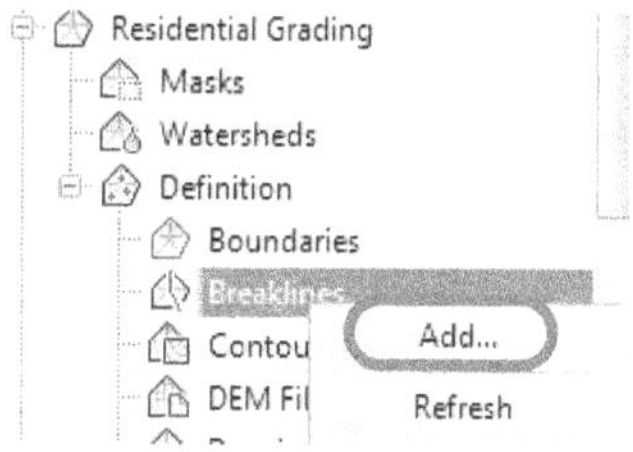

Figure 2–28

4. In the Add Breaklines dialog box, type a description and set the type to **Standard** if elevations are already assigned to the parcels. Add weeding and supplementing factors as required. Click **OK** to close the dialog box.
5. Select the parcel segments in the drawing. Press <Enter> when done.

How To: Add Wall Breaklines to a Surface

1. Draw a feature line, parcel line, survey figure, or 3D Polyline.
2. In the *Prospector* tab>expand Surfaces>[Surface you are working with]>Definition. Right-click on Breaklines and select **Add**, as shown in Figure 2–29.

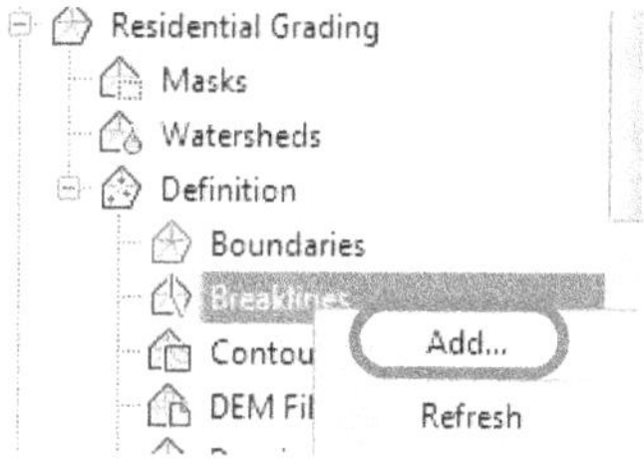

Figure 2–29

3. In the Add Breaklines dialog box, type a description and set the type to **Wall**, as shown in Figure 2–30.

Figure 2–30

4. Add weeding and supplementing factors as required. Click **OK** to close the dialog box.
5. In the drawing, select the object you drew in Step 1. Press <Enter> when done.
6. Pick a point on the side to offset the original feature line.
7. Type **I** to set the height of the wall at each individual vertex or press <Enter> to accept the default **All** to set the height of all of the vertices at the same time.
8. In the Command Line, type a value for the difference in elevation or type **E** to set the actual elevation.

2.3 Editing Surfaces

Once the basic information has been added to a surface definition, you might need to edit the surface to make it more accurate. Surface edits can be done by selecting the surface. Then, in the *Tin Surface* contextual tab>Modify panel, expand

(Edit Surface) to display the available tools, as shown in Figure 2–31.

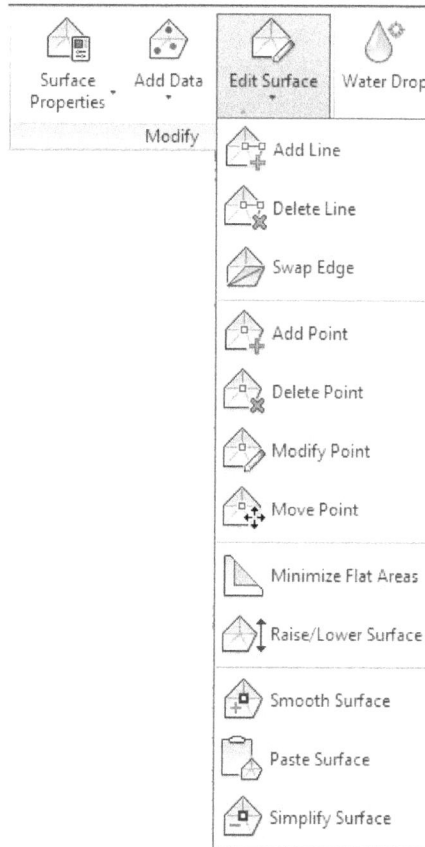

Figure 2–31

The tools in the Edit Surface drop-down list are as follows:

Icon	Command	Description
	Add Line	Adds additional triangle line to a surface to modify how the surface triangulates. Note that the surface triangles must be visible in the style to use this command.

	Delete Line	Removes triangle or grid lines from a surface to modify how the surface triangulates. Note that the surface triangles or grid lines must be visible in the style to use this command.
	Swap Edge	Changes the direction of two triangle faces within a surface to modify how the surface triangulates. Note that the surface triangles must be visible in the style to use this command.
	Add Point	Adds a point to a surface to modify how the surface triangulates. Note that the surface points must be visible in the style to use this command.
	Delete Point	Removes unnecessary or inaccurate points from a surface to modify how the surface triangulates. Note that the surface points must be visible in the style to use this command.
	Modify Point	Modifies the elevation of a surface point to modify how the surface triangulates. Note that the surface points must be visible in the style to use this command.
	Move Point	Moves a surface point to a new location without changing its elevation to modify how the surface triangulates. Note that the surface points must be visible in the style to use this command.
	Minimize Flat Areas	Reduces the number of adjacent triangles containing the same elevation and modifies how the surface triangulates to make it more accurately represent a real-world surface.
	Raise/Lower Surface	Adds/Subtracts a specified distance to a surface and changes the elevations of every triangle by the same amount.
	Smooth Surface	Adds points at system-determined elevations using Natural Neighbor Interpolation (NNI) or Kriging methods to smooth contour lines without making them overlap.
	Paste Surface	Combines two surfaces by overriding triangles in the destination surface with triangles from the pasted surface. Note that the paste order is key because elevations are taken from the last surface pasted.
	Simplify Surface	Removes unnecessary points from a surface to reduce its size while preserving its accuracy.

How To: Paste Surfaces Together

1. In the drawing, select the destination surface (it is going to be overridden by another surface.
2. In the *Tin Surface* contextual tab>Modify panel, expand the Edit Surface drop-down list and click ⬚ (Paste Surface).
3. In the Select Surface dialog box, select the surface(s) to paste into the destination surface, as shown in Figure 2–32.

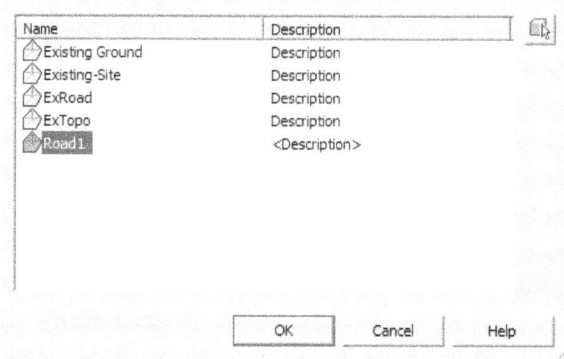

Figure 2–32

4. Click **OK** to close the dialog box.

Practice 2b

Estimated time for completion: 10 minutes

Create and Edit the Surface to Add Retaining Walls

Practice Objective

- Create wall breaklines to display drastic grade breaks and create a 7 foot minimum wall.

In this practice you will create a finish ground surface to grade the single-family area. You will then paste the surfaces together and add wall breaklines to the surface.

Task 1 - Create a finish ground surface to grade the single-family area.

1. Continue working in the drawing from the previous practice or open **PARCELS-B1-Grading.dwg** from the *C:\Civil3D-Grading\Parcels* folder.

2. In the *View* tab>Views panel, select **Single Family Lots** as the view to zoom into the residential area.

3. In the *Home* tab>Create Ground Data panel, click ✍ (Create Surface).

4. In the Create Surface dialog box, for the *Name* type **Residential Grading**, for the *Description* type **Grading from parcel segment elevations and additional breaklines**, and for the *Style* select **Temporary Grading View**, as shown in Figure 2–33.

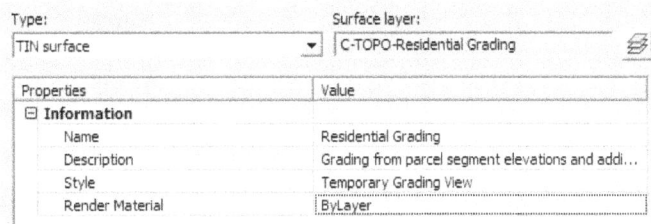

Type:	Surface layer:	
TIN surface	C-TOPO-Residential Grading	🗁

Properties	Value
⊟ **Information**	
Name	Residential Grading
Description	Grading from parcel segment elevations and addi...
Style	Temporary Grading View
Render Material	ByLayer

Figure 2–33

5. Click **OK** to close the dialog box.

6. In the *Prospector* tab, expand **Surfaces>Residential Grading>Definition**. Right-click on Breaklines and select **Add**. In the Add Breaklines dialog box, for the *Description* type **Residential Parcels**, as shown in Figure 2–34. Click **OK** to accept the other defaults and close the dialog box.

Description:
Residential Parcels

Type:
Standard

File link options:
Break link to file

□ Weeding factors

Distance:
5.000

Angle:
4.0000 (d)

Supplementing factors

□ Distance:
100.000'

Mid-ordinate distance:
1.000'

| OK | Cancel | Help |

Figure 2–34

7. Select the 15 single-family parcel segments and the one Multi-Family parcel segment to the north (16 total), as shown in Figure 2–35. Press <Enter> to end the selection.

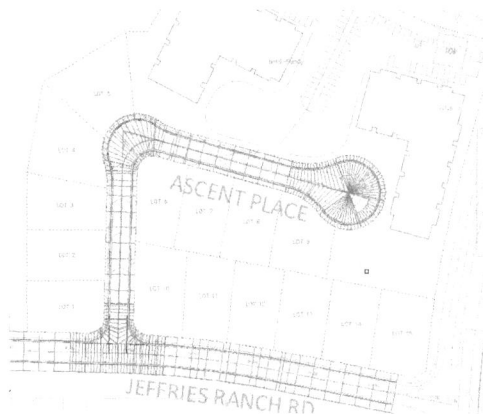

Figure 2–35

8. Save the drawing.

Task 2 - Paste the surfaces together.

1. Continue working in the drawing from the previous task or open **PARCELS-B2-Grading.dwg** from the *C:\Civil3D-Grading\Parcels* folder.

2. In the drawing, select the **Residential Grading** surface.

3. In the *Tin Surface* contextual tab>Modify panel, expand the Edit Surface drop-down list and click 🗐 (Paste Surface).

4. In the Select Surface dialog box, select the **Road1** surface, as shown in Figure 2–36.

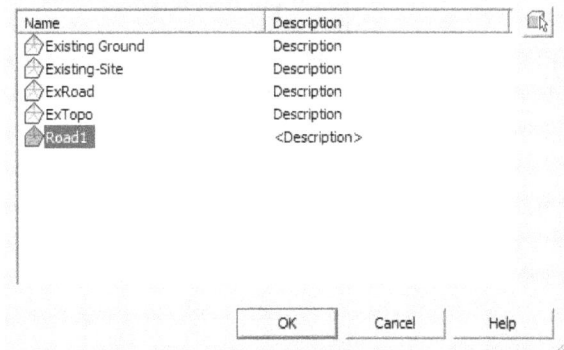

Name	Description	
Existing Ground	Description	
Existing-Site	Description	
ExRoad	Description	
ExTopo	Description	
Road1	<Description>	

Figure 2–36

5. Click **OK** to close the dialog box.

6. Save the drawing. The drawing display as shown in Figure 2–37.

Figure 2–37

Task 3 - Add wall breaklines to the surface.

1. Continue working in the drawing from the previous task or open **PARCELS-B3-Grading.dwg** from the *C:\Civil3D-Grading\Parcels* folder.

The feature lines for the top of walls have already been created for you to speed up the process. This was done by creating stepped offsets of the parcels lines 55' from the back of lot at a positive 2% slope to ensure that the water drains away from the house toward the back property line and 30' from the street at a positive 4% grade to ensure that the water drains toward the street in front. At the front of the property, the wall is a minimum of 7' and tapers down from there. Figure 2–38 shows a cross section of a typical wall breakline.

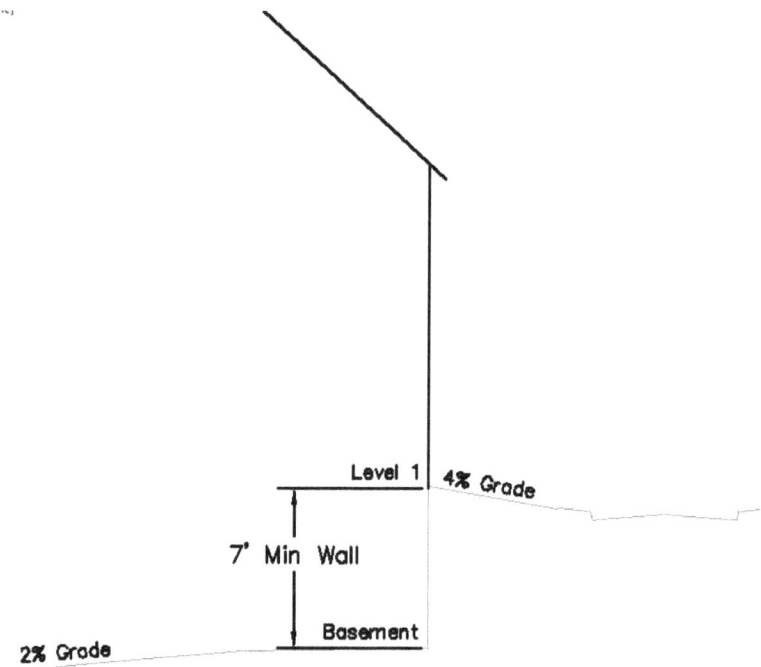

Figure 2–38

2. In the *Insert* tab>Block panel, click 🔲 (Insert)>**More Options**.

3. In the Insert dialog box, browse for **RetainingWalls.dwg** in the *C:\Civil3D-Grading\Parcels* folder. Clear all of the insertion options except **Explode**, as shown in Figure 2–39.

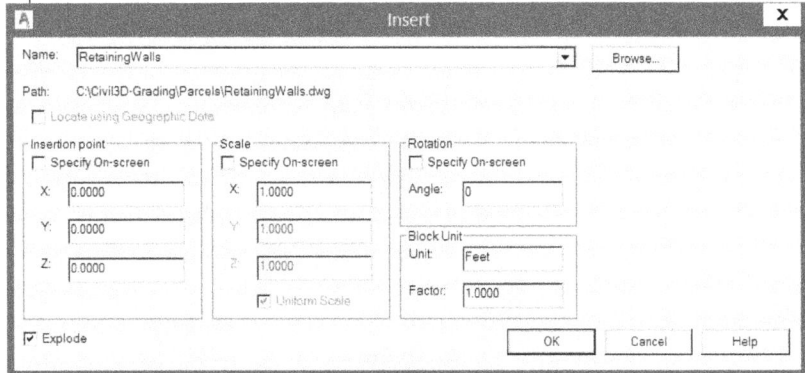

Figure 2–39

4. Click **OK** to close the dialog box.

5. In the *View* tab>Views panel, select **Lot1** as the view to zoom into the first lot to grade.

6. Select the Residential Grading surface in the drawing. In the *Tin Surface* contextual tab>Modify panel, expand the Add Data drop-down list and click ⬠ (Breaklines), as shown in Figure 2–40.

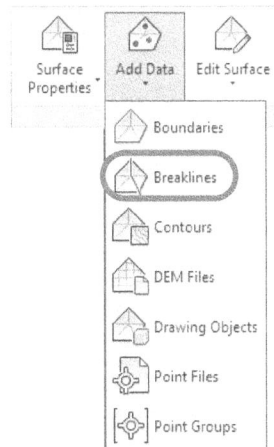

Figure 2–40

7. In the Add Breaklines dialog box, for the *Description* type **Wall Lot 1**. For the type select **Wall**, as shown in Figure 2–41. Click **OK** to accept all of the other defaults and close the dialog box.

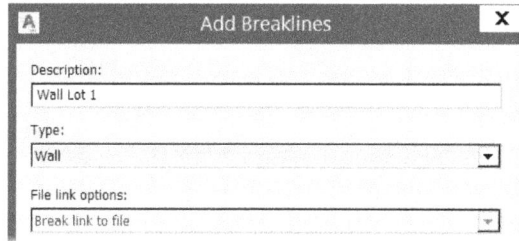

Figure 2–41

8. In the drawing, select the blue feature line inside Lot 1 and press <Enter>.

9. Pick a point to the inside of the building area (left side) for the offset side. Press <Enter> to accept the **All** option to set the height for all of the vertices at the same time.

10. In the Command Line, select the **Elevation** option.

11. For the elevation value type **196**. Note that the arrows on the surface indicate the direction in which the water will flow, as shown in Figure 2–42.

Figure 2–42

12. Repeat Steps 5 to 11 to add a retaining wall to Lots 2 to 5 using the following value for the target elevation in each lot.

Area	Target Elevation
Lot 2	188
Lot 3	186
Lot 4	183
Lot 5	182

Once all of the wall breaklines are in the surface, add the back of lot breaklines to set the back yard grades at 2%.

13. In the *View* tab>Views panel, select **Single Family Lots** as the view to zoom into.

14. Select the Residential Grading surface in the drawing. In the *Tin Surface* contextual tab>Modify panel, expand the Add Data drop-down list and click ⬠ (Breaklines).

15. In the Add Breaklines dialog box, for the *Description* type **Backyard Grade** and for the *Type* select **Standard**. Click **OK** to accept all of the other defaults and close the dialog box.

16. In the drawing, select the black feature lines in each lot, as shown in Figure 2–43. Press <Enter> to end the selection.

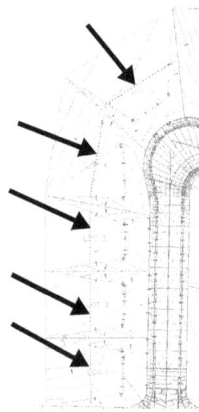

Figure 2–43

17. Press <Esc> to release the surface and then save the drawing.

2.4 Feature Line Interactions With Parcel Lines

When parcel lines and feature lines reside in the same site and intersect each other or share vertices, one line overrides the elevations of the other and creates a split point at the shared point of intersection. The last object edited automatically edits the elevations of the first. This is called the *last one wins* rule. Therefore, it is recommended that you create multiple sites for a grading plan. Keeping parcels in one site and feature lines in another site ensures that they do not unintentionally override each other as you are working.

When parcels share line segment(s), any edits to the elevations of one parcel affect the elevations of the second parcel along the shared segment(s). This includes any elevation points that might be added. Figure 2–44 shows the elevations of two lots that share a common segment. Elevation points have been inserted along the shared segment in Lot 1 (marked with circular symbols). Note that Lot 2 automatically picked up the same elevation points (marked with empty triangles) along the shared segment. These are known as split points.

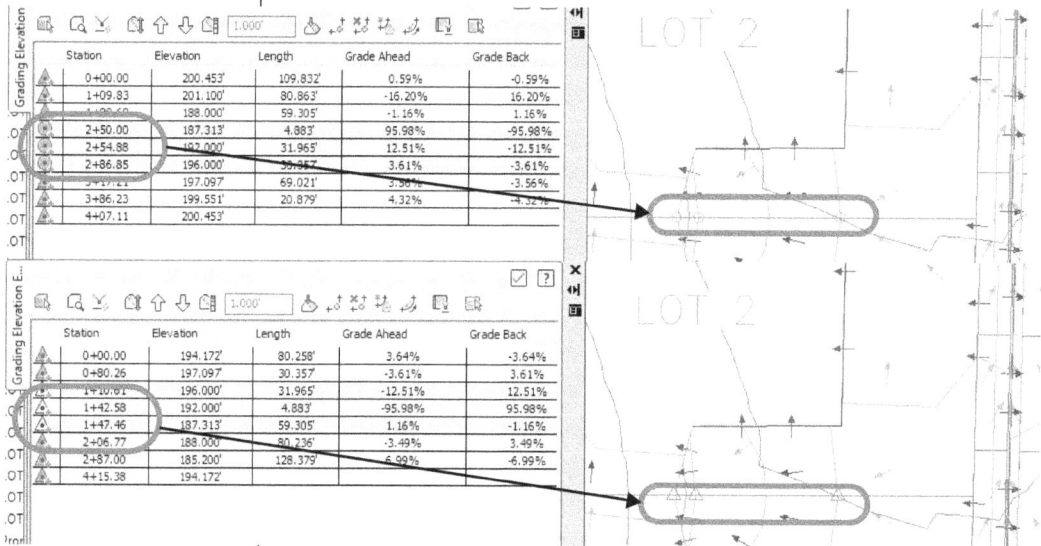

Figure 2–44

Practice 2c

Add Elevation Points to Parcels

Practice Objective

- Create split points along parcel lines by adding elevations to adjacent parcel segments.

Estimated time for completion: 10 minutes

In this practice you will insert elevation points along the parcel segments.

1. Continue working in the drawing from the previous practice or open **PARCELS-C1-Grading.dwg** from the *C:\Civil3D-Grading\Parcels* folder.

2. In the *View* tab>Views panel, select **Lot1** as the view to zoom into the first lot to grade.

3. In the *Prospector* tab, expand Surfaces, right-click on Residential Surface and select **Rebuild - Automatic**, as shown in Figure 2–45.

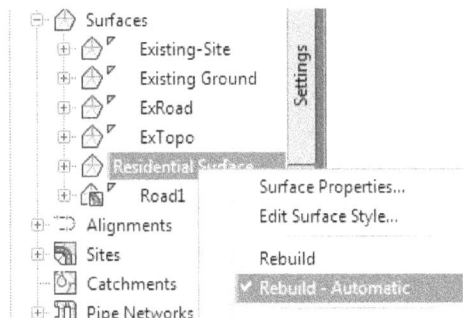

Figure 2–45

4. In the drawing, select the Lot 1 parcel segments. In the *Parcel Segments* contextual tab>Modify panel, click ⬚ (Edit Elevations). In the Edit Elevations panel, click ⬚ (Elevation Editor).

5. In the Elevation Editor vista, click ⬚ (Insert Elevation Point).

6. In the drawing, pick the endpoint of the walls at the front corner of the house in Lot 1, as shown in Figure 2–46.

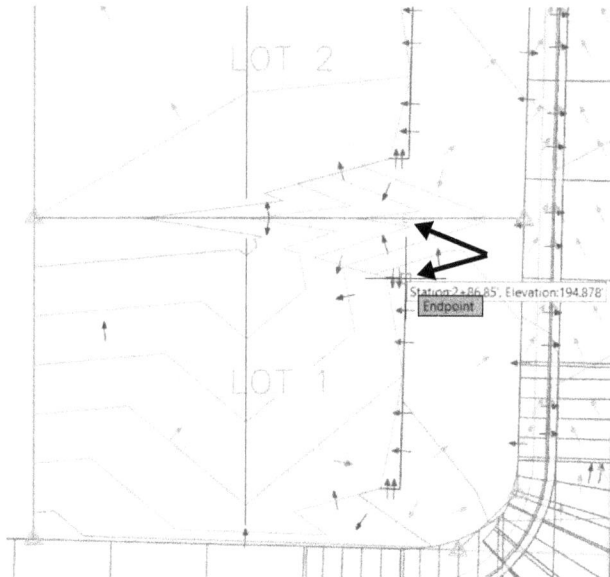

Figure 2–46

7. In the Insert PVI dialog box, for the *Elevation* type **198**. Click **OK**. (This dialog box might not open. If it does not, keep an eye on the Command Line because it will prompt you for the elevation instead.)

8. Repeat Steps 4 to 7 to add an elevation at the endpoint of the backyard feature lines for Lot 1 with an elevation of **190**.

When finished, the Lot 1 elevations in the Elevation Editor vista should be as shown in Figure 2–47.

	Station	Elevation	Length	Grade Ahead	Grade Back
	0+00.00	200.453'	109.832'	0.59%	-0.59%
	1+09.83	201.100'	80.863'	-16.20%	16.20%
	1+90.69	188.000'	55.000'	3.64%	-3.64%
	2+45.69	190.000'	41.155'	19.44%	-19.44%
	2+86.85	198.000'	30.356'	-3.13%	3.13%
	3+17.21	197.050'	69.021'	3.64%	-3.64%
	3+86.23	199.565'	20.879'	4.26%	-4.26%
	4+07.11	200.453'			

Figure 2–47

9. In the Elevation Editor vista, click 🔲 (Select Feature).

10. In the drawing, select the Lot 2 parcel segments. Note the three split points marked with triangles along the south boundary line, as shown in Figure 2–48.

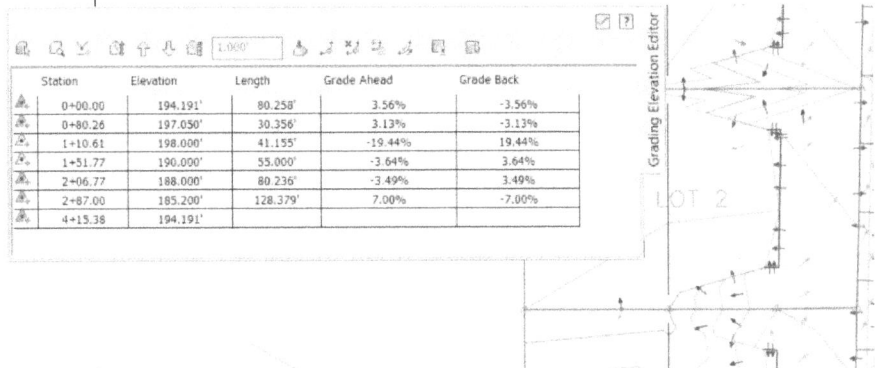

Station	Elevation	Length	Grade Ahead	Grade Back
0+00.00	194.191'	80.258'	3.56%	-3.56%
0+80.26	197.050'	30.356'	3.13%	-3.13%
1+10.61	198.000'	41.155'	-19.44%	19.44%
1+51.77	190.000'	55.000'	-3.64%	3.64%
2+06.77	188.000'	80.236'	-3.49%	3.49%
2+87.00	185.200'	128.379'	7.00%	-7.00%
4+15.38	194.191'			

Figure 2–48

11. Repeat Steps 4 to 8 to add elevation points to the north line of Lot 2, as shown in Figure 2–49.

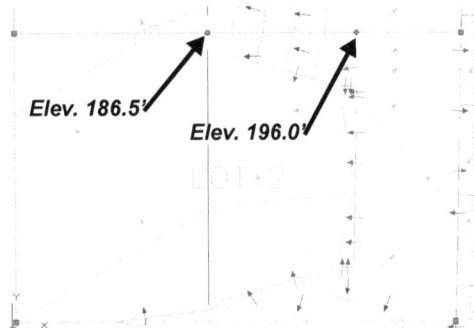

Elev. 186.5'

Elev. 196.0'

Figure 2–49

12. Repeat Steps 4 to 8 to add elevation points to the north line of Lot 3, as shown in Figure 2–50.

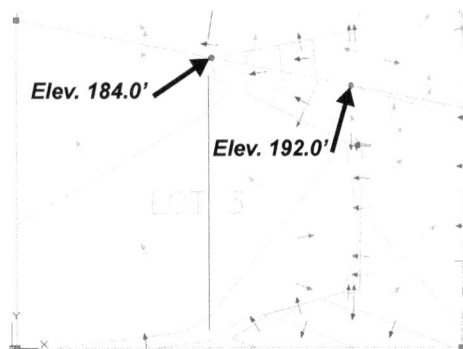

Elev. 184.0'

Elev. 192.0'

Figure 2–50

13. Repeat Steps 4 to 8 to add elevation points to the north line of Lot 4, as shown in Figure 2–51.

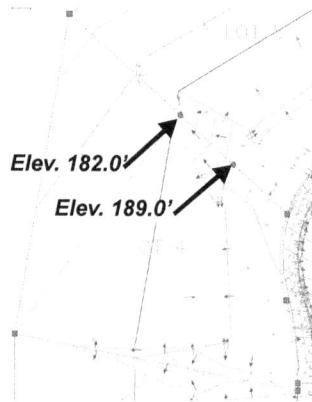

Elev. 182.0'

Elev. 189.0'

Figure 2–51

14. Save the drawing.

Chapter Review Questions

1. Where do you set the option to use parcel elevations in the drawing?

    a. Parcel Properties

    b. Site Properties

    c. Drawing Properties

    d. Feature Line Properties

2. When using (Edit Elevations) in the *Parcel Segments* contextual tab>Edit Elevations panel, how many vertices' elevations do you set at a time?

    a. One

    b. Any selected

    c. All

3. When using (Set Elevations by Reference) in the *Parcel Segments* contextual tab>Edit Elevations panel, how many vertices' elevations do you set at a time?

    a. One

    b. Any selected

    c. All

4. When creating a wall breakline, you can use the following to set the elevations of the offset points at each vertex? (Select all that apply.)

    a. Elevation

    b. Difference in Elevation

    c. By Reference

    d. Surface

5. When feature lines, parcel segments, or survey figures cross each other, what is the elevation point assigned called?

    a. Point of Intersection

    b. Crossing Point

    c. Elevation Point

    d. Split Point

Command Summary

Button	Command	Location
	Breakline	• **Ribbon**: *Tin Surface* contextual tab> Modify panel, expanded Add Data drop-down list • **Command Prompt:** AddSurfaceBreaklines
	Bring to Front	• **Ribbon**: *Parcel Segments* contextual tab>expanded General Tools panel • **Command Prompt:** DrawOrder
	Edit Elevations	• **Ribbon**: *Parcel Segments* contextual tab>Edit Elevations panel • **Command Prompt:** EditFeatureElevs
	Elevations from Surface	• **Ribbon**: *Parcel Segments* contextual tab>Edit Elevations panel • **Command Prompt:** FeatureElevsFromSurf
	Move to Site	• **Ribbon**: *Parcel* contextual tab> Modify panel • **Command Prompt:** MoveToSite
	Paste Surface	• **Ribbon**: *Tin Surface* contextual tab> Modify panel, expanded Edit Surface drop-down list • **Command Prompt:** EditSurfacePaste
	Send to Back	• **Ribbon**: *Parcel Segments* contextual tab>expanded General Tools panel • **Command Prompt:** DrawOrder
	Set Elevations by Reference	• **Ribbon**: *Parcel Segments* contextual tab>Edit Elevations panel • **Command Prompt:** SetFeatureRefElev

Building Pad Design

Setting the elevation of a building pad and grading out from that pad a specified slope is important to fully understand how much cut and fill a site is going to have. In this chapter, you learn how to assign elevations to a building footprint, and then create a simple grading object to calculate how much cut/fill is going to be required for the building at that elevation.

Learning Objectives in this Chapter

- List the five ways in which feature lines can be created.
- Create a feature line from objects in a drawing or external reference file.
- Project a specific slope from a baseline to a specific target in a drawing.
- Change the grading criteria of an existing grading solution.
- Calculate the earthwork volumes for a grading group or a single grading object using the Grading Volume Tools.

3.1 Feature Lines Overview

The AutoCAD® Civil 3D® software uses 3D polylines known as *Feature Lines* for grading footprints, corridor modeling, and surface breaklines. A feature line could represent a building footprint, parking lot perimeter, swale, or ridgeline. The benefit of using a feature line over an AutoCAD 3D polyline is its ease of editing and its ability to support arcs without tessellation. Tessellated curves are undesirable in grading because of their many small grading faces around radial corners. To access commands for creating feature lines, select the *Home* tab> Create Design panel and select **Feature Line**, as shown in Figure 3–1.

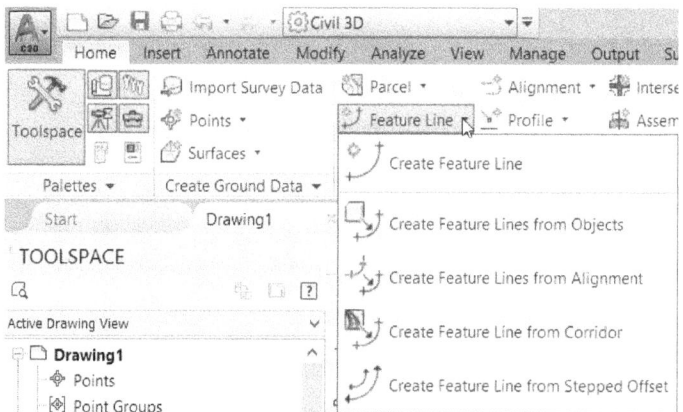

Figure 3–1

Feature Lines can be created in five different ways:

1. Create Feature Line manually.
2. Create Feature Lines from Objects.
3. Create Feature Lines from Alignment.
4. Create Feature Lines from Corridor.
5. Create Feature Line from Stepped Offset.

3.2 Create Feature Lines from Objects

Designs often start out as 2D conceptual drawings to help determine where to locate design components. In these cases, you can easily convert existing 2D or 3D polylines, lines, or arcs into feature lines. During the conversion process, a name and style are assigned to the feature line along with elevations for each of the vertices. To edit the elevations of a feature line, you use the same tools used for editing parcel segment elevations.

How To: Create a Feature Line from Existing Objects

1. In the *Home* tab>Create Design panel, in the Feature Line drop-down list, select ⬚↲ (Create Feature Lines From Objects).
2. Select the arcs, lines, or polylines in the drawing to convert or type **X** and press <Enter> to select objects in an external reference file.
3. In the Create Feature Lines dialog box, set the **Site** to ensure that other feature lines, parcels, and grading groups interact with the new feature line. Type a name for the feature line. Set the style, layer, and conversion options, as shown in Figure 3–2.

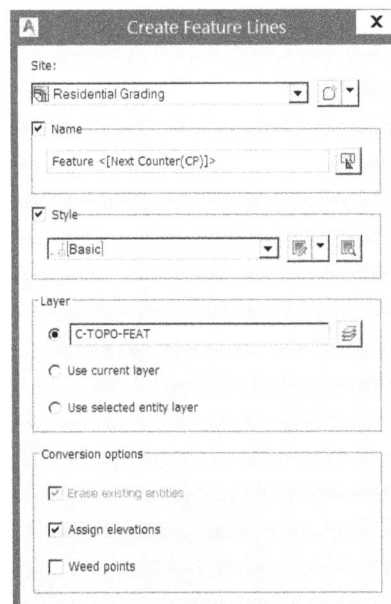

Figure 3–2

4. If the option to assign elevations is selected in the Conversion options, a dialog box opens that enables you to assign elevations to the vertices, as shown in Figure 3–3.

   • Select the **Elevation** option and type the required elevation value or set the vertex elevations to be assigned from other gradings or surfaces that exist in the drawing.

   • By selecting the option to insert intermediate grade break points, additional elevation points are added to the feature line anywhere the line crosses a surface triangle.

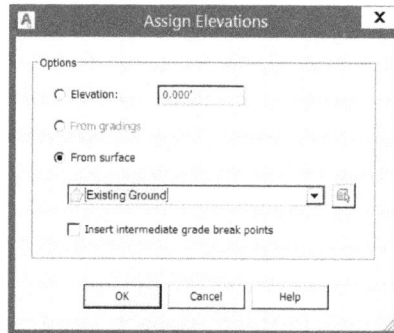

Figure 3–3

5. If the **Weed Points** option is selected under Conversion options, a third dialog box opens, as shown in Figure 3–4.

   • Set the minimum angle, grade, or length that is required between the elevation points. This causes any points closer than the set minimums to be removed.

   • You can also set the minimum 3D distance between elevation points.

   • At the bottom of the dialog box, an information line indicates how many vertices are going to be weeded out.

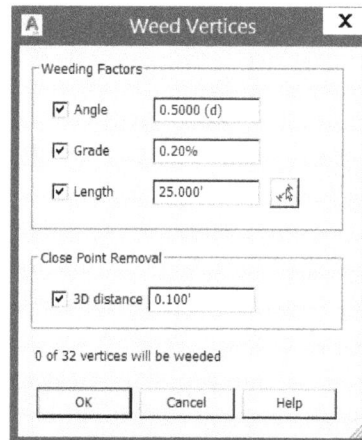

Figure 3–4

Practice 3a

Estimated time for completion: 10 minutes

Create a Feature Line from Objects in an XREF

Practice Objective

- Create a feature line from objects in an external reference file.

In this practice you will create a feature line from objects and then edit the feature line elevations.

Task 1 - Create a feature line from objects.

In this task you will convert a drawing's polyline into a grading feature line. The feature line is the basis for the future grading object baseline.

1. Open **BLDG-A1-Grading.dwg** from the *C:\Civil3D-Grading\ BLDG Pad* folder.

2. In the *View* tab>Views panel, select **Building 1** as the view to zoom into the L-shape that represents the building footprint, as shown in Figure 3–5.

[−][Building 1][2D Wireframe]

Figure 3–5

3. In the *Home* tab>Create Design panel, expand the Feature Line drop-down list and select 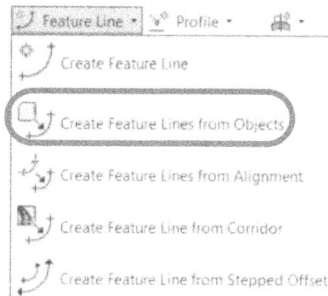 (Create Feature Lines from Objects), as shown in Figure 3–6.

Figure 3–6

4. In the Command Line, select **Xref** to select linework from the XREF.

5. Select the L-shaped polyline representing the building footprint, as shown in Figure 3–7. Press <Enter> to end the object selection process.

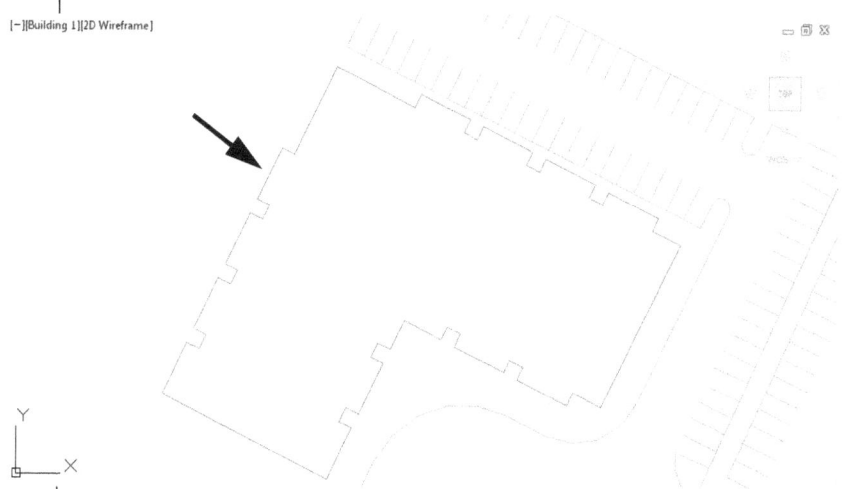

Figure 3–7

6. In the Create Feature Lines dialog box, complete the following, as shown in Figure 3–8:
   - Set the *Site* to **Multi-Family Site**.
   - In the *Name* field, type **Building1**.
   - Set the *Style* to **Building Pad**,
   - Set the *Conversion options* to **Assign elevations**.
   - Click **OK** to close the dialog box.

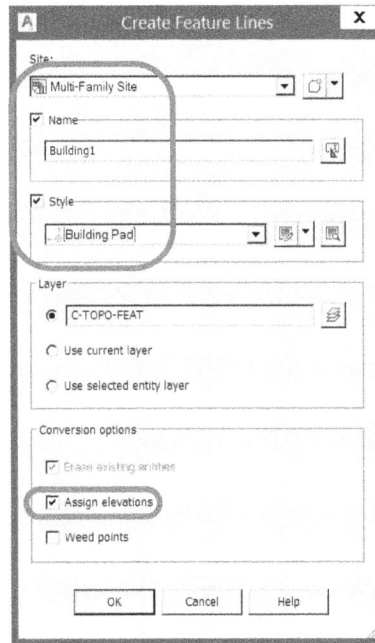

Figure 3–8

7. In the Assign Elevations dialog box, complete the following, as shown in Figure 3–9:

- Select **From Surface** for the surface
- Select **Existing Ground**
- Clear the **Insert intermediate grade break points** option.
- Click **OK** to close the dialog box.

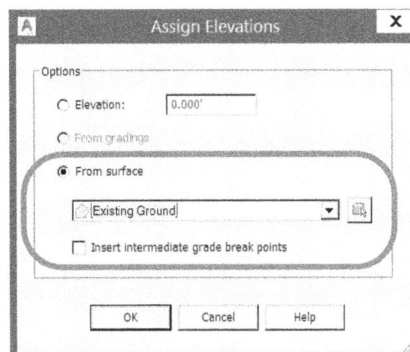

Figure 3–9

8. Save the drawing.

Task 2 - Edit the feature line elevations.

1. Continue working in the drawing or open
   BLDG-A2-Grading.dwg from the *C:\Civil3D-Grading\
   BLDG Pad* folder.

2. Select the feature line created in the previous task (the blue
   building footprint). In the *Feature Line* contextual tab>Modify
   panel, select **Edit Elevations**, as shown in Figure 3–10.

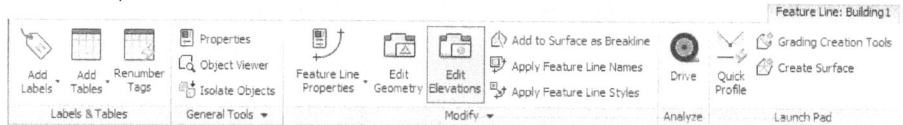

Figure 3–10

3. In the Edit Elevations panel, select **Elevation Editor**, as
   shown in Figure 3–11.

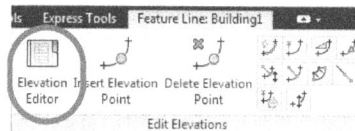

Figure 3–11

4. In the Elevation Editor panorama, select any row and hold
   down <Ctrl> as you type **A** to select every row, as shown in
   Figure 3–12.

Station	Elevation	Length	Grade Ahead	Grade Back
5+92.81	173.762'	27.108'	3.62%	-3.62%
6+19.91	174.745'	90.114'	2.33%	-2.33%
7+10.03	176.846'	27.108'	-3.07%	3.07%
7+37.14	176.014'	6.631'	-3.88%	3.88%
7+43.77	175.756'	7.272'	-3.80%	3.80%
7+51.04	175.480'	6.631'	4.41%	-4.41%
7+57.67	175.772'	27.108'	-2.81%	2.81%
7+84.78	175.012'	6.631'	-3.16%	3.16%
7+91.41	174.802'	7.272'	-2.77%	2.77%
7+98.68	174.601'	6.631'	3.03%	-3.03%
8+05.31	174.802'	15.253'	-3.72%	3.72%
8+20.56	174.234'	20.481'	2.36%	-2.36%
8+41.05	174.718'	6.631'	-5.08%	5.08%
8+47.68	174.381'	7.272'	2.44%	-2.44%
8+54.95	174.559'	6.631'	5.02%	-5.02%
8+61.58	174.892'	27.108'	2.66%	-2.66%
8+88.69	175.612'			

Figure 3–12

5. In the Elevation Editor, click ⬇ (Flatten Grade or Elevation). Select **Constant Elevation**, as shown in Figure 3–13. Click **OK** to close the dialog box.

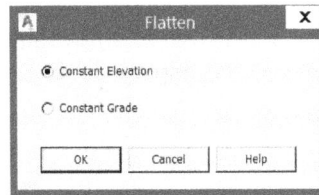

Figure 3–13

6. In the Elevation Editor, click ⬍ (Raise/Lower). In the *Input* field, type **172** and press <Enter>, as shown in Figure 3–14.

Figure 3–14

7. Click ☑ to close the Elevation Editor panorama.

8. Save the drawing.

3.3 Grading Creation Tools

This section focuses on grading to a surface. To start the **Grading** command, go to the *Home* tab>Create Design panel, expand the Grading drop-down list, and select a command in the Grading Creation Tools toolbar, as shown at the top of Figure 3–15.

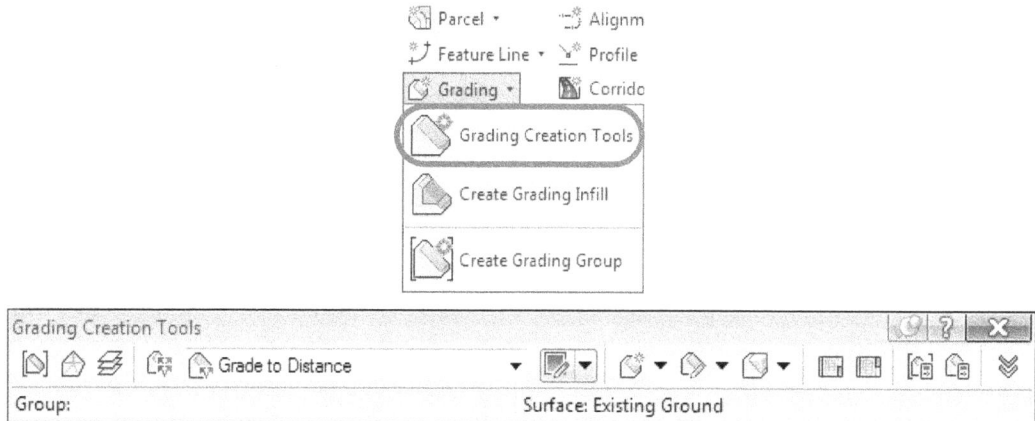

Figure 3–15

It is recommended that you start on the left and work to the right in command specific toolbars. The Grading Creation Tools toolbar is no exception to this recommended process. Therefore, the first thing you need to do is define or set the Grading Group.

Grading Groups

A grading object consists of a base line, projection lines, target lines, and faces. Combining multiple grading objects into a group enables you to create complex grading schemes. A grading group calculates a volume for an entire grading area, rather than one object at a time, unlike the AutoCAD® Civil 3D® Land Desktop software. Figure 3–16 shows each part of a grading group. Each time a grading object is created, a new feature line is created as a projected target line. The resulting target line can then be used as a baseline for a new grading object within the same group.

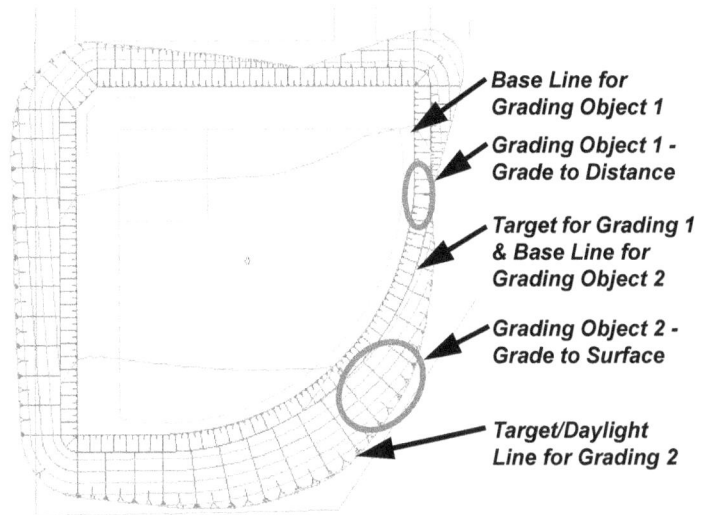

Figure 3–16

To create a new grading group, click ⬡ (Set Grading Group) in the Grading Creation Tools toolbar. The first entry is the site in which you want to work, as shown in Figure 3–17. Sites can be created in the template to keep constancy across all of the projects. If a site does not already exist, one called Site 1 is created automatically.

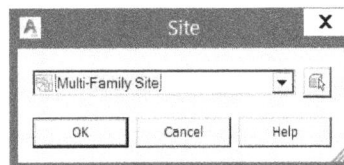

Figure 3–17

Once the site has been set, another dialog box opens enabling you to create a grading group, as shown in Figure 3–18. The first task is to type a name and a description. Next you decide whether you want to predefine a surface for the grading group. If simple grading groups are being created with one or two projections, creating a surface immediately should not be a problem. However, if a grading group is complex with three or more grading objects, it is recommended that you wait until the grading group is complete before creating the group's surface.

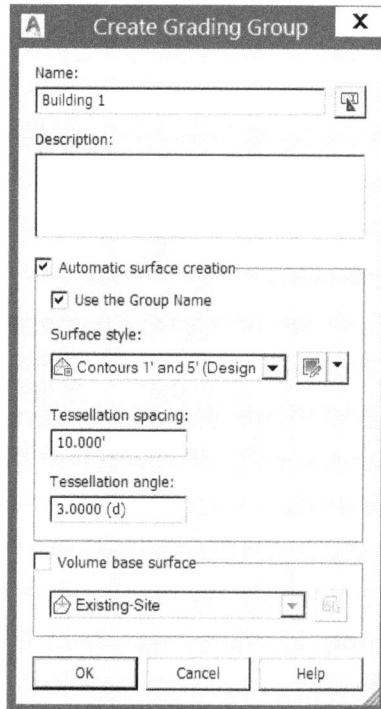

Figure 3–18

The last option to consider in the Create Grading Group dialog box is whether or not to set a Volume base surface. By selecting this option, a volume for the entire grading group can be calculated between this base surface and the grading group's surface. The base surface is usually set to the existing ground surface.

If the **Automatic surface creation** option is selected, a Create Surface dialog box opens, as shown in Figure 3–19. If you also selected the **Use the Group Name** option, the surface name field is already filled in with the grading group's name. Using the grading group's name as the surface ensures consistency and makes communication between other team members easy because they recognize that the grading group and surface are the same. As with any AutoCAD Civil 3D surface, you can assign a style to the grading group surface.

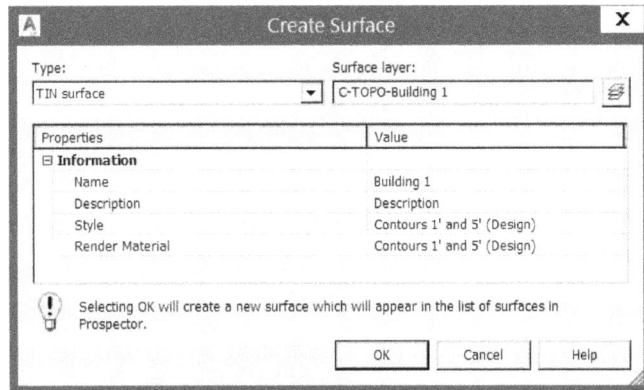

Figure 3–19

Grading Setup

The next task in the Grading Creation Tools toolbar is to set the target surface ⬠. This is especially important if you want to grade to a surface because this surface is the Grade to Surface criteria's target. If a volume base surface was set in the Create Grading Group dialog box, the surface is set in the Grading Creation Tools toolbar, as shown in Figure 3–20.

Figure 3–20

The next tool in the Grading Creation Tools toolbar is ▤ (Set Grading Layer). Although you can use this tool to set the Layer for the grading objects, it is recommended that you use the drawing settings and grading styles to set the layer.

The next tool is 🗔 (Select a Criteria Set). The standard AutoCAD Civil 3D template includes a Basic criteria set that incorporates all four grading criteria without any locks toggled on. If you or someone in your company has added additional grading criteria sets to prevent unnecessary parameter entries, you can select the grading criteria set that you want to use, as shown in Figure 3–21.

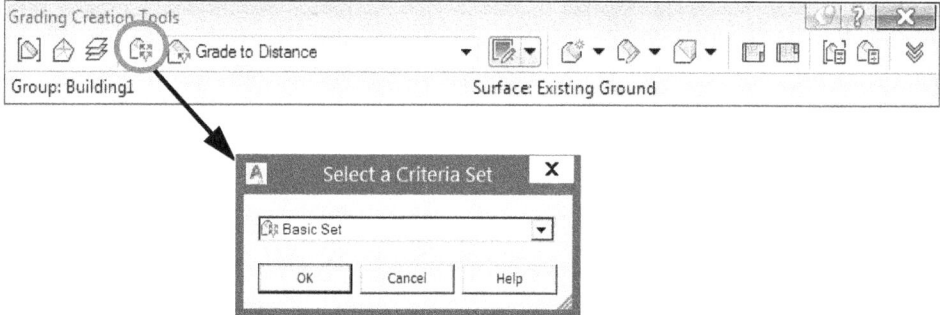

Figure 3–21

Depending on the selected Criteria Set, different grading criteria might be available. Figure 3–22 shows the available criteria from the Basic Set. Select the required criteria for the type of project you are doing. If the required criteria is not available, you can create new criteria on the fly by clicking 🗔▼ (Create New Criteria).

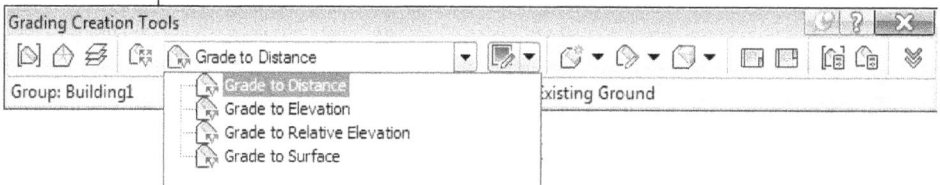

Figure 3–22

Create Grading

After setting the above parameters, you are ready to start grading. Click ☁️ (Create Grading) and select the feature line that you want to use as the baseline. Next you are prompted for the side to which to grade if you want the grading to apply to the entire length of the feature line. After you have set the length to apply the grading criteria, the next prompt is for the grading parameters. This only occurs if the criteria you are using is not locked. Grading can be done on either side even if you have an open feature line or a closed feature line. If grading to the inside of a closed feature line, projections continue until the target is reached or the grading grades to itself, as shown in Figure 3–23.

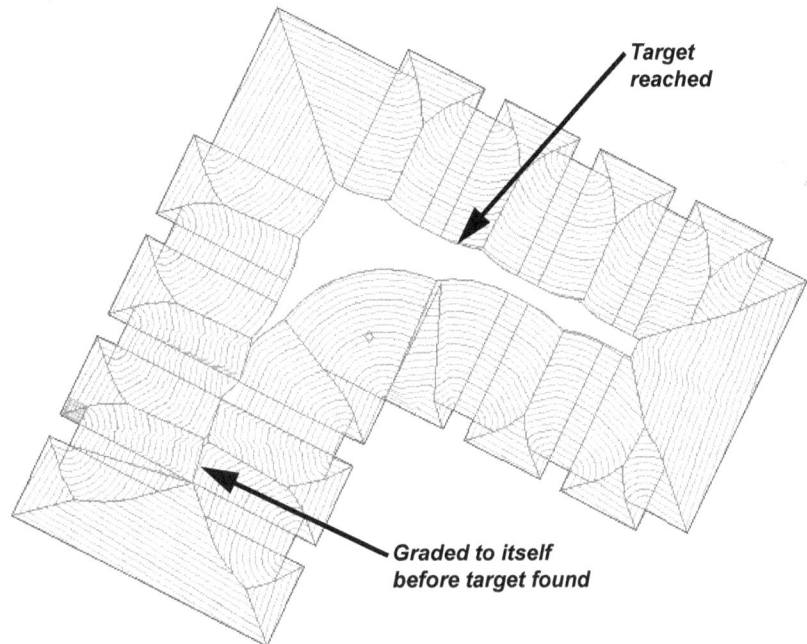

Target reached

Graded to itself before target found

Figure 3–23

Grading Infill

Sometimes there is a need to fill in an area between two grading objects or feature lines. A grading infill is a grading face that eliminates holes in grading groups and ensures that the finished ground surface covers the entire grading area. To create an infill, click 🖻 (Create Infill) in the Create Grading drop-down list in the Grading Creation toolbar. The routine prompts you to pick a point in the open area to infill with a grading face (similar to picking a point to hatch an area), as shown in Figure 3–24.

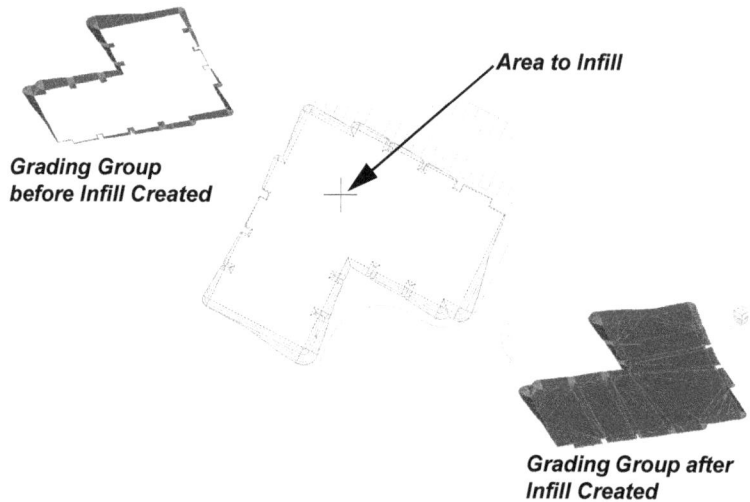

Area to Infill

Grading Group before Infill Created

Grading Group after Infill Created

Figure 3–24

3.4 Editing the Grading

After creating a grading group, you might need to change one or more of the grading parameters. Some changes are required due to a mistake when creating the original grading place or due to a design change. In either case, the grading criteria used during the creation of the grading object determines what can change. If you used a Grade to Distance criteria but meant to use a Grade to Surface criteria, then you must delete the original grading object and replace it with a new grading object.

Delete Grading Objects

To delete a grading object and not corrupt your drawing, you should first select the grading object and, in the *Grading* contextual tab>Modify panel, click ⬠ (Delete Grading), as shown in Figure 3–25. It is important that you delete the outer most grading object before deleting the interior grading objects. This is because if an interior grading object is used by other grading objects as a baseline, the exterior grading object becomes corrupt and unusable.

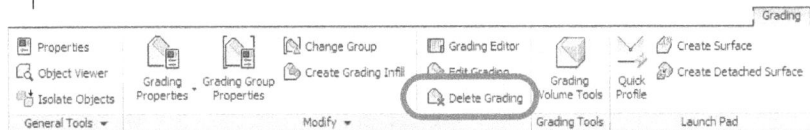

Figure 3–25

Modify Grading Object Criteria

To modify the input parameters of a grading object, you must first ensure that the criteria used was not locked; locks prevent editing. To check this and make the required changes at the same time, you use the Grading Editor. In the *Grading* contextual tab>Modify panel, click ⬛ (Grading Editor), as shown in Figure 3–26.

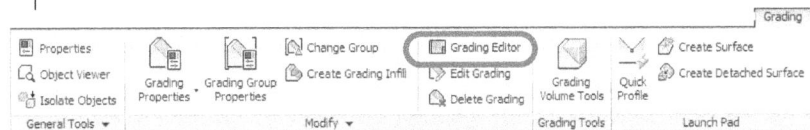

Figure 3–26

The Panorama's Grading Editor vista enables you to modify a grading's parameters. Any parameters that were locked when creating the grading object have a lock symbol to the left indicating that they cannot be changed. Anything without a lock can be changed by selecting the value field to the right of the parameter, as shown in Figure 3–27.

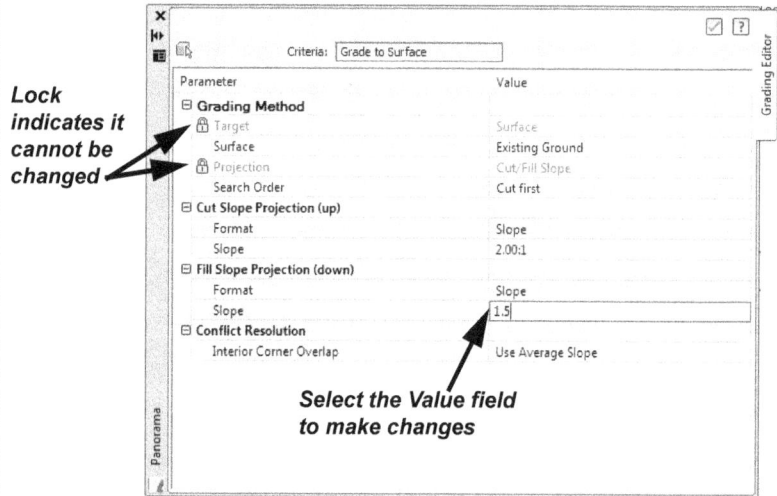

Lock indicates it cannot be changed

Select the Value field to make changes

Figure 3–27

Alternatively, you can click ✎ (Edit Grading) on the *Grading* contextual tab>Modify panel to use the Grading Editor to change the grading parameters, as shown in Figure 3–28. This routine prompts you for the parameters in the Command Line. Note that you are only prompted for parameters that are not locked.

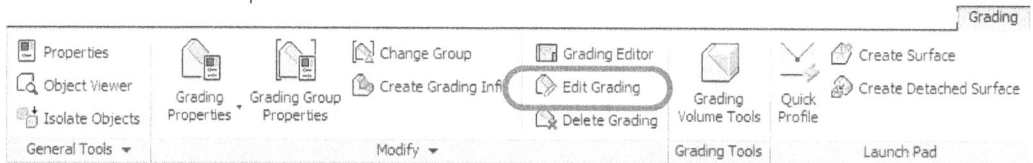

Figure 3–28

Practice 3b

Estimated time for completion: 10 minutes

Grading Creation Tools

Practice Objective

- Project a feature line at a specific slope to a surface.

In this practice you will, grade to a surface, create infill, and modify the grading criteria.

Task 1 - Grade to a surface.

In this task you will use the feature line as a baseline for your Grading Object and use the Grading Creation Tools toolbar to create a grading that slopes into the existing ground surface.

1. Continue working in the drawing from the last practice or open **BLDG-B1-Grading.dwg** from the *C:\Civil3D-Grading\ BLDG Pad* folder.

2. In the *Home* tab>Create Design panel, expand the Grading drop-down list and click 🖫 (Grading Creation Tools). The Grading Creation Tools toolbar displays.

3. In the Grading Creation Tools toolbar, click 🖾 (Set Group). Select **Multi-Family Site** as shown in Figure 3–29. Click **OK** to close the dialog box.

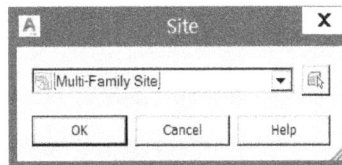

Figure 3–29

4. In the Create Grading Group dialog box, do the following, as shown in Figure 3–30:

   - For the *Name*, type **Building1**.
   - Select the option to automatically create a surface
   - Set the *Volume base surface* to **Existing Ground**.
   - Click **OK** to close the dialog box.

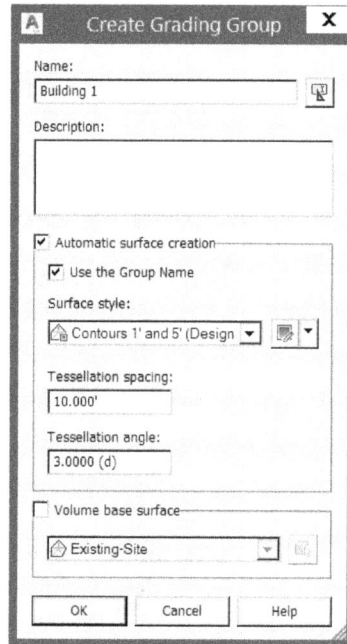

Figure 3–30

5. In the Create Surface dialog box, leave all of the default values and click **OK**.

6. In the Grading Creation Tools toolbar, verify that the *Criteria Set* is set to **Basic Set** by hovering over (Select a Criteria Set). Set the grading criteria to **Grade to Surface**, as shown in Figure 3–31.

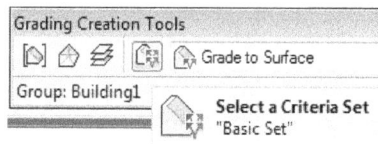

Figure 3–31

7. In the Grading Creation Tools toolbar, click ⬚ (Create Grading). Select the blue building feature line that was created in the last practice, as shown in Figure 3–32.

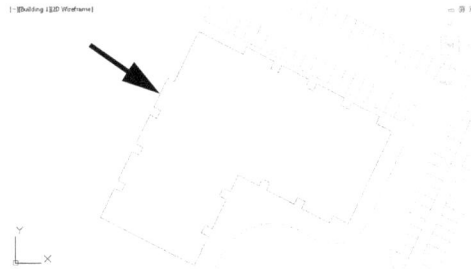

Figure 3–32

8. When prompted for a grading side, pick a point outside the building footprint.

9. When prompted to apply it to the entire length, press <Enter> to accept the default of **Yes**.

10. Press <Enter> to accept the default format of slope for both cut and fill.

11. Press <Enter> to accept the default 2:1 Slopes for both cut and fill.

12. Click ☑ to close the Events Vista. Press <Esc> to end the command. The drawing should display as shown in Figure 3–33.

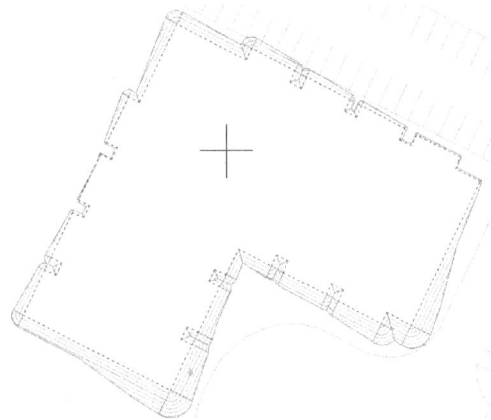

Figure 3–33

13. Save the drawing.

Task 2 - Create infill.

1. Continue working on the drawing from the previous task or open **BLDG-B2-Grading.dwg** from the C:\Civil3D-Grading\ BLDG Pad folder.

2. In the Grading Creation Tools toolbar, verify that the Grading Group is set to **Building1** as shown in Figure 3–34.

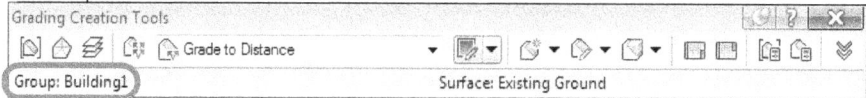

Figure 3–34

3. In the Grading Creation Tools toolbar, expand the Create Grading drop-down list and click 🖆 (Create Infill). Pick a point in the center of the building footprint as shown in Figure 3–35.

A green diamond indicating that the area now has a grading face should display.

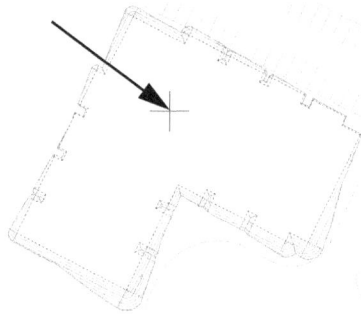

Figure 3–35

4. Click ☑ to close the Events Vista. Press <Esc> to end the command.

5. Save the drawing.

Task 3 - Modify the grading criteria.

After completing the grading, note that the fill slope on the north side of the building is encroaching on the parking lot. Rather than moving the building or the parking lot, you will increase the fill slope to 1.5:1.

1. Continue to work in the drawing from the previous task or open **BLDG-B3-Grading.dwg** from the C:\Civil3D-Grading\ BLDG Pad folder.

2. Select the grading object center mark (diamond symbol) created by grading to the surface, as shown in Figure 3–36.

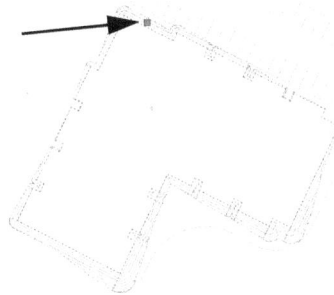

Figure 3–36

3. In the *Grading* contextual tab>Modify panel, click (Grading Editor).

4. In the Grading Editor panorama, change the *Fill Slope* to **1.5** and press <Enter>, as shown in Figure 3–37.

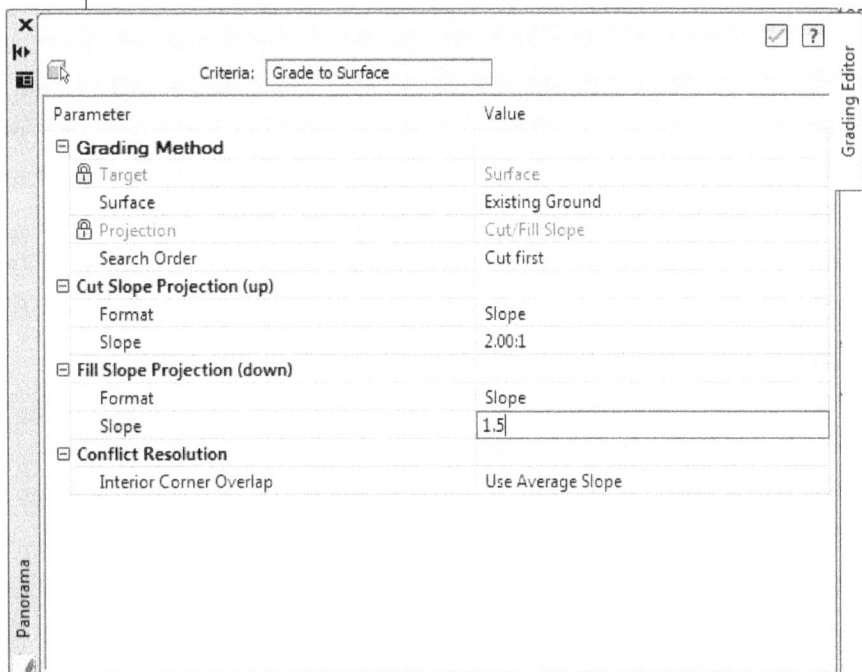

Parameter	Value
Grading Method	
Target	Surface
Surface	Existing Ground
Projection	Cut/Fill Slope
Search Order	Cut first
Cut Slope Projection (up)	
Format	Slope
Slope	2.00:1
Fill Slope Projection (down)	
Format	Slope
Slope	1.5
Conflict Resolution	
Interior Corner Overlap	Use Average Slope

Criteria: Grade to Surface

Figure 3–37

5. Click ☑ to close the Grading Editor panorama. Press <Esc> to release the grading object.

6. Save the drawing.

3.5 Grading Volume Tools

The biggest benefit to using grading groups to create future grading plans is the ease in which they can be modified and their volumes calculated. The Grading Volume Tools assist in calculating the earthwork volumes for the grading group and assist in balancing the cut and fill volumes.

Calculate Volumes

Selecting a grading object displays the *Grading* contextual tab. You also access this tab by going to the *Modify* tab>Design panel and clicking ◻ (Grading). In the *Grading* tab>Grading Tools panel, click ◻ (Grading Volume Tools) to access the Grading Volume Tools toolbar, as shown in Figure 3–38.

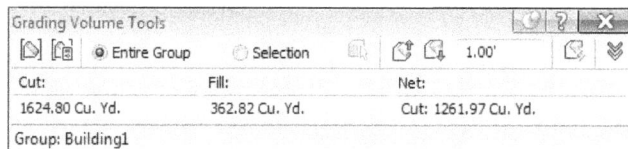

Figure 3–38

The group whose calculation displays in the toolbar is listed in the bottom left corner. To change which group is being calculated, click ◻ (Set Group) at the top left. By default, the **Entire Group** option is set so that the volume for all of the grading objects within the group is calculated as one item. To find the volume of a single grading object, change the option to **Selection** and pick a grading object in the drawing by clicking ◻, as shown in Figure 3–39.

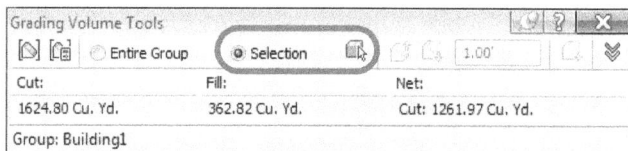

Figure 3–39

Balance Volumes

Grading Groups can be adjusted vertically using the Grading Volume Tools to balance the cut and fill volumes and reduce the cost of hauling material in or out of the site. To do so, the **Entire Group** option must be selected. The option to raise or lower the group becomes available, as shown in Figure 3–40.

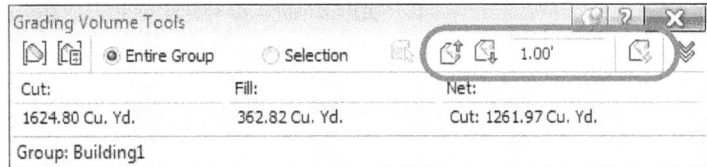

Figure 3–40

Incremental Changes

Typing an increment in the input field and clicking (Raise Entire Group) or (Lower Entire Group) enables you to incrementally raise or lower the entire grading group. Clicking

displays the history of how the incremental changes affect the volume calculations, as shown in Figure 3–41.

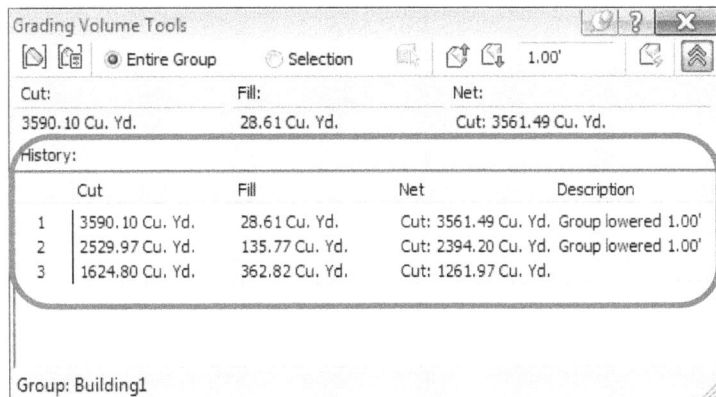

Figure 3–41

Automatically Balance Cut and Fill

Many projects require that the cut and fill for the project be minimized as much as possible to reduce costs. If that is the case on your project, you can use ⬚ (Auto Balance) to automatically raise or lower the entire grading group to balance the volumes. If this option is selected, a dialog box opens prompting you to set the required volume, as shown in Figure 3–42.

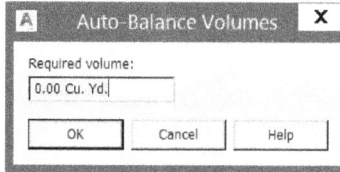

Figure 3–42

If you enter a specific volume in the *Required volume* field and click **OK** but the resulting volume does not match your entered target volume, you can click ⬚ (Auto Balance) again to get it closer. There might be times when you need to click this option more than once to get the required result.

Practice 3c

Estimated time for completion: 5 minutes

Grading Volume Tools

Practice Objective

- Calculate and balance the cut and fill volumes of a grading group.

In this practice you will, calculate the grading group volume.

1. Continue working in the drawing from the previous practice or open **BLDG-C1-Grading.dwg** from the *C:\Civil3D-Grading\ BLDG Pad* folder.

2. In the *Home* tab>Create Design panel, expand the Grading drop-down list and click ⬢ (Grading Creation Tools).

3. In the Grading Creation Tools toolbar, click ⬢ (Grading Volume Tools), as shown in Figure 3–43.

Figure 3–43

4. In the Grading Volume Tools toolbar, verify that the Building1 group is set to be **Current**, as shown in Figure 3–44. If not, click ⬢ (Set Grading) to and select it.

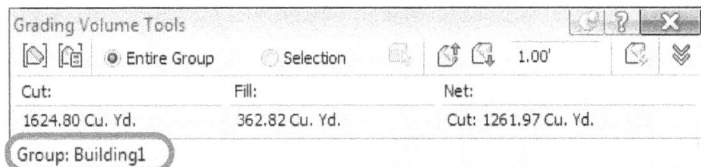

Figure 3–44

5. Click ⬢ (Raise Group) to raise the entire group by **1'**.

6. Click ⬢ (Expand Toolbar) to display the grading calculation history.

7. Click (Auto-Balance) to automatically balance the cut and fill volumes for the entire group. Take the default of 0 (zero), as shown in Figure 3–45. Click **OK** to close the dialog box.

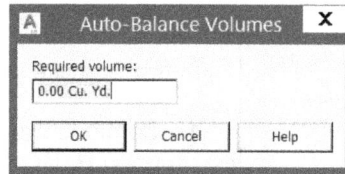

Figure 3–45

8. Review the final volume calculation.

9. Save the drawing.

Chapter Review Questions

1. Which is not an option for creating a feature line?

    a. **Create Feature Lines from Objects**

    b. **Create Feature Lines from Alignment**

    c. **Create Feature Lines from Corridor**

    d. **Create Feature Lines from Profile**

2. When creating a feature line from objects, which object cannot be used?

    a. Lines

    b. Circles

    c. Arcs

    d. Polylines or 3D Polylines

3. Which icon in the Elevation Editor represents an elevation point?

    a. (Circle)

    b. (Triangle)

4. Which icon fills in an area that has not been graded with a grading face?

    a.

    b.

    c.

    d.

5. Which icon in the Grading Volume Tools toolbar enables you to display a history of the grading volume calculations?

    a.

    b.

    c.

    d.

Command Summary

Button	Command	Location
	Auto-Balance	• **Toolbar**: Grading Volume Tools (*contextual*)
	Create Feature Lines From Objects	• **Ribbon**: *Home* tab>Create Design panel, expand Feature Line drop-down list and click Create Feature Lines From Objects • **Command Prompt:** CreateFeatureLines
	Create Grading	• **Toolbar**: Grading Creation Tools (*contextual*)
	Create Grading Infill	• **Toolbar**: Grading Creation Tools (*contextual*) • **Ribbon**: *Home* tab>Create Design panel, expand Grading drop-down list and click Create Grading Infill • **Command Prompt:** CreateGradingInfill
	Elevation Editor	• **Ribbon**: *Feature Line* contextual tab> Edit Elevations panel>Elevation Editor • **Command Prompt:** GradingElevEditor
	Grading Creation Tools	• **Ribbon**: *Home* tab>Create Design panel, expand Grading drop-down list and click Grading Creation Tools • **Command Prompt:** GradingTools
	Grading Volume Tools	• **Ribbon**: *Grading* contextual tab> Grading Tools panel>Grading Volume Tools • **Command Prompt:** GradingVolumeTools
	Lower Grading Features	• **Toolbar**: Grading Volume Tools (*contextual*)
	Raise Grading Features	• **Toolbar**: Grading Volume Tools (*contextual*)
	Set Group	• **Toolbar**: Grading Volume Tools (*contextual*)
	Set Surface	• **Toolbar**: Grading Volume Tools (*contextual*)

4

Parking Lot Design

Parking lots can be a bit more difficult to grade than a building since you need to ensure that it drains properly across the parking surface. In this chapter, you learn how to easily set slopes along a parking lot perimeter using temporary surfaces. Then you create curb returns and grade to the existing ground at various slopes to accommodate the large quantities of fill that are required to set the parking lot at the required elevations. The buildings act as retaining walls at specific locations and access to the building from the parking lot is at the second level.

Learning Objectives in this Chapter

- Draw a feature line from scratch.
- Create a temporary surface to assist in setting feature line elevations and slopes.
- Edit feature lines using the geometry editing tools.
- Copy or Move feature lines from one site to another.
- Create a grading group that transitions from one grade to another along a feature line.
- Create a surface from a grading group.
- Create feature lines that affect the grading group surface.

4.1 Draw Feature Lines

When creating feature lines, ⌐ (Create Feature Line) creates both straight and curved segments. Elevations are assigned at each vertex by typing an elevation value or by assigning an elevation from a surface that exists in the drawing.

How To: Draw a Feature Line

1. In the *Home* tab>Create Design panel, click ⌐ (Create Feature Line).
2. In the Create Feature Line dialog box, set the site, enter a name for the feature line, and select a style for the feature line, as shown in Figure 4–1. Click **OK**.

Note that the conversion options are unavailable.

Figure 4–1

3. In the Command Line you are prompted to *Specify start point:*. Pick a point in the drawing or type a coordinate value where the feature line starts.
4. In the Command Line you are prompted to *Specify elevation*. You can either type an elevation value or type **S** and press <Enter> to obtain a surface elevation at that point.
5. In the Command Line you are prompted to *Specify the next point*. Pick a point in the drawing or type a coordinate value to define the next end point.
6. Type the capital letter(s) from the following options to set the elevation:

Option	Description
Grade	A grade percentage is applied between the previous point and the next point.
SLope	A rise:run slope is applied between the previous point and the next point.
Elevation	The typed elevation is given to the next point.
Difference	An elevation is calculated for the next point by adding an amount to the previous point's elevation value.
SUrface	Obtain the elevation from a selected surface at the next point in the drawing.
Transition	Skips setting the elevation of the next point and subsequent points by pressing <Enter> until an elevation is assigned to the last point. The elevations for all intermediate vertices is calculated from a grade based on the distance between the first and last point and the change in elevation.

7. In the Command Line you are prompted to *Specify the next point*. Type **A** and press <Enter> to draw an arc.
8. Type the capitol letter from the following options to create the arc according to the required design parameters.

Option	Description
Arc end point	Pick an arc end point to complete the arc. The arc is automatically tangential to the previous segment.
Radius	Enter a radius and then pick the end point of the arc or type **L** to enter the arc length. The arc is automatically tangential to the previous segment.
Secondpnt	Pick a point to specify the second point through which the arc must pass. Then specify the arc endpoint by picking another point or typing **L** to set the arc length. This enables the arc to not be tangential to the previous segment.
Line	Returns to drawing straight line segments.
Undo	Undoes the last segment of the feature line.

Using feature line arcs avoids creating tessellated arcs. This is preferred when working with grading footprints because it creates many small grading faces joined by radial corners. If you use 3D polylines as surface breaklines for grading, tessellation occurs and slows down your drawing. You can use the **Fit Curve** command to convert tessellated arcs to true arcs.

4.2 Create a Temporary Surface

Creating a temporary surface can help set elevations of a complex feature line. For example, a feature line that has to follow a specific slope across a site. Parking lots are examples of this strategy because they often slope to one side or to the center for drainage management.

To create a temporary surface, it is recommended that you create a temporary site for the temporary feature lines and grading groups. Once the design feature line has been created it is used for the final grading and the elevations are obtained from the temporary surface. You can then delete the temporary site without losing any design information. This helps to keep the drawing clean and to run faster.

How To: Create a Temporary Surface

1. Create a temporary site for all of the feature lines and grading groups that are going to be deleted later. Define the site by going to the *Prospector* tab, right-clicking on Sites, and selecting **New**.
2. Decide whether you start from the center and grade out in both directions or start on one side and create multiple grading objects going in the same direction at different slopes. Figure 4–2 shows an example of grading from the center out in both directions.

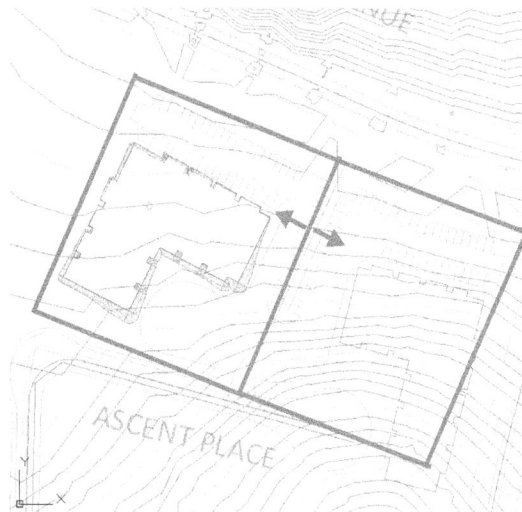

Figure 4–2

3. Create the base feature line.

4. Create a grading group with the **Automatic surface creation** option selected, as shown in Figure 4–3.

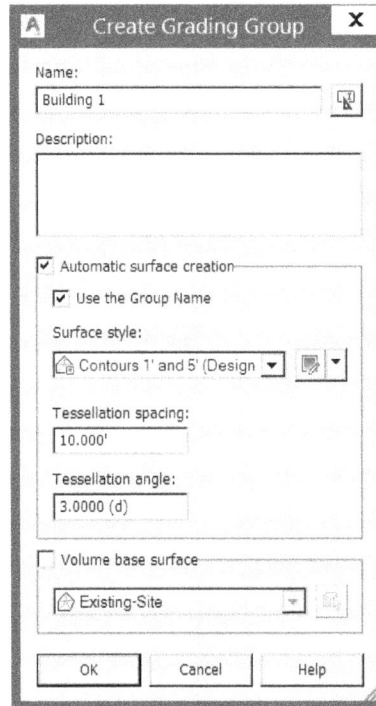

Figure 4–3

5. Create grading from the base feature line out each side at a required distance to cover the entire site. Set a grade in each direction to provides the required slopes.

6. Use the surface elevations from this temporary surface to assign elevations for the actual grading design feature line.

Practice 4a

Draw a Feature Line and Create a Temporary Surface

Practice Objective

- Create a feature line and temporary surface which will be used to assign elevations to the vertices of another feature line.

Estimated time for completion: 10 minutes

In this practice you will create a temporary site, draw a feature line, create a temporary surface, and create a feature line and set elevations by grading.

Task 1 - Create a temporary site.

1. Open **PKLOT-A1-Grading.dwg** from the *C:\Civil3D-Grading\Parking Lot* folder.

2. In the *View* tab>Views panel, select **Parking Lot** as the view to zoom into the parking lot area, as shown in Figure 4–4.

Figure 4–4

3. In the *Prospector* tab, right-click on Sites and select **New**, as shown in Figure 4–5.

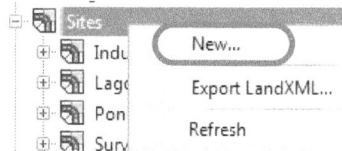

Figure 4–5

4. In the *Information* tab, for the *Name* type **Temp**, and click **OK**.

Task 2 - Draw a feature line.

1. Continue working in the drawing from the previous task or open **PKLOT-A2-Grading.dwg** from the *C:\Civil3D-Grading\ Parking Lot* folder.

2. In the *Home* tab>Create Design panel, click ⤴ (Create Feature Lines).

3. In the Create Feature Lines dialog box, complete the following, as shown in Figure 4–6:
   - For the *Site*, select **Temp**.
   - For the feature line *Name,* type **CenterLine**.
   - For the *Style,* select **Basic Feature Line**.
   - Click **OK**.

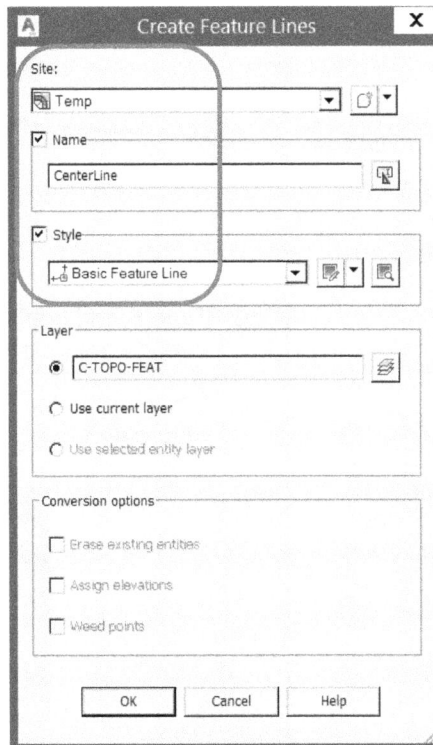

Figure 4–6

4. At the Command Prompt you will be prompted to pick a point. Using the **Endpoint** Osnap, click point one on the parking lot center line, as shown in Figure 4–7.

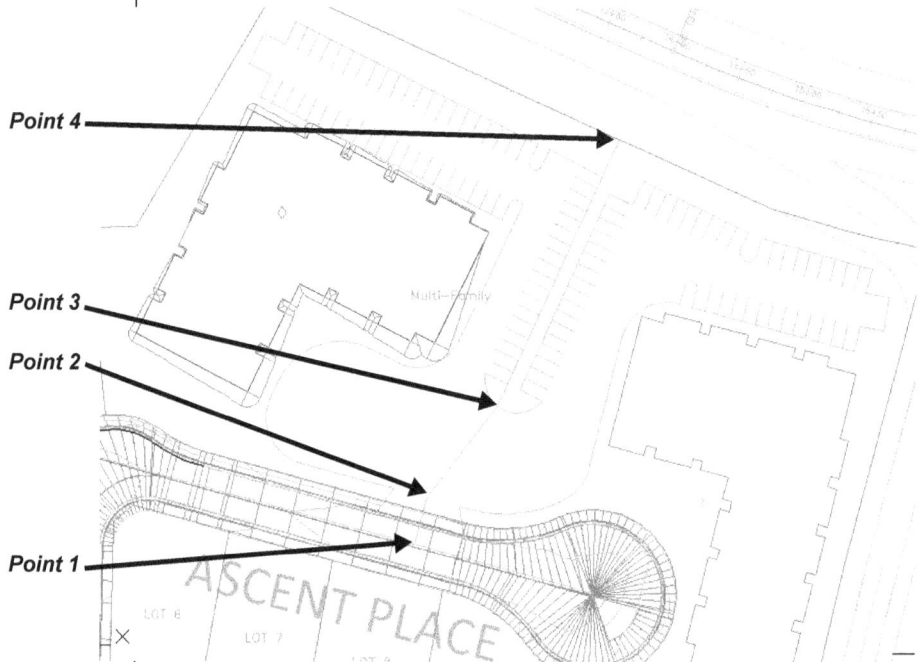

Point 4

Point 3

Point 2

Point 1

Figure 4–7

5. Type **S** and press <Enter> to have it find the elevation of a surface at that point.

6. When prompted for the surface, select **Road1**, as shown in Figure 4–8.

*If this dialog box does not open, type **S** and press <Enter> to select the surface.*

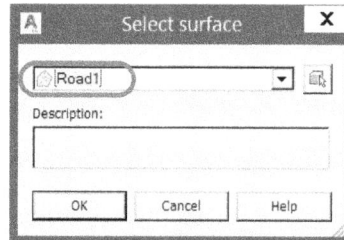

Figure 4–8

7. Press <Enter> to accept 188.719.

8. For the next point, use the **Endpoint** Osnap to pick point 2, as shown in Figure 4–7.

*If grade is not the default, type **G** and press <Enter> before setting the negative 2% grade.*

9. For the elevation, the default will be to set the grade. Type **-2** and press <Enter> to set the grade at 2% going down.

10. For the next point, use the **Endpoint** Osnap to pick point 3, as shown in Figure 4–7.

11. For the elevation, the default will be to set the grade. Type **-2** and press <Enter> to set the grade at 2% going down.

12. For the next point, use the **Endpoint** Osnap to pick point 4, as shown in Figure 4–7.

13. For the elevation, the default will be to set the grade. Type **4** and press <Enter> to set the grade at 4% going up.

14. Press <Enter> to end the command.

15. Save the drawing.

Task 3 - Create a temporary surface.

1. Continue working in the drawing from the previous task or open **PKLOT-A3-Grading.dwg** from the *C:\Civil3D-Grading\ Parking Lot* folder.

2. In the *Home* tab>Create Design panel, click ⌖ (Grading Creation Tools).

3. In the Grading Creations Tools toolbar, click ◹ (Set Group).

4. In the Site dialog box, for the *Site name* select **Temp**, as shown in Figure 4–9. Click **OK**.

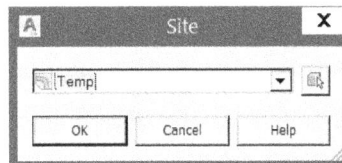

Figure 4–9

5. In the Create Grading Group dialog box, do the following, as shown in Figure 4–10:

- For the *Name*, type **Temp Parking Lot**.
- Select the **Automatic surface creation** option.
- Click **OK** twice to accept all of the other defaults.

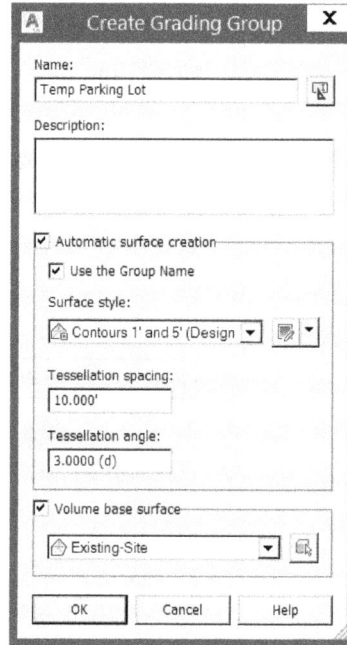

Figure 4–10

6. In the Grading Creation Tools toolbar, select **Grade to Distance** for the criteria, as shown in Figure 4–11.

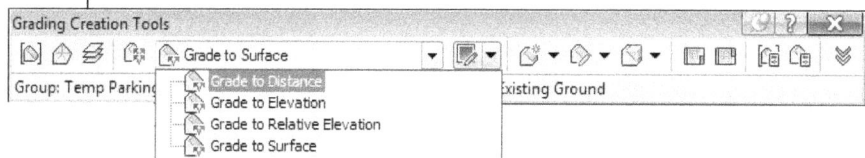

Figure 4–11

7. In the Grading Creation Tools toolbar, click ⟨ (Create Grading.

8. In the drawing, select the CenterLine feature line that you created in the last task, as shown in Figure 4–12.

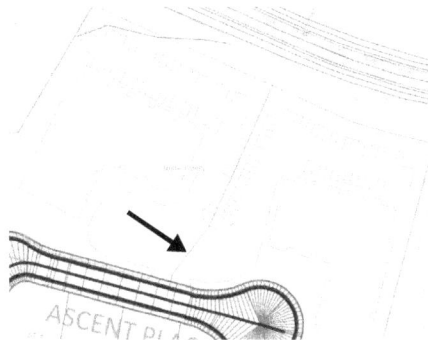

Figure 4–12

9. When prompted for a side to which to grade, pick a point in the drawing to the right of the feature line. Press <Enter> to accept the default to grade the entire length of the feature line.

- For the *Distance*, type **235** and press <Enter>.
- For the *Format*, type **G** and press <Enter> for grade.
- For the *Grade* type **2** for a positive 2% slope.

10. Repeat Steps 2 to 9 to grade to the left side **265'** at a **2%** grade.

11. Press <Esc> to end the command.

12. Close the Grading Creation Tools toolbar.

13. Save the drawing.

Note: If selecting the feature line is difficult, you might need to set the drawing order of the grading surface to the back.

Task 4 - Create a feature line and set elevations by grading.

1. Continue working in the drawing from the previous task or open **PKLOT-A4-Grading.dwg** from the *C:\Civil3D-Grading\ Parking Lot* folder.

2. In the *Home* tab>Create Design panel, expand the Feature Line drop-down list and click (Create Feature Line from Objects).

3. Type **X** and press <Enter> to select linework from the external reference file. Select the magenta line that represents the parking lot perimeter, as shown in Figure 4–13. Press <Enter> to continue.

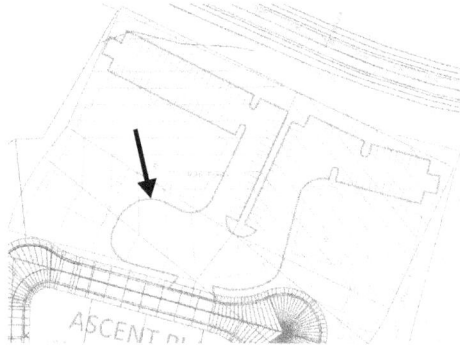

Figure 4–13

4. In the Create Feature Lines dialog box, complete the following, as shown in Figure 4–14:

   • Leave the *Site* set to **Temp**.

   • For the *Name*, type **ParkingEOP**.

   • Set the *Style* to **Parking Lot**.

   • Verify that **Assign elevations** is selected.

   • Click **OK**.

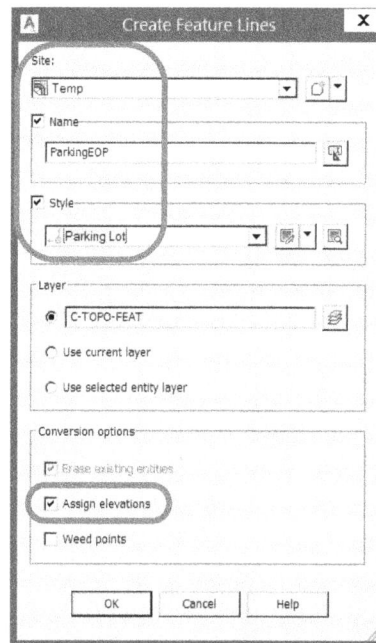

Figure 4–14

5. In the Assign Elevations dialog box, select **From gradings**, as shown in Figure 4–15. Click **OK**.

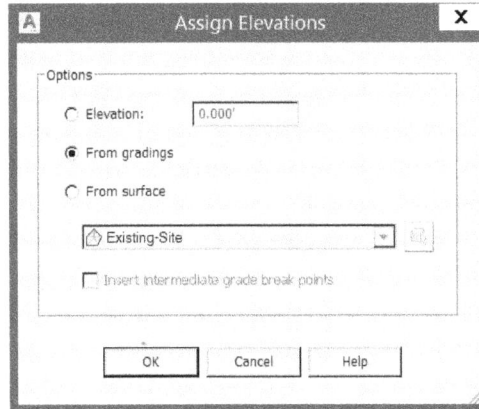

Figure 4–15

6. Save the drawing.

4.3 Edit Feature Line Geometry

Working with feature lines is similar to working with standard AutoCAD lines and polylines. The differences are with the tools that are used to make the required changes. To access the tools, select a feature line. In the *Feature Line contextual tab*>Modify panel, click ⬚ (Edit Geometry). The Edit Geometry panel displays, as shown in Figure 4–16.

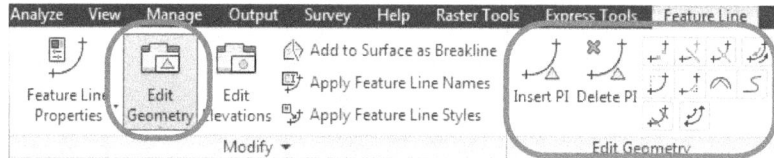

Figure 4–16

The tool functions are as follows:

Icon	Command	Description
	Insert PI	Adds a new vertex to a feature line, survey figure, parcel line, polyline, or 3D polyline, giving you additional horizontal and vertical control.
	Delete PI	Removes a selected vertex from a feature line, survey figure, parcel line, polyline, or 3D polyline.
	Break	Creates a gap or break in a feature line, survey figure, or parcel line. The location selected when picking the object is the first point of the break, unless otherwise specified.
	Trim	Removes part of a feature line, survey figure, or parcel line at the specified boundary edge.
	Join	Combines two feature lines, survey figures, parcel lines, polylines, or 3D polylines that fall within the tolerance distance set in the command settings.
	Reverse	Changes the direction of the stationing along a feature line, survey figure, parcel line, polyline, or 3D polyline.
	Edit Curve	Changes the radius of a feature line arc, parcel line arc, or survey figure arc.
	Fillet	Creates a curve between two segments of selected feature line(s), survey figures, parcel lines, or 3D polylines.

	Fit Curve	Places a curve between the selected vertices of a feature line, survey figure, parcel line, or 3D polyline while removing vertices between the selected vertices. Useful for converting tessellated lines to true arcs.
	Smooth	Adds multiple arcs to feature lines or survey figures to assist in smoothing tessellated lines.
	Weed	Removes unnecessary vertices along feature lines, polylines, or 3D polylines based on defined angle, grade, length, and 3D distance values.
	Stepped Offset	Creates copies of a selected feature line, survey figure, polyline, or 3D polyline at a specified horizontal and vertical distance away from the original object.

Delete PI

Reshaping a feature line is easily done by removing vertices where lines intersect or where lines connect to arcs. When you delete a PI from a feature line, it is just like using the straighten command within the Polyline Edit command.

How To: Modify a Feature Line Using the Delete PI Command

1. In the Drawing, select a feature line.
2. In the *Feature Line contextual tab*>Modify panel, click

   (Edit Geometry). In the Edit Geometry panel that

   displays, click (Delete PI).
3. In the drawing, click near the vertex you wish to remove.

Stepped Offsets

When working in the standard AutoCAD® software, you can use the **Offset** command to quickly make copies of lines, arcs, and polylines at a specific horizontal distance away from the original object. However, when working in 3D, a horizontal and vertical offset is often required. That is why the **Stepped Offset** command is available. You can use it to make copies of feature lines, survey figures, and parcel lines a specified distance away from the original object both horizontally and vertically.

How To: Create Stepped Offsets

1. In the *Home* tab>Create Design panel, expand the Feature Line drop-down list and click (Stepped Offset), as shown in Figure 4–17.

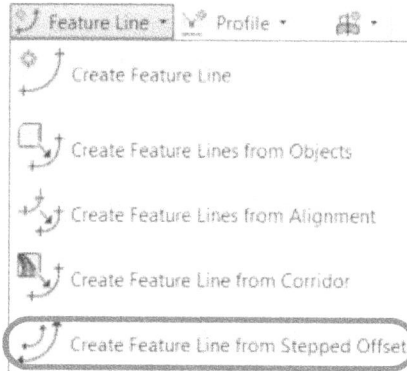

Figure 4–17

2. Specify the distance to offset the new object by typing a numeric value or type **T** to specify the point the new object should pass through.
3. Select the feature line, survey figure, or parcel line to offset from the drawing.
4. Specify which side to offset to by picking a point in the drawing.
5. Type the capitol letter from the following options to set the elevation of the new object.

Option	Description
Grade	A grade percentage is applied between the original object and the newly offset object.
SLope	A rise:run slope is applied between the original object and the newly offset object.
Elevation	The typed elevation is assigned to the new object.
Difference	An elevation is calculated for the new object's vertices by adding the amount entered to the original feature line, parcel line, or survey figure's vertice elevations.
Variable	Enables you to enter a new elevation or a difference in elevation for each vertex along the new feature line, survey figure, or parcel line.

- The default option is set to **Difference** or the last option used.

4.4 Copy or Move Feature Lines from One Site to Another

Feature lines must reside in a site to be created and used. If you use feature lines for grading, it is important that they reside in the same site as their grading group. Sometimes feature lines are created in the wrong site or need to be reused in other sites. In these cases you can move or copy a feature line from one site to another. You are able to copy or move the contents of an entire site (alignments, grading groups, parcels, and feature lines) to another site.

How To: Move or Copy Feature Lines

1. Select the object(s) to move or copy.
2. Right-click and select **Move to Site** or **Copy to Site**, as shown in Figure 4–18.

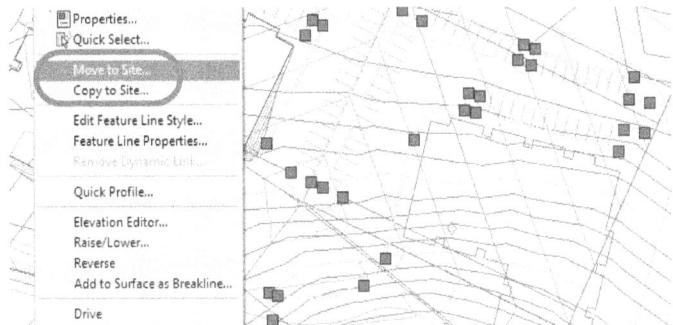

Figure 4–18

3. In the dialog box, select an option for the *Destination site*, as shown in Figure 4–19.

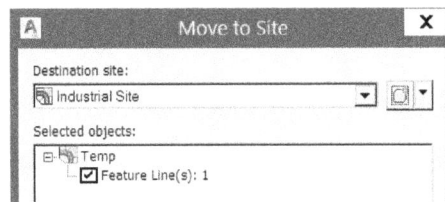

Figure 4–19

4.5 Create a Transitional Grading Group

So far you have only created grading groups that follow the same slope the entire length of the feature line. Some designs require a transition from one slope to another to accommodate large differences in elevation without a large amount of grading area. For example, you have a target slope for a site of 5:1, but can grade as steep as 2:1 if needed. You might need to use a 2:1 slope to ensure that you do not encroach on an easement, another building, or a property line. To fit a building on the property, you can grade the front to the preferred slope of 5:1, and then grade the back at 2:1 to ensure that you stay within the property line. In between the two slopes, you use a transitional grading object and have the computer calculate the transitional slopes between the building's front and back, as shown in Figure 4–20. In this example, you had to change grading slopes to ensure that the building to the north is not encroached on by the cut or fill slopes from the building to the south.

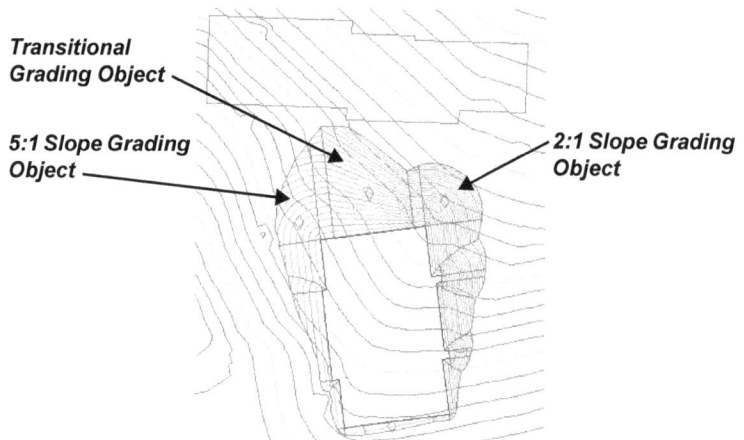

Transitional Grading Object

5:1 Slope Grading Object

2:1 Slope Grading Object

Figure 4–20

How To: Create Transitional Grading Groups

1. In the *Home* tab>Create Design panel, expand the Grading drop-down list and click 🖋 (Grading Creation Tools).

2. In the Grading Creation Tools toolbar, click 🔲 (Set Group) on the far left. Select the **Site** in which you want to work, as shown in Figure 4–21.

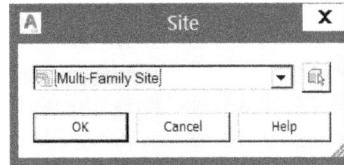

Figure 4–21

3. In the Create Grading Group dialog box, type a name in the *Name* field. Do not select the **Automatic surface creation** option, as shown in Figure 4–22. Click **OK**.

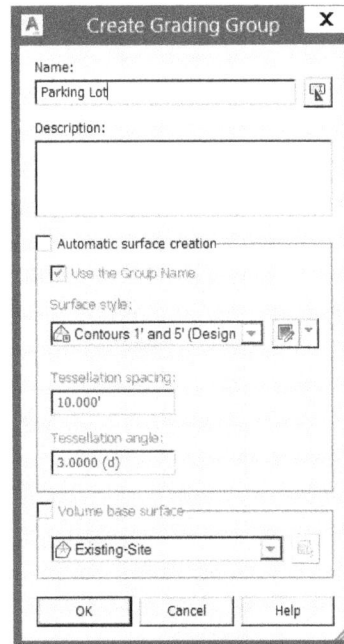

Figure 4–22

4. In the Grading Creation Tools toolbar, click 🔲 (Select a Criteria Set) to select the grading criteria set that is required for the project.
5. Set the required grading criteria, as shown in Figure 4–23.

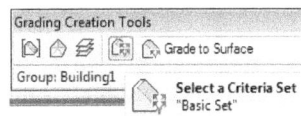

Figure 4–23

6. In the Grading Creation Tools toolbar, click 🔲 (Create Grading). Select the feature line to use as the baseline.

7. When prompted for a grading side, pick a point in the drawing.
8. When prompted to apply it to the entire length, type **N** and press <Enter>.
9. In the Command Line, the routine prompts you to *Select the start point:*. In the drawing, an arrow displays pointing in the direction of the feature line stations to help you pick the point to start your first slope, as shown in Figure 4–24.

You can use any Osnap commands or type the feature line station value.

Station:1+92.50', Elevation:237.00'

Figure 4–24

10. In the Command Line, the station you selected displays for your verification (this occurs even if you are typing the station). Press <Enter> to accept.
11. In the Command Line, you are prompted to specify the end point for the grading. You can either pick a point in the drawing (as you did in Step 10), or proceed as follows:
    - Type a feature line station.
    - Or type **L** and press <Enter> to set the length of the grading.
    - In the drawing, an arrow displays pointing in the opposite direction as the starting point for the grading, as shown in Figure 4–25.

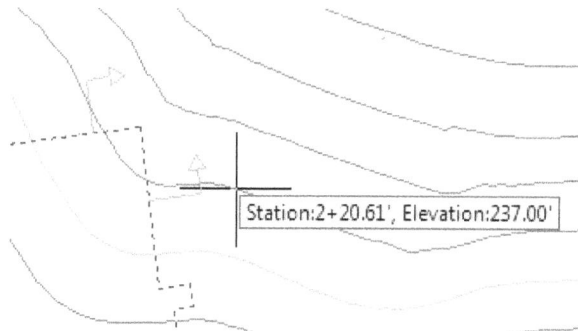

Station:2+20.61', Elevation:237.00'

Figure 4–25

12. In the Command Line, the station displays for verification even if you are typing the station value. Press <Enter> to accept it.

13. Repeat Steps 1 to 12 to set another grading criteria on the same feature line. Your results should be similar to those shown in Figure 4–26.

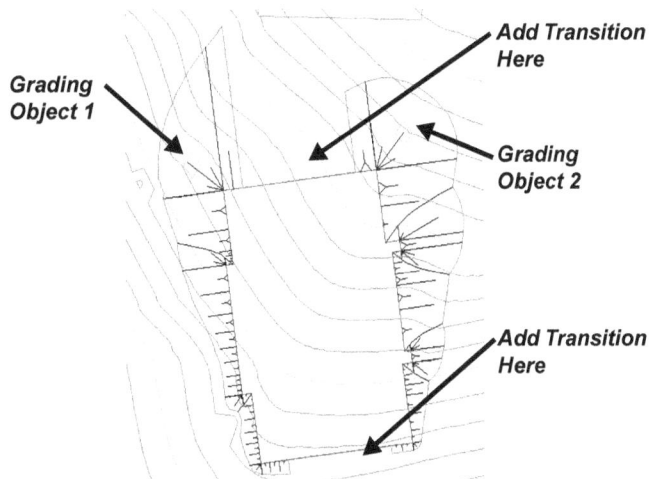

Figure 4–26

14. In the Grading Creation Tools toolbar, expand the Create Grading drop-down list and click ⬡ (Create Transition).
15. In the Command Line, you are prompted to *Select the feature:* Select the feature line that has been partially graded.
16. In the Command Line, you are prompted to pick a point between the gradings. Select between any previously created grading objects, as shown in Figure 4–26.
17. Repeat Steps 15 to 16 as needed to complete all of the transitions.
18. Press <Esc> to end the command.

Practice 4b

Create Stepped Offsets and Transitional Gradings

Practice Objective

* Create curb returns using stepped offsets and incorporate them into a parking lot grading group.

Estimated time for completion: 30 minutes

In this practice you will create stepped offsets. You will also move feature lines to a different site, grade to a surface with varying slopes along one feature line, and create transitions between predefined grading objects along the same feature line.

Task 1 - Create stepped offsets.

1. Continue working in the drawing from the last practice or open **PKLOT-B1-Grading.dwg** from the *C:\Civil3D-Grading\ Parking Lot* folder.

2. In the *Prospector* tab, expand **Sites>Temp** and select the feature lines. In the preview window, select **Parking EOP**, right-click and select **Select**, as shown in Figure 4–27.

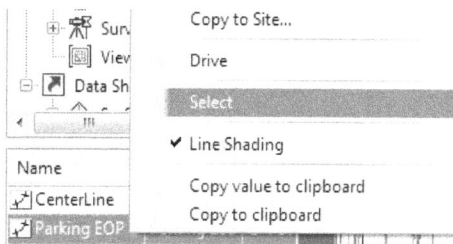

Figure 4–27

If the Edit Geometry panel is not displayed,

click ▣ (Edit Geometry) in the Feature Line contextual tab>Modify panel.

3. In the *Feature Line* contextual tab>Edit Geometry panel, click ⤵ (Stepped Offset).

4. For the *Offset Distance*, type **2** and press <Enter>.

5. In the drawing, pick a point inside the parking area for the side to which to offset.

6. To set the elevation, type **G** and press <Enter> for grade.

7. For the grade, type **2** to set the grade at 2%. (This will act as the lip of curb.)

8. Press <Esc> to end the command.

You are going to start the command again in the next Step, but first you have to exit and then restart the command to set a different offset value for the next feature line.

9. In the *Prospector* tab, expand **Sites>Temp**, and select the feature lines. In the preview window, select **Parking EOP**, right-click and select **Select**, as shown in Figure 4–28.

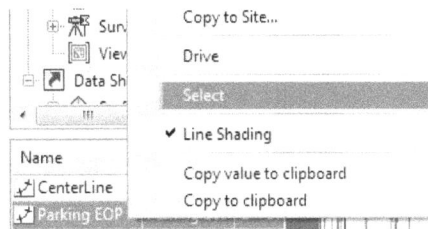

Figure 4–28

10. In the *Feature Line* contextual tab>Edit Geometry panel, click ↲ (Stepped Offset).

- For the *Offset Distance*, type **0.1**.
- In the drawing, pick a point outside the Parking EOP feature line for the side to which to offset.
- To set the elevation, type **D** and press <Enter> for *Difference*.
- For the difference in elevation, type **0.5** to set the new feature line 6" above the other one. (This creates the curb face for the parking lot.)
- Press <Esc> to end the command.
- Press <Esc> again to release the selection.

11. In the *Prospector* tab, expand **Sites>Temp**, and select the feature lines. In the preview window, select the last feature line without a name, right-click and select **Select**, as shown in Figure 4–29.

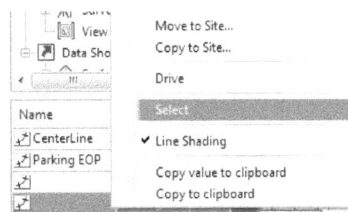

Figure 4–29

12. In the *Feature Line* contextual tab>Edit Geometry panel, click

    🕊 (Stepped Offset).

- For the *Offset Distance*, type **0.5**.
- In the drawing, pick a point outside the Parking EOP feature line for the side to which to offset.
- To set the elevation, type **D** and press <Enter> for *Difference*.
- For the difference in elevation, type **0** to set the new feature line at the same elevation as the other one. (This creates the top back of curb for the parking lot.)
- Press <Esc> to end the command.

13. If you zoom in the four lines representing the curb are displayed, as shown in Figure 4–30.

Figure 4–30

14. Save the drawing.

Task 2 - Move feature lines to a different site.

You now have all of the necessary feature lines in the Temp site. However, you need to move them to the Multi-Family site so they interact with the Building1 grading group that was previously created.

1. Continue working in the drawing from the previous task or open **PKLOT-B2-Grading.dwg** from the *C:\Civil3D-Grading\ Parking Lot* folder.

2. Select the last feature line created from the stepped offset (the top back of the curb), as shown in Figure 4–31.

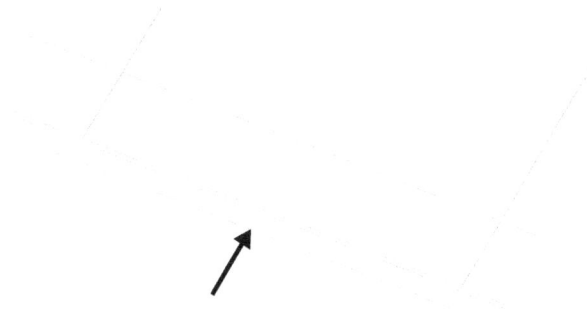

Figure 4–31

3. Right-click and select **Move to Site**, as shown in Figure 4–32.

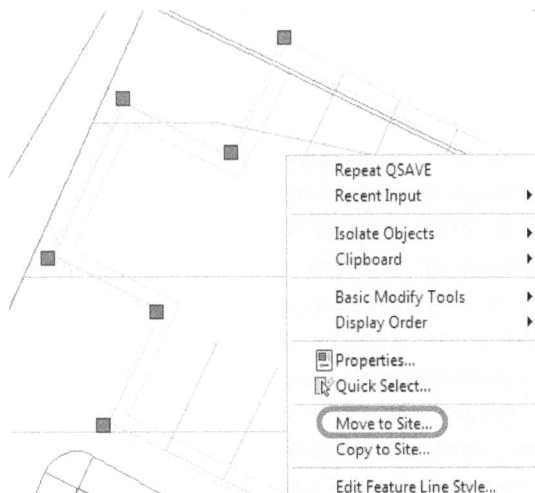

Figure 4–32

4. Set the *Destination site* to **Multi-Family Site**, as shown in Figure 4–33. Click **OK**.

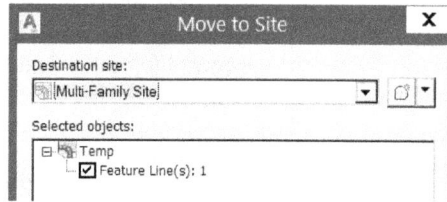

Figure 4–33

5. In the drawing, select the top back of curb feature line in the Muti-Family Site.

If the Edit Geometry panel is not displayed, in the Feature Line contextual tab>Modify panel, click ⬚ (Edit Geometry).

6. In the Edit Geometry panel that displays, click ⬚ (Delete PI).

7. In the drawing, remove the four vertices circled in Figure 4–34.

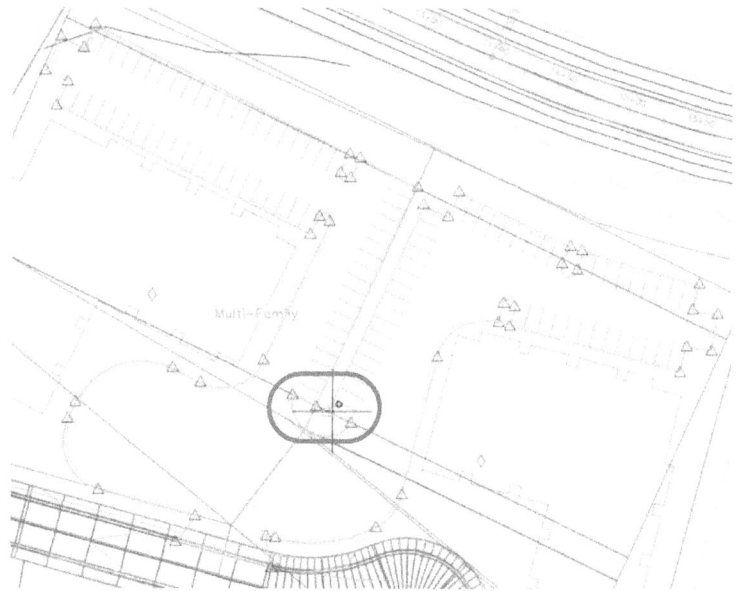

Figure 4–34

8. Press <Esc> and save the drawing.

Task 3 - Grade to a surface with varying slopes along one feature line.

1. Continue working in the drawing from the previous task or open **PKLOT-B3-Grading.dwg** from the *C:\Civil3D-Grading\ Parking Lot* folder.

2. In the *Home* tab>Create Design panel, expand the Grading drop-down list, and click ⬥ (Grading Creation Tools).

3. In the Grading Creation Tools toolbar, click ⬥ (Set Group) on the far left to open the Select Grading Group dialog box.

4. In the Select Grading Group dialog box, select the **Multi-Family Site** and click ⬥ (Create Grading Group), as shown in Figure 4–35.

Figure 4–35

5. In the Create Grading Group dialog box, complete the following, as shown in Figure 4–36:
   - In the *Name* field, type **Parking Lot**.
   - Do not select the **Automatic surface creation** option.
   - Click **OK** twice to return to the Grading Creation Tools toolbar.

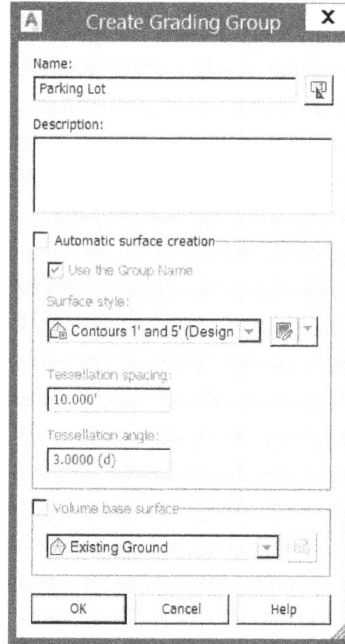

Figure 4–36

6. In the Grading Creation Tools toolbar, click ⬧ (Set Surface) In the Select surface dialog box, select **Existing Ground**. Click **OK**.

7. In the Grading Creation Tools toolbar, verify that the grading criteria set is set to **Basic Set**. Then set the grading criteria to **Grade to Surface**, as shown in Figure 4–37.

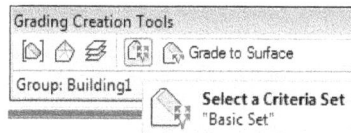

Figure 4–37

8. In the Grading Creation Tools toolbar, click ⬡ (Create Grading). Select the top back of curb feature line to use as the baseline, as shown in Figure 4–38.

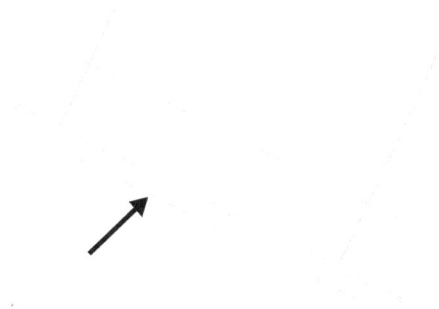

Figure 4–38

9. When prompted for a grading side, pick a point on the outside of the parking lot.

10. When prompted to apply it to the entire length, type **N** and press <Enter>.

11. Using the **Endpoint** Osnap, select the endpoint at the beginning of the feature line. Press <Enter> to accept <0+00.00> as the beginning value.

12. Using the **Midpoint** Osnap, select the midpoint of the first curve, as shown in Figure 4–39. Press <Enter> to accept <0+62.77'> as the ending value.

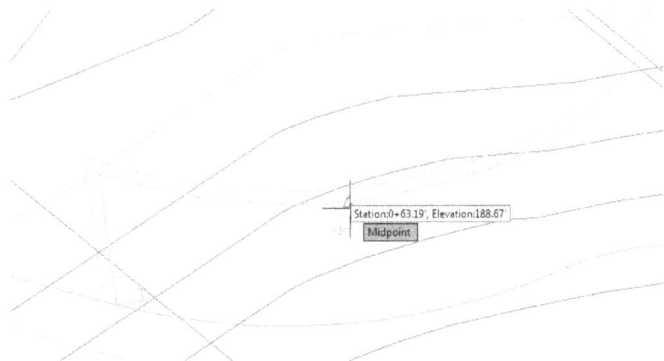

Station:0+63.19', Elevation:188.67'

Midpoint

Figure 4–39

13. Press <Enter> to accept **Slope** as the cut format. Type **2** for a 2:1 slope.

The command continues until you press <Esc>. Rather than end the command, select the same feature line again to continue grading until prompted to press <Esc>.

14. Press <Enter> to accept **Slope** as the fill format. Type **2** for a 2:1 slope.

15. Select the curb feature line again.

16. Select a point on the outside of the parking lot to which to grade.

17. In the Command Line, type **135** for the start point. Press <Enter> to accept the beginning value. This is near the beginning of the building 2 footprint.

18. Using the **Endpoint** Osnap, select the south corner of the parking lot north of building 2 for the endpoint, as shown in Figure 4–40. Press <Enter> to accept <4+34.16'> as the end value.

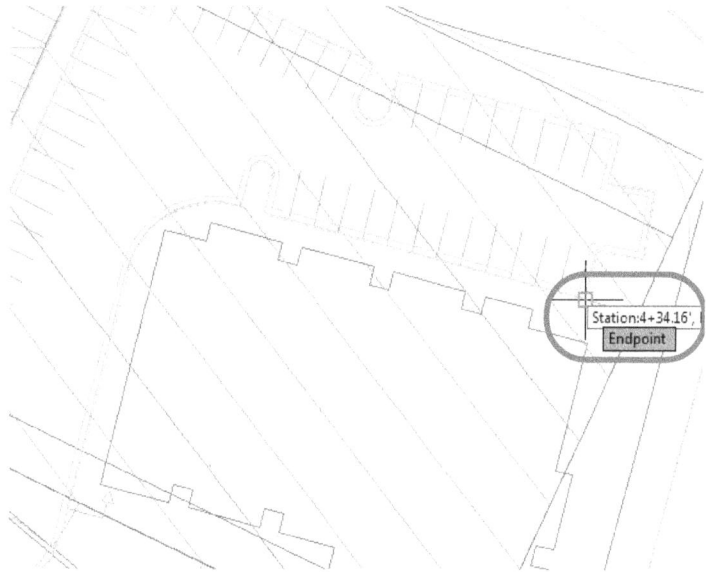

Figure 4–40

19. Press <Enter> to accept **Slope** as the cut format. Type **0.1** for a 0.1:1 slope.

20. Press <Enter> to accept **Slope** as the fill format. Type **0.1** for a 0.1:1 slope.

21. Select the curb feature line again.

22. Select a point on the outside of the parking lot to which to grade.

23. For the beginning point, select the endpoint at the top right corner of the parking lot north of the last endpoint selected, as shown in Figure 4–41.

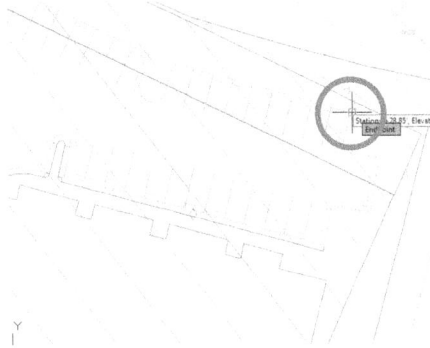

Figure 4–41

24. Press <Enter> to accept <5+28.85'> as the station.

25. For the ending point, select the endpoint at the top left corner on the far north west side of the parking lot, as shown in Figure 4–42.

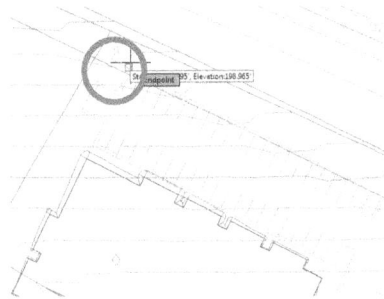

Figure 4–42

26. Press <Enter> to accept <10+67.74'> as the station.

27. Press <Enter> to accept **Slope** as the cut format. Type **2** for a 2:1 slope.

28. Press <Enter> to accept **Slope** as the fill format. Type **2** for a 2:1 slope.

29. Select the curb feature line again and select a point on the outside of the parking lot to which to grade.

30. Using the **Endpoint** Osnap, select the south corner of the parking lot north of building 1 as the start point, as shown in Figure 4–43. Press <Enter> to accept <11+62.68'> as the start point.

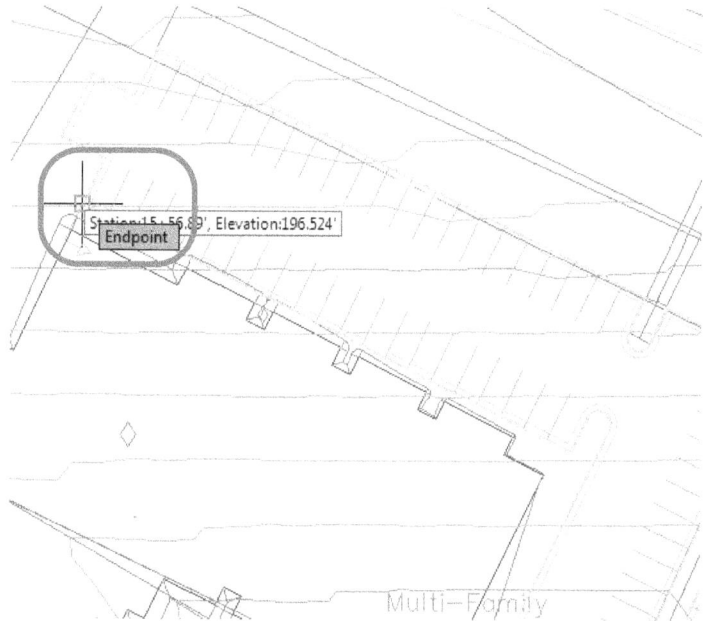

Station:15+56.89', Elevation:196.524'
Endpoint

Multi-Family

Figure 4–43

31. In the Command Line, type **1650** for the end point. Press <Enter> to accept it.

32. Press <Enter> to accept **Slope** as the cut format. Type **0.1** for a 0.1:1 slope.

33. Press <Enter> to accept **Slope** as the fill format. Type **0.1** for a 0.1:1 slope.

34. Select the curb feature line again and pick a point on the outside to which to grade.

35. Using Osnaps, select the endpoint of the last curve near the parking lot entrance, as shown in Figure 4–44.

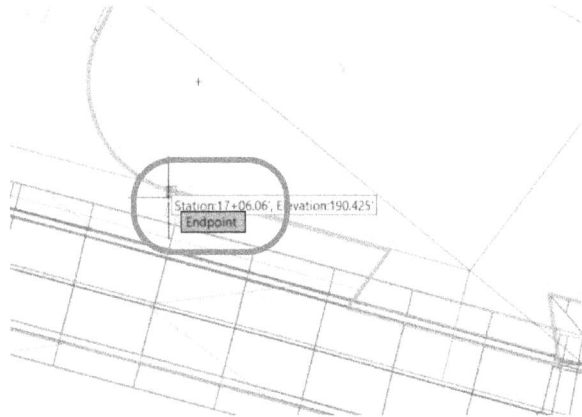

Figure 4–44

36. Press <Enter> to accept <17+06.06'> as the station.

37. Using Osnaps, select the endpoint of the feature line at the parking lot entrance, as shown in Figure 4–45.

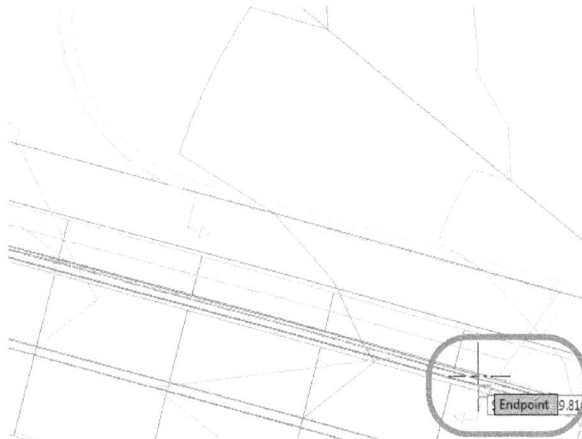

Figure 4–45

38. Press <Enter> to accept <17+95.60'> as the station.

39. Press <Enter> to accept **Slope** as the cut format. Type **2** for a 2:1 slope.

40. Press <Enter> to accept **Slope** as the fill format. Type **2** for a 2:1 slope.

41. Press <Esc> to end the command.

42. Save the drawing.

Task 4 - Create Transitions between predefined grading objects along the same feature line.

1. Continue working in the drawing from the previous task or open **PKLOT-B4-Grading.dwg** from the *C:\Civil3D-Grading\ Parking Lot* folder.

2. In the Grading Creation Tools toolbar, expand the Create Grading drop-down list and click 🏵 (Create Transition).

3. Select the curb feature line that contains the previously created grading objects.

4. In the Command Line, you are prompted to pick a point between the gradings. Select between two previously created grading objects, as shown in Figure 4–46.

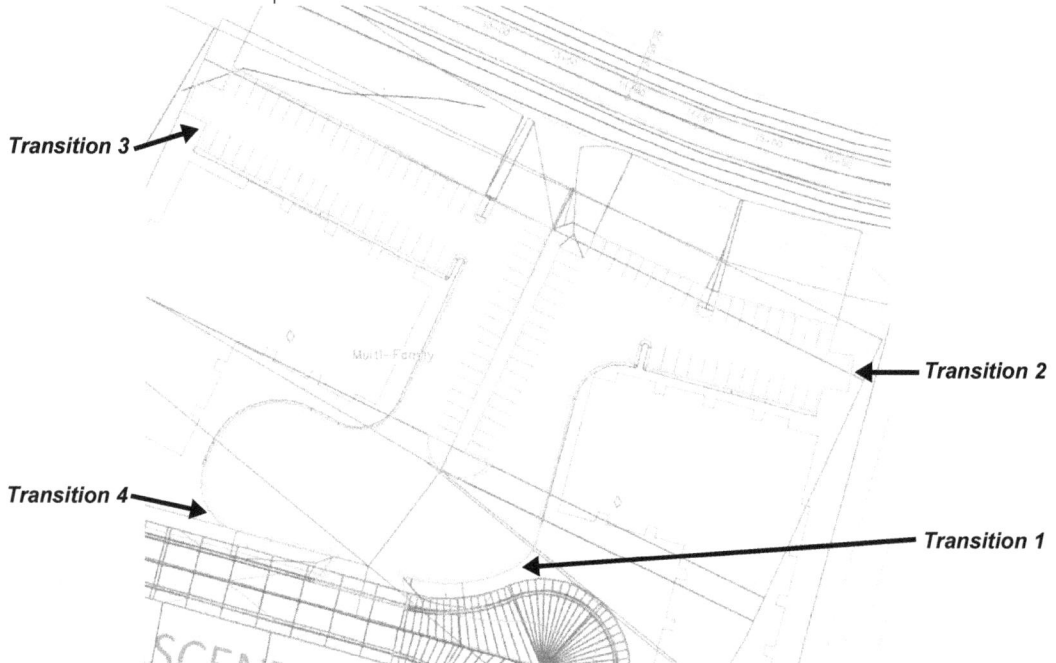

Figure 4–46

5. Repeat Steps 3 to 4 as needed to complete all four transitions.

6. Press <Esc> to end the command.

7. Save the drawing.

4.6 Create a Grading Surface

When working with complex grading objects, it is better to completely design the grading group before creating its surface. In most design workflows, as you first create the grading group, you clear the option to create a surface automatically and then build a surface from the grading group at a later time.

When you are ready to build the surface, you can select any part of the grading group. In the *Grading* contextual tab, click

(Grading Group Properties). In the Grading Group Properties dialog box, select the **Automatic Surface Creation** option to create a surface and click **OK**, as shown in Figure 4–47. You can also select the **Volume Base Surface** option if needed.

Figure 4–47

The Create Surface dialog box opens and you enter a surface name (the grading group name is the default surface name), type a description, set a style, and set a render material. Clicking **OK** creates the surface and displays the contours.

4.7 Add Feature Lines to a Grading Surface

After creating a grading group, any feature lines in the same area affects the surface that was created by the grading group. The key to making this work is to ensure that the grading group and feature lines are in the same site. Figure 4–48 shows what happens when feature lines are drawn on top of a grading object in the same site.

Before adding a feature line

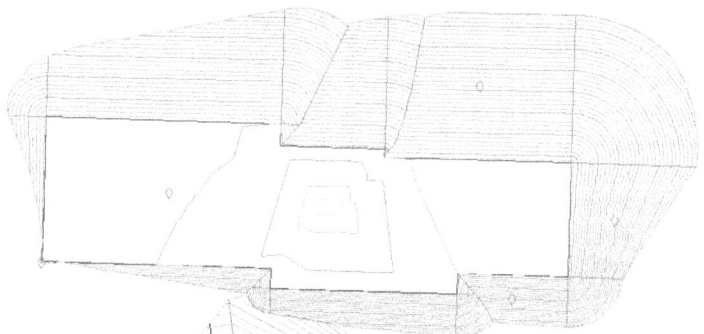

After adding a feature line

Figure 4–48

Practice 4c

Estimated time for completion: 10 minutes

Create a Surface with Proper Drainage

Practice Objective

- Create a grading group surface and add feature lines for proper drainage.

In this practice you will prepare to create a grading surface, create the grading surface, and add feature lines to a grading surface.

Task 1 - Prepare to create a grading surface.

Before creating a finished ground surface, you need to clean up and finish the grading group. So far you have created multiple feature lines to represent the curb and gutter of the parking area. You have also created grading objects all the way around the parking lot. Next you need to infill the center of the parking lot to add the pavement's grading.

1. Continue working in the drawing from the previous practice or open **PKLOT-C1-Grading.dwg** from the *C:\Civil3D-Grading\ Parking Lot* folder.

2. In the *Home* tab>Create Design panel, expand the Grading drop-down list and click (Create Infill).

3. Pick a point in the center of the parking lot area, as shown in Figure 4–49.

Figure 4–49

4. Press <Esc> to end the command and save the drawing.

Task 2 - Create the grading surface.

1. Continue working in the drawing from the previous task or open **PKLOT-C2-Grading.dwg** from the *C:\Civil3D-Grading\ Parking Lot* folder.

2. Select the diamond shape representing the infill center mark of the parking lot (or any part of the grading group). In the *Grading* contextual tab>Modify panel, click ▣ (Grading Group Properties).

3. In the Grading Group Properties dialog box, in the *Information* tab, select the **Automatic Surface Creation** option, as shown in Figure 4–50.

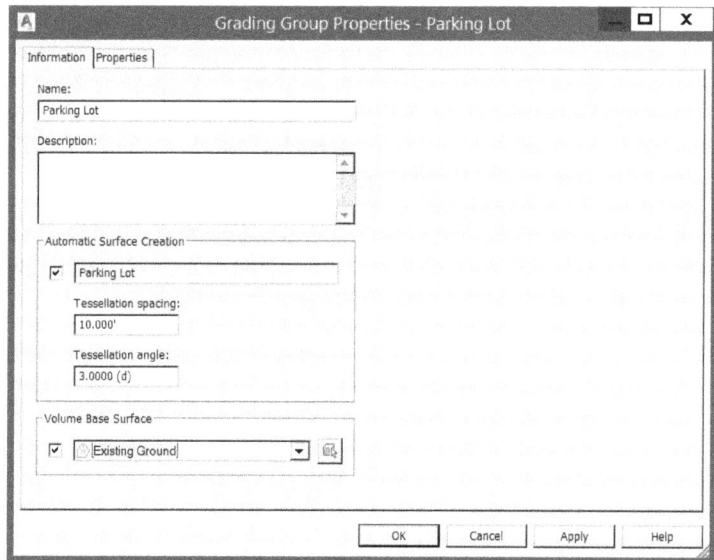

Figure 4–50

4. When the Create Surface dialog box opens, click **OK** to accept the defaults.

5. Select the **Volume Base Surface** option and select **Existing Ground** for the base surface.

6. Click **OK** and save the drawing.

Task 3 - Add feature lines to a grading surface.

1. Continue working in the drawing from the previous task or open **PKLOT-C3-Grading.dwg** from the *C:\Civil3D-Grading\ Parking Lot* folder.

2. In the *Prospector* tab, expand **Sites>Temp**. Select the Feature Lines collection to view them in the preview. Select all of the feature lines except **CenterLine**, right-click and select **Move to Site**, as shown in Figure 4–51.

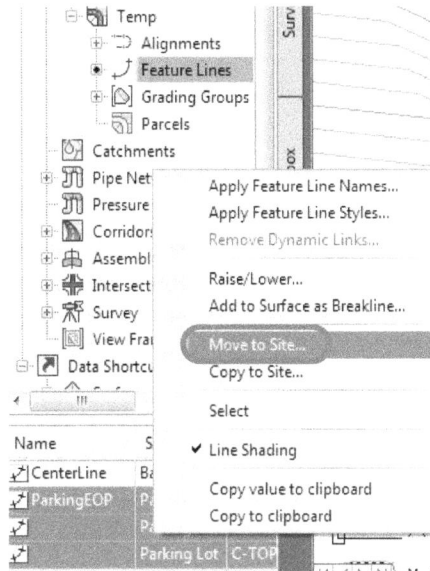

Figure 4–51

3. In the Move to Site dialog box, select **Multi-Family Site** as the destination site, as shown in Figure 4–52.

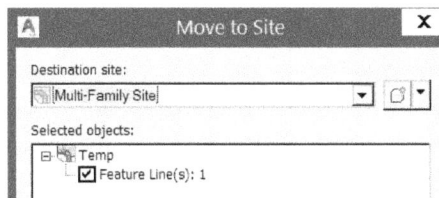

Figure 4–52

The original infill grading object automatically fills in the center island of the parking lot. You need to add additional infill grading objects to fill in the surface of the asphalt and the curbs.

4. In the *Home* tab>Create Design panel, expand the Grading drop-down list and click (Create Infill).

5. Pick a point in the center of the parking lot area, as shown in Figure 4–53.

Figure 4–53

6. Repeat Steps 4 and 5 to add infill between each of the curb lines. When you are done, you should see that the grading is slightly affected along the edge of the parking lot where the feature lines have caused more definition, as shown in Figure 4–54.

Figure 4–54

7. You can now delete the Temp Site. In the *Prospector* tab, expand **Sites**. Right-click on Temp and select **Delete**, as shown in Figure 4–55.

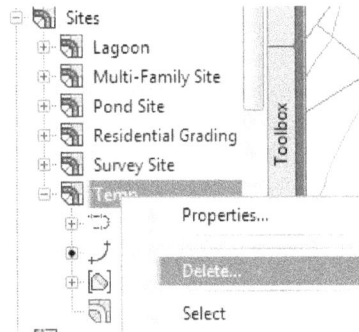

Figure 4–55

8. Save the drawing.

Chapter Review Questions

1. Which of the following is NOT an option for setting the elevation a feature line vertex as you draw it?

    a. Slope

    b. Transition

    c. Surface

    d. Grading Object

2. Which of the following is NOT an option for creating curves within feature lines as you draw them?

    a. Secondpnt

    b. Diameter

    c. Radius

    d. Arc end point

3. The **Stepped Offset** command is the same as the AutoCAD **Offset** command. These commands can be used interchangeably.

    a. True

    b. False

4. Which of the following is not an option for setting elevations when using the **Stepped Offset** command?

    a. Grade

    b. Slope

    c. Difference

    d. Surface

5. Which icon in the Grading Creation Tools toolbar enables you to create transitions between two grading objects of varying slopes?

    a.

    b.

    c.

    d.

Command Summary

Button	Command	Location
	Create Feature Line	• **Ribbon**: *Home* tab>Create Design panel, expand Feature Line drop-down list
		• **Command Prompt:** DrawFeatureLine
	Create Infill	• **Ribbon**: *Home* tab>Create Design panel, expand Grading drop-down list
		• **Toolbar**: Grading Creation Tools (*contextual*), expand Create Grading drop-down list
	Delete PI	• **Ribbon**: *Grading* contextual tab> Edit Geometry panel
		• **Command Prompt:** DeleteFeaturePI
	Grading Group Properties	• **Ribbon**: *Grading* contextual tab> Modify panel
	Stepped Offset	• **Ribbon**: *Feature Line* contextual tab> Edit Geometry panel
		• **Command Prompt:** GradingElevEditor

Pond Design

Pond grading can be some of the most difficult grading projects. They often require grading one object from another and combining various feature lines to use as a baseline. In this chapter you learn more feature line editing tools and work with complex grading groups.

Learning Objectives in this Chapter

- Review what you have already learned about creating feature lines.
- Change the elevations of a feature line using the Elevation Editor panel tools.
- Create feature lines from corridors to take advantage of existing design data.
- Edit feature lines using geometry editing tools, such as break, trim, join, etc.
- Create a grading object from another, previously created grading object.

5.1 Feature Line Review

There are times when you cannot create a simple grading object. For example, the design criteria required for the pond cross-section shown in Figure 5–1 is too complex for just a grading group.

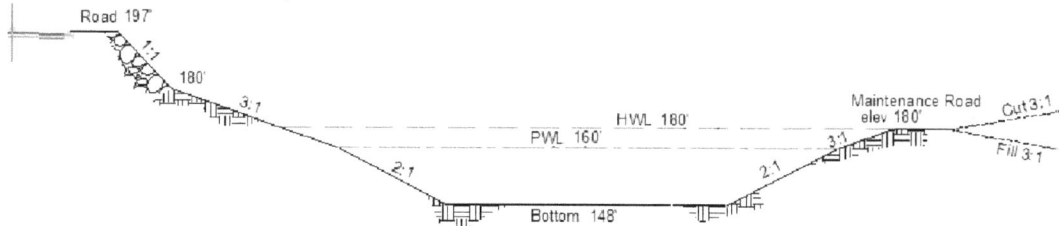

Figure 5–1

Each side of the pond requires different grading criteria:

- At the **South end** of the pond site is a road which has an elevation of 197'. The road is elevated at an average of 20' above the adjacent parcels. As a result, you use a 1:1 slope from the road so that you can create a pond base elevation of 180'.

- At the **North end** of the pond site, a maintenance access road is designed that is elevated 3' above the Permanent Water Level (PWL).

To grade the pond as shown in the cross-section, you must establish a base feature line that uses a common grading criteria. This involves the following:

- Creating a base feature line to the South (1:1 to elev 180').

- Creating a base feature line to the North (3:1 to elev 164').

- Joining the trimmed east and west feature lines to the north and south control feature lines.

- Grading the pond based on this new combined feature line.

Feature Line Contextual Tab

The *Feature Line* contextual tab (shown in Figure 5–2), contains commands that enable you to edit and modify feature lines. These include tools to edit feature line elevations and feature line geometry, such as **Break**, **Trim**, **Join**, and **Fillet** (which creates a true, 3D curve).

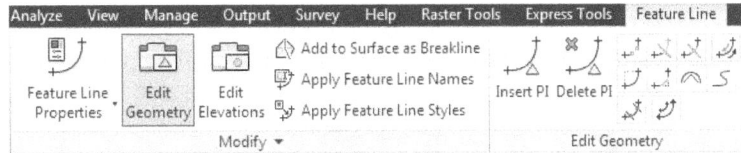

Figure 5–2

The **Create Feature Line** and **Create Feature Lines from Objects** commands are accessed in the *Home* tab>Create Design panel, expanded Feature Line drop-down list, as shown in Figure 5–3.

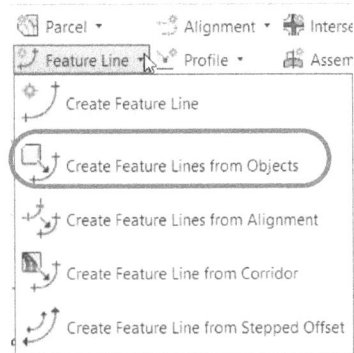

Figure 5–3

These commands can be used to draw feature lines from scratch and to establish an elevation at each vertex. You can also use existing objects to create feature lines and set the elevations of their vertices from surfaces and grading objects.

Practice 5a

Feature Lines I

Practice Objective

• Create and edit feature lines using various tools.

Estimated time for completion: 10 minutes

In this practice you will define the perimeter of the pond using two methods of defining a feature line. You will create a feature line from a surface and then create a feature based on design elevations.

Task 1 - Create a feature line from a surface.

Mission Avenue is the northern boundary of the site and an existing subdivision bounds the western side. To establish a design control line for the north and west perimeters of the site, you will create a feature line that extracts elevations from the existing surface.

1. Open **POND-A1-Grading.dwg** from the *C:\Civil3D-Grading\ Pond* folder.

2. In the *View* tab>Views panel, select the preset view **Storm Pond**. A red polyline displays along the north and west property lines, as shown in Figure 5–4.

You might need to type **Regen** *in the Command Line to display this polyline.*

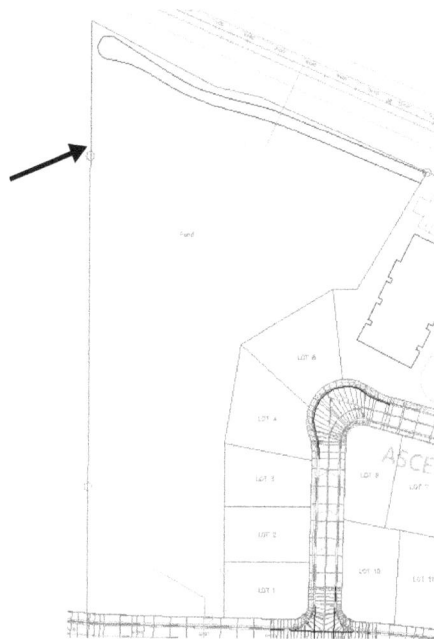

Figure 5–4

3. In the *Home* tab>Create Design panel, expand the Feature Line drop-down list and click ⬚ (Create Feature Lines from Objects).

4. When prompted to *Select the object:*, select the red polyline shown in Figure 5–4. Press <Enter> when done.

5. In the Create Feature Lines dialog box, complete the following, as shown in Figure 5–5:

   • For the *Site,* select **Pond Site**

   • For the *Name,* type **North-West-Boundary**

   • In the *Conversion options* area select the **Erase existing entities**, **Assign elevations**, and **Weed Points** options.

   • Accept all of the other defaults and click **OK** when done.

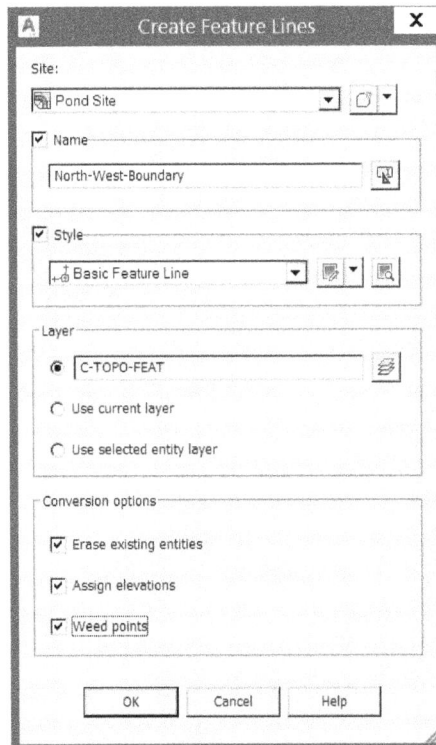

Figure 5–5

6. In the Assign Elevations dialog box, complete the following, as shown in Figure 5–6.

   - Select the **From surface** option.
   - In the drop-down list, select **Existing Ground**.
   - Select the **Insert intermediate grade break points** option.
   - Click **OK** to accept the changes and close the dialog box.

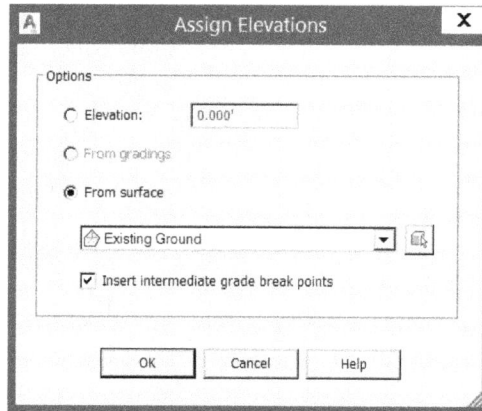

Figure 5–6

7. In the Weed Vertices dialog box, accept the defaults and click **OK**, as shown in Figure 5–7.

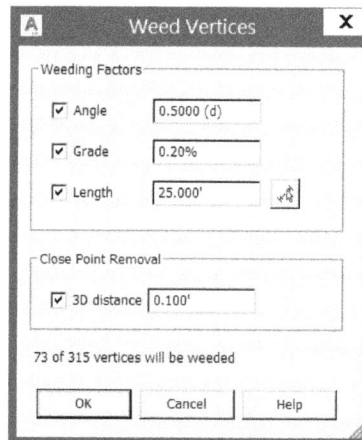

Figure 5–7

8. A feature line has been created for the north and west property lines of the site, with elevations matching the existing ground surface. Save the drawing.

Task 2 - Create a feature based on design elevations.

In this task you will create a feature line of the east perimeter of the pond. The grades at the east perimeter of the pond are governed by the rear grades of the lots or parcels.

1. Continue working with the drawing from the previous task or open **POND-A2-Grading.dwg** from the *C:\Civil3D-Grading\ Pond* folder.

   Based on the street grades and types of lots that are required (Walkout Basements), elevations for the east property line have been roughly calculated. The last point (pt7) ties into the existing ground elevation that is controlled by Mission Avenue, as shown in Figure 5–8.

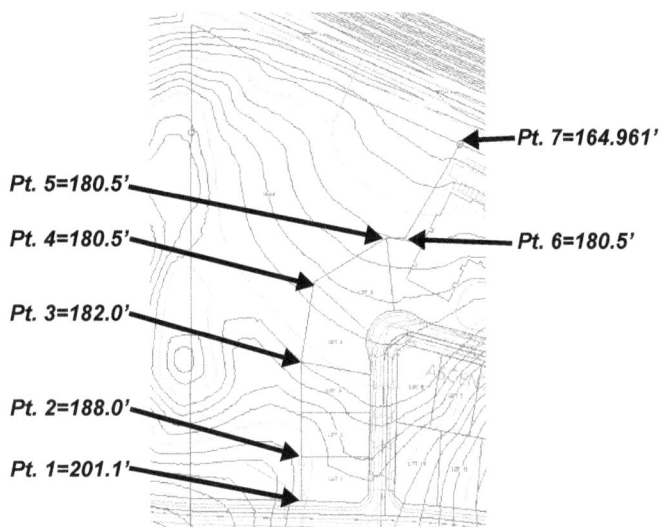

Figure 5–8

2. In the *Home* tab>Create Design panel, expand the Feature Line drop-down list and click ⌁ (Create Feature Line).

3. In the Create Feature Lines dialog box, complete the following:
   - Select **Pond Site** for the site and select the option to name it.
   - For the *Name* type **East-Boundary**.
   - Accept all of the other defaults.
   - Click **OK**.

4. When prompted for the feature line points, using the **Endpoint** Osnap, select **Pt1**, as shown in Figure 5–8.

5. When prompted to *Specify elevation or [surface] <0.000>:* type **201.1** and press <Enter>.

6. When prompted for the next point, using the **Endpoint** Osnap, select **Pt2**, as shown in Figure 5–8.

7. You are prompted to *Specify grade or [SLope/Elevation/ Difference/SUrface/Transition] <0.00>:*. If the option is not set to accept elevations, type **E** and press <Enter> to set the default as the elevation.

8. Once the option has been set to accept elevations, you are prompted to *Specify elevation or [Grade/SLope/Difference/ SUrface/ Transition] <61.300>*. Type **188.0** and press <Enter>.

9. Continue selecting endpoints and entering elevations for all of the points as shown in Figure 5–8. When finished entering the elevation for the last point, pt7, (**164.961**), press <Enter> to exit the command.

10. Save the drawing.

5.2 Edit Elevations

The Grading Elevation Editor vista (shown in Figure 5–9) enables you to add, modify, or vary the elevations of a feature line. The feature line data is organized into rows, where one row lists the data for an individual vertex.

Station	Elevation	Length	Grade Ahead	Grade Back
0+00.00	60.000'	729.550'	0.00%	0.00%
7+29.55	60.000'	82.272'	0.00%	0.00%
8+11.82	60.000'	0.643'	0.00%	0.00%
8+12.47	60.000'	63.341'	0.00%	0.00%
8+75.81	60.000'	91.491'	0.00%	0.00%
9+67.30	60.000'	2.995'	0.00%	0.00%
9+70.29	60.000'	103.000'	0.00%	0.00%

Figure 5–9

Other elevation editing tools are available on the *Feature Line* contextual tab>Edit Elevations panel. To access this panel, in the

Modify tab>Design panel, click ↲ (Feature Line). The *Feature Line* contextual tab displays, click ⬚ (Edit Elevations). The Edit Elevations panel displays as shown in Figure 5–10.

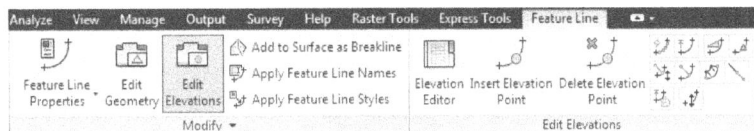

Figure 5–10

Each icon's function is as follows:

Icon	Command	Description
	Elevation Editor	Opens the Elevation Editor vista where you edit the vertex elevations of feature lines, survey figures, and parcel lines.
	Insert Elevation Point	Adds an elevation control to the feature line. Elevation points provide an elevation control without creating a new vertex. These points are Z-controls without X- or Y-components.
	Delete Elevation Point	Vertical grade breaks are anywhere other than horizontal vertices.

	Quick Elevation Edit	Displays elevation values at vertices and elevation points along a feature line or parcel line. Selecting one of these points enables you to edit it in the Command Line.
	Edit Elevations	Edits elevations at vertices along a feature line, parcel line, or 3D polyline as you step through each vertex in the Command Line.
	Set Grade/Slope Between Points	Sets the grade or slope between two points on a feature line, parcel line, or 3D polyline. The elevations between the two selected points are interpolated to maintain the grade/slope/elevation/elevation difference entered.
	Insert High/Low Elevation Point	Inserts a high or low break point where two grades intersect on a feature line, survey figure, parcel line, or 3D polyline.
	Raise/Lower by Reference	Raises or lowers a feature line, survey figure, parcel line, or 3D polyline a specified grade or slope from a selected COGO point or surface elevation.
	Set Elevation by Reference	Sets a single vertex elevation on a feature line, survey figure, parcel line, or 3D polyline a specified grade or slope from a selected COGO point or surface elevation.
	Adjacent Elevations by Reference	Sets elevations of one feature line, survey figure, parcel line, or 3D polyline based on a grade/slope/elevation/elevation difference from points on another feature running alongside the first feature.
	Grade Extension by Reference	Extends the grade of one feature line, survey figure, parcel line, or 3D Polyline across a gap to set the elevations of another feature and maintain the same slope.
	Elevations from Surface	Takes the elevations of all vertices from the surface if no vertices are selected. If a vertex is selected, it takes the surface elevation for just that vertex.
	Raise/Lower	Raises or lowers all of the feature line vertices by the elevation entered.

- You can edit the elevations of a feature line or parcel line before or after it becomes part of a grading group.

How To: Insert Elevation Points

1. In the *Feature Line contextual tab*>Modify panel, click

   ⬚ (Edit Elevations).

2. In the Elevation Editor or in the *Feature Line contextual tab*>

   Edit Elevations panel, click ⬚ (Insert Elevation Point).

3. Either pick a point along the feature line or enter a station where you want the new elevation point to be located.

4. At the Command line, type the station and press <Enter>. Then type the elevation and press <Enter>.

5. In the Grading Elevation Editor vista, the new station should be displayed, as shown in Figure 5–11.

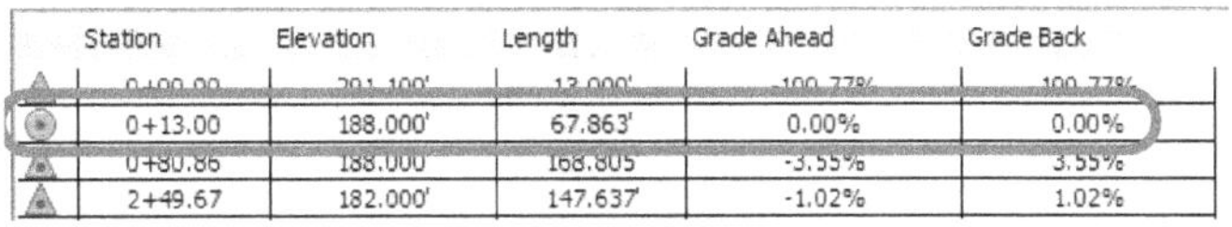

Station	Elevation	Length	Grade Ahead	Grade Back
0+00.00	201.100'	13.000'	-100.77%	100.77%
0+13.00	188.000'	67.863'	0.00%	0.00%
0+80.86	188.000	168.805	-3.55%	3.55%
2+49.67	182.000'	147.637'	-1.02%	1.02%

Figure 5–11

5.3 Create Feature Lines From Corridors

When corridors are created, the sub-assemblies point codes create feature lines. These feature lines can be used in grading groups but they must be extracted from the corridor for the

Grading command to recognize them. (Create Feature Line from Corridor) in the Feature Line drop-down list in the *Home* tab>Create Design panel extracts the feature lines from a corridor model. During the extraction process, you determine whether the new feature line automatically updates if the corridor changes. The **Create dynamic link to the corridor** option in the Create Feature Line from Corridor dialog box creates this dynamic link.

How To: Create a Feature Line from a Corridor

1. In the *Home* tab>Create Design panel, expand the Feature

    Line drop-down list and click (Create Feature Line from Corridor), as shown in Figure 5–12.

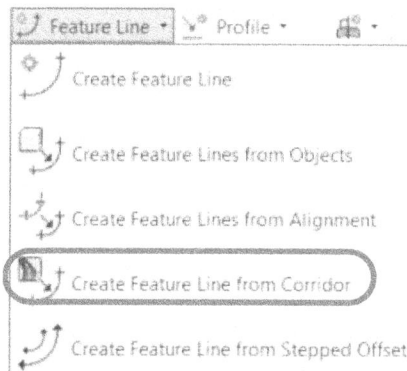

Figure 5–12

2. When prompted, select the corridor that you want to use.
3. When prompted, select the corridor feature line that you want to use, as shown in Figure 5–13.
4. In the Extract Corridor Feature Line dialog box, select a *Site*.

5. Click **Settings** and determine whether you want to have the feature line automatically update or not with the **Create dynamic link to the corridor** option, as shown in Figure 5–13.

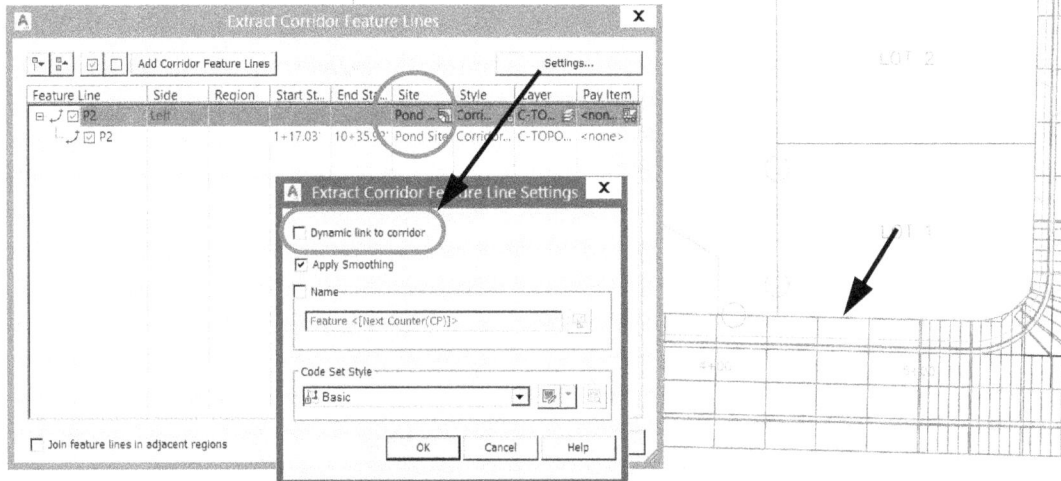

Figure 5–13

6. If you want to give the feature line a name, select the **Name** option and type a name in the *Name* field.
7. Click **OK** to accept and close the dialog box.
8. A message displays in the Command Line indicating that a feature line has been created. Press <Enter> to exit the **Selection** command.

5.4 Edit Geometry

The Edit Geometry panel (shown in Figure 5–14) enables you to modify feature lines, survey figures, parcel lines, polylines, and 3D polylines. When working with feature lines, you must use these commands to make edits to feature line geometry, rather than the **Polyline Edit** command. To open the Edit Geometry panel, in the *Feature Line contextual tab>*Modify panel, click 🖻 (Edit Geometry).

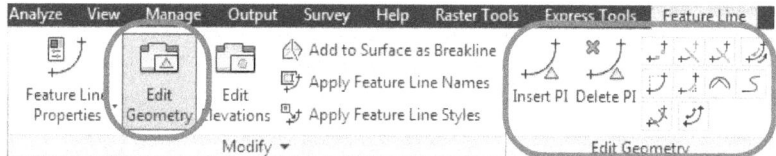

Figure 5–14

The tool functions are as follows:

Icon	Command	Description
	Insert PI	Adds a new vertex to a feature line, survey figure, parcel line, polyline, or 3D polyline giving you additional horizontal and vertical control.
	Delete PI	Removes a selected vertex from a feature line, survey figure, parcel line, polyline, or 3D polyline.
	Break	Creates a gap or break in a feature line, survey figure, or parcel line. The location selected when picking the object is the first point of the break unless otherwise specified.
	Trim	Removes part of a feature line, survey figure, or parcel line at the specified boundary edge.
	Join	Combines two feature lines, survey figures, parcel lines, polylines, or 3D polylines that fall within the tolerance distance set in the command settings.
	Reverse	Changes the direction of the stationing along a feature line, survey figure, parcel line, polyline, or 3D polyline.
	Edit Curve	Changes the radius of a feature line arc, parcel line arc, or survey figure arc.
	Fillet	Creates a curve between two segments of selected feature line(s), survey figures, parcel lines, or 3D polylines.

	Fit Curve	Places a curve between selected vertices of a feature line, survey figure, parcel line, or 3D polyline while removing vertices between the selected vertices. Useful for converting tessellated lines to true arcs.
	Smooth	Adds multiple arcs to feature lines or survey figures to assist in smoothing tessellated lines.
	Weed	Removes unnecessary vertices along feature lines, polylines, or 3D polylines based on defined angle, grade, length, and 3D distance values.
	Stepped Offset	Creates copies of a selected feature line, survey figure, polyline, or 3D polyline a specified horizontal and vertical distance away from the original object.

Break Feature Lines

Feature lines can be broken into two or more segments in order to have more control over surface elevations. It is common for existing ground surface contours or corridor feature lines to be used in a finish ground grading plan. However, the entire feature line might not be required. It is in these instances that it becomes

necessary to use the feature line ⤙ (Break) or ⤝ (Trim) commands. The **Break** command allows you to break the feature line at selected points, as shown in Figure 5–15.

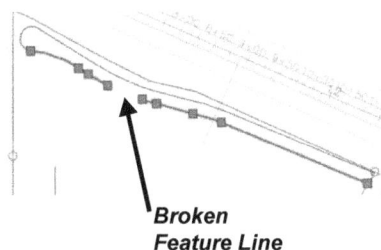

Broken Feature Line

Figure 5–15

How To: Break a Feature Line

1. In Model Space, select the feature line that needs to be split into two feature lines.
2. In the *Feature Line* contextual tab>Modify panel, click (Edit Geometry) to display the Edit Geometry panel.

3. In the Edit Geometry panel, click ⤙ (Break), as shown in Figure 5–16.

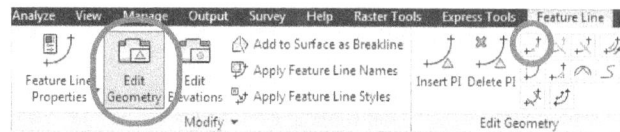

Figure 5–16

4. When prompted to select an object to break, select the feature line at the location where you want to place the first break point.
5. When prompted to select the second break point, click on the line at the second point.

    • If you need to provide a different first point, type **F** and press <Enter>. Click on the feature line to re-select the first break point, and then click on the feature line at the second break point location.

Trim Feature Lines

Feature lines can be trimmed at specified cutting edges. This allows you to ensure that feature lines do not go beyond a specific boundary. The specified boundary becomes the cutting edge, and then the feature line is removed up to the cutting edge, as shown in Figure 5–17.

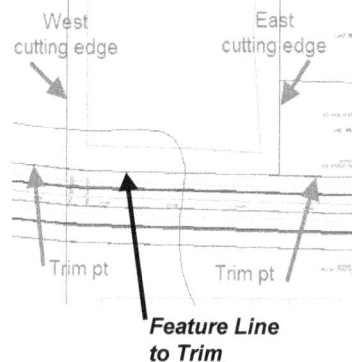

Feature Line to Trim

Figure 5–17

How To: Trim a Feature Line

1. In Model Space, select the feature line requiring trimming.
2. In the *Feature Line* contextual tab>Modify panel, click

    ▢ (Edit Geometry) to display the Edit Geometry panel.

3. In the Edit Geometry panel, click ⊹ (Trim), as shown in Figure 5–18.

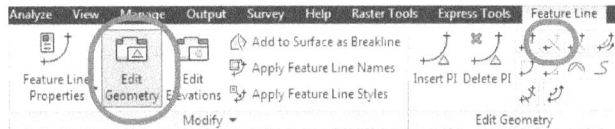

Figure 5–18

4. When prompted to select the cutting edge, select an object to trim to and press <Enter>.
5. When prompted to select the object to trim, select the feature line to trim on the side you wish to remove from the drawing.

Join Feature Lines

When two feature lines touch each other, end to end, at the same elevation, you can join them into one feature line, as shown in Figure 5–19. This is especially useful when you have used various commands to create the base feature lines, such as *Create Feature Line From Objects* or *Create Feature Line From Corridors*.

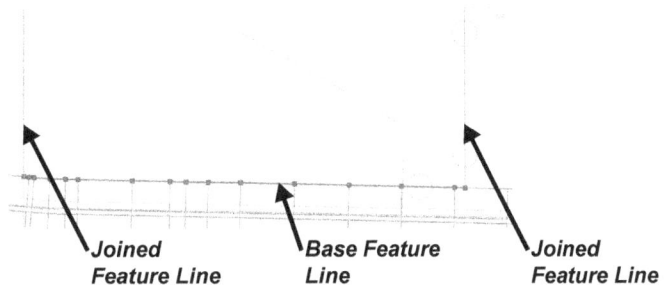

Joined Feature Line   *Base Feature Line*   *Joined Feature Line*

Figure 5–19

How To: Join Feature Lines Together

1. In the *Feature Line* contextual tab>Modify panel, click ⊡ (Edit Geometry) to display the Edit Geometry panel.

2. In the Edit Geometry panel, click ⊹ (Join), as shown in Figure 5–20.

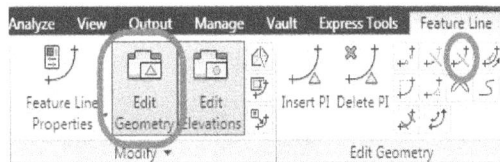

Figure 5–20

3. When prompted, select all the feature lines in the drawing that you want to join.
4. Press <Enter> to end the command
5. Press <Esc> to exit the feature line selection.

Hint: Fixing Feature Lines Which Fail to Join.

If the ⊀ (Join) command does not join the selected feature lines, some grip editing might be required where lines do not intersect perfectly.

Alternatively, you can change the command settings to set a tolerance factor. Changing the tolerance factor allows feature lines with a gap between them to join together as long as the gap is within the selected tolerance.

Practice 5b

Feature Lines II

Estimated time for completion: 15 minutes

Practice Objectives

- Edit feature line elevations by adding additional elevation points at locations other than the vertices.
- Create feature lines from corridors to speed up the creation process and ensure design coordination.

In this practice you will modify feature line elevations, create a feature line from a corridor and edit feature line geometry.

Task 1 - Modify feature line elevations.

In the Grading Elevation Editor vista you can make changes to the feature line design. Due to the grade difference between Jeffries Ranch Rd and the adjacent lot grade, the start of the feature line must be adjusted to display a 1:1 slope.

1. Continue working with the drawing from the previous practice or open **POND-B1-Grading.dwg** from the *C:\Civil3D-Grading\Pond* folder.

2. In Model Space, select the East-Boundary feature line you created in the last practice. In the *Feature Line* contextual tab>Modify panel, click 📷 (Edit Elevations) to display the Edit Elevations panel, and then click 🔳 (Insert Elevation Point).

3. When prompted for a point, type **13** and press <Enter> at the Command Line (this is the station along the feature line).

4. When prompted for the *Elevation*, type **188.0'** and press <Enter>.

5. In the *Feature Line* contextual tab>Edit Elevations panel, click 🔲 (Elevation Editor) to open the vista. The new station should display with a circle icon indicating that it is an elevation point rather than a vertex, as shown in Figure 5–21.

Station	Elevation	Length	Grade Ahead	Grade Back
0+00.00	204.100'	13.000'	100.77%	100.77%
0+13.00	188.000'	67.863'	0.00%	0.00%
0+80.86	188.000'	100.815'	0.00%	0.00%
2+49.67	182.000'	147.637'	-1.02%	1.02%

Figure 5–21

6. Save the drawing.

Task 2 - Create a feature line from corridor.

The grades at the south end of the pond are controlled by Jeffries Ranch Rd. In this task you will extract a feature from the corridor to establish the elevation of the south property line.

1. Continue working with the drawing from the previous task or open **POND-B2-Grading.dwg** from the *C:\Civil3D-Grading\ Pond* folder.

2. In the *View* tab>Views panel, select the preset view **Storm Pond**.

3. In the *Home* tab>Layers panel, ensure that the **C-ROAD-CORR** layer is toggled on. Regen all by typing **REA** in the Command Line.

4. In Model Space, select the Jeffries Ranch Rd corridor object, right-click, and select **Display Order>Bring to Front**.

5. In the *Home* tab>Create Design panel, expand the Feature Line drop-down list and click 🖳 (Create Feature Line from Corridor), as shown in Figure 5–22.

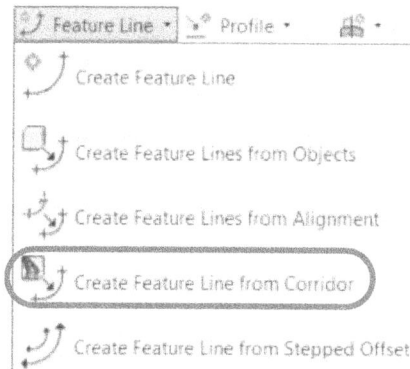

Figure 5–22

If it is difficult to select the corridor feature line, you can toggle on the selection cycling.

6. When prompted to select the corridor, click on Jeffries Ranch Rd.

7. When prompted to select the feature line, select the **north edge** (green or magenta) line, as shown in Figure 5–23. Press <Enter> to indicate that you are finished selecting feature lines.

8. In the Extract Corridor Feature Line dialog box, complete the following, as shown in Figure 5–23:
   - In the *Site* column, select **Pond Site**.
   - Click **Settings**.
   - Clear the **Dynamic link to the corridor** option.
   - Accept the remaining defaults.
   - Click **OK** to close the Settings dialog box.
   - Click **Extract**.

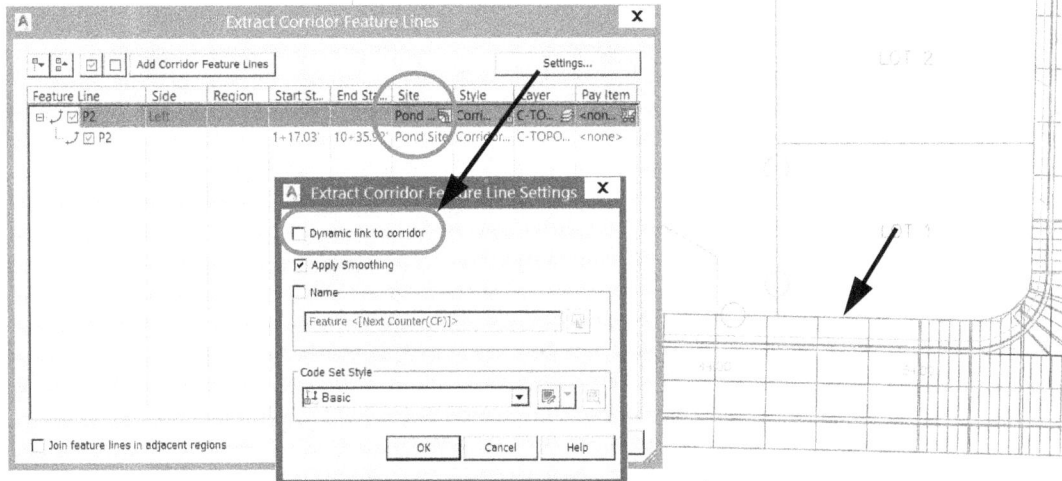

Figure 5–23

A message displays at the Command Line indicating that a feature line from <P2> has been created.

9. Save the drawing.

Task 3 - Edit feature line geometry.

1. Continue working with the drawing from the previous task or open **POND-B3-Grading.dwg** from the *C:\Civil3D-Grading\ Pond* folder.

2. In Model Space, select the newly created feature line, as shown in Figure 5–24. In the *Feature Line* contextual tab> Modify panel, click 🗀 (Edit Geometry). In the Edit Geometry panel, click ⤬ (Trim).

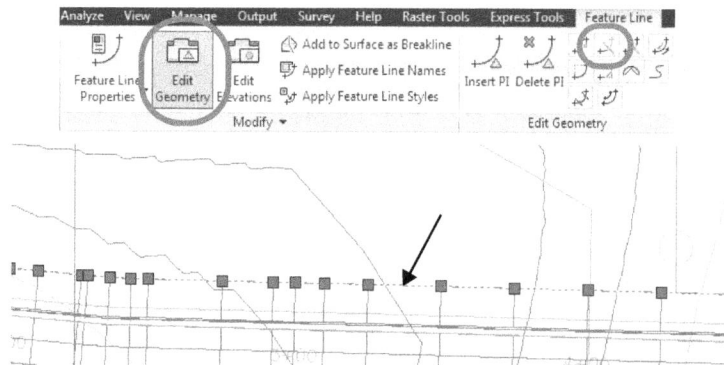

Figure 5–24

3. When prompted to select the cutting edge, select the east and west property lines of the pond and press <Enter> when done.

4. When prompted to select the object to trim, select the feature line at a point outside the pond property lines, west of the west cutting edge and east of the east cutting edge, as shown in Figure 5–25. Press <Enter> when done and press <Esc> to exit the feature object selection.

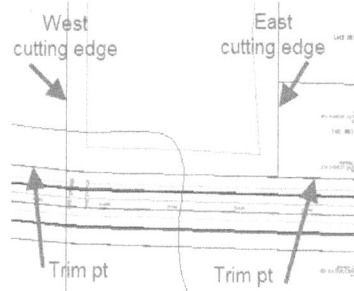

Figure 5–25

A feature line based on the corridor road design has now been created.

5. To join the three feature lines, select the feature line at the west side of the pond.

6. In the Feature Line contextual tab>Modify panel, click

    ⬚ (Edit Geometry) to display the Edit Geometry panel, and

    then click ⬚ (Join), as shown in Figure 5–26.

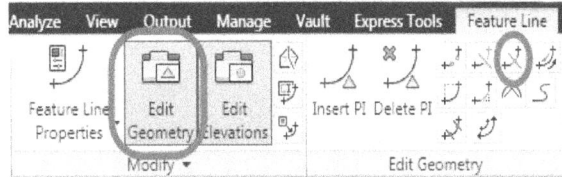

Figure 5–26

If the feature line fails to join any lines in this process, some grip editing might be required where lines do not intersect completely.

7. When prompted, select the feature line to the south and select the feature line to the east. Press <Enter> to end the command and press <Esc> to exit the feature line selection.

8. Save the drawing.

5.5 Creating Complex Grading Groups

An example of grading groups that use one baseline and project specific slopes until they find daylight (called *grading to a surface*) is shown in Figure 5–27.

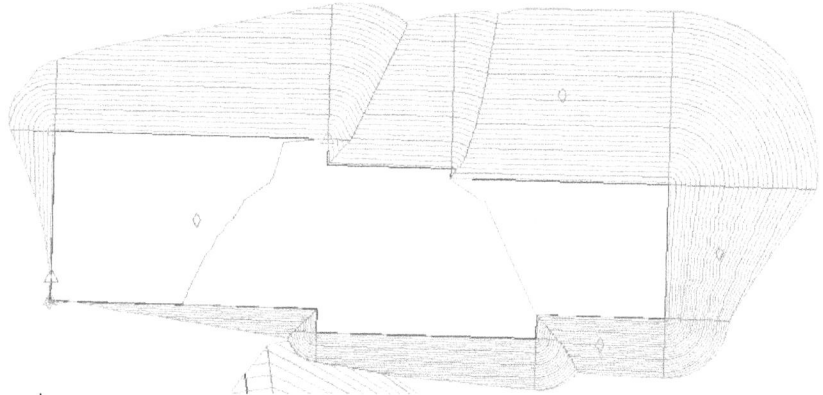

Figure 5–27

Unfortunately, real world grading projects are not always that simple. That is why the AutoCAD® Civil® 3D provides a way to grade one grading object from another within the same site. When reviewing the pond grading parameters for the project, note that you need multiple grades for the interior of the pond, a maintenance road running along part of the pond, and then daylight from the maintenance road, as shown in Figure 5–28.

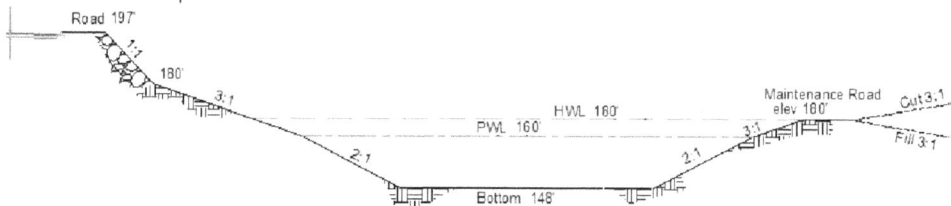

Figure 5–28

It is quite typical that pond grading projects use a minimum of three or four different grading criteria. Four types of grading criteria are available.

Grade to Elevation

When you need to keep a specific grade or slope to a specified elevation, the Grade to Elevation criteria is used. This enables you to set the target to be a specific elevation. It is often used in pond grading because the top of the pond needs to be level, as shown in Figure 5–29. Note in the Front View that the pond bottom is sloped while the top is level.

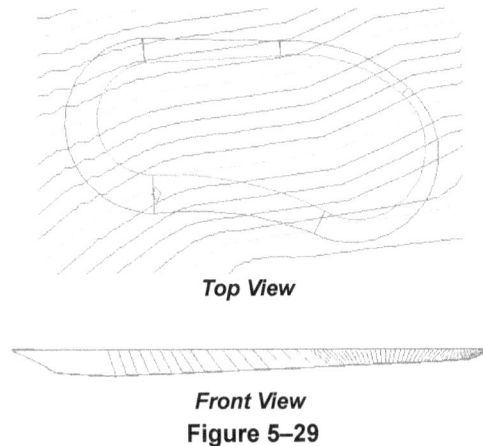

Top View

Front View

Figure 5–29

Grade to Relative Elevation

Sometimes you need too project a grade up or down a specific vertical distance. In this case you would use the Grade to Relative Elevation criteria, as shown in Figure 5–30. Note that in the front view, both the top and bottom have the same slope unlike the Grade to Elevation in which they had differing slopes.

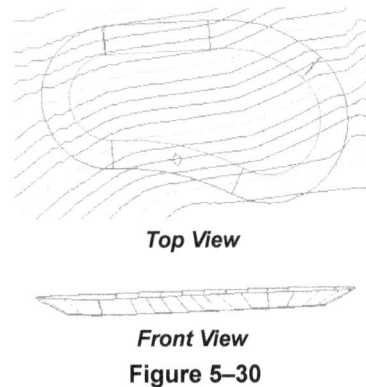

Top View

Front View

Figure 5–30

Grade to Distance

When you need to keep a specific grade or slope for a specified horizontal distance, you can use the Grade to Distance criteria. In pond grading, you might need to use this criteria to grade a maintenance road around the perimeter of the pond, as shown in Figure 5–31.

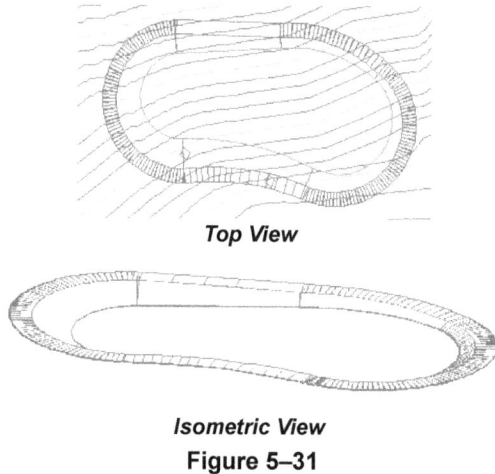

Top View

Isometric View

Figure 5–31

Grade to Surface

When you need to keep a specific slope until the projection finds daylight, you can use the Grade to Surface criteria, as shown in Figure 5–32. In pond grading, this is sometimes the first grading object that you create if you are starting from the outside and grading in. The pond in Figure 5–32 was graded from the inside out.

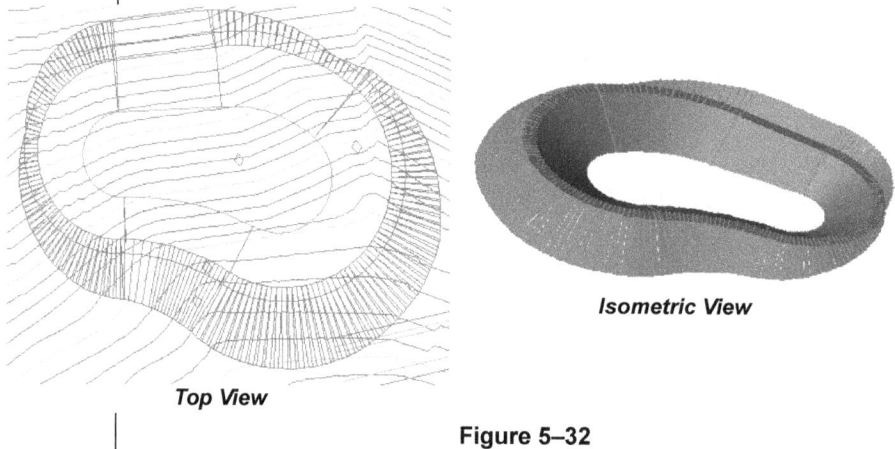

Isometric View

Top View

Figure 5–32

Practice 5c

(Optional) Pond Grading I - Feature Line (Create Base Line)

Practice Objective

- Create and modify feature lines using grading objects and feature line editing tools.

Estimated time for completion: 30 minutes

In this practice you will establish control feature lines at the north and south ends, as shown in Figure 5–33, and then create the pond outside rim feature line.

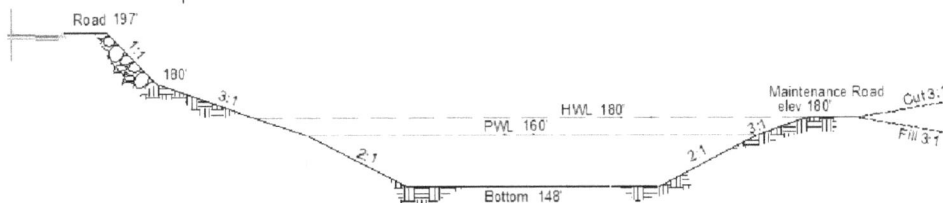

Figure 5–33

Task 1 - Establish control feature lines (south end).

1. Continue working with the drawing from the previous practice or open **POND-C1-Grading.dwg** from the *C:\Civil3D-Grading\Pond* folder.

2. In the *View* tab>Views panel, select the preset view **Storm Pond**.

3. In the *Home* tab>Create Design panel, expand the Grading drop-down list and click ⬚ (Grading Creation Tools).

4. In the Grading Creation Tools toolbar, click ⬚ (Set the Grading Group). Select **Pond Site** for the site and click **OK**, as shown in Figure 5–34.

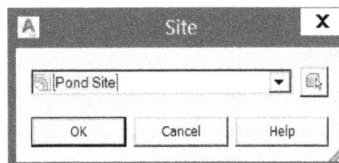

Figure 5–34

You will create a temporary grading object that creates pre-design information.

5. In the Create Grading Group dialog box, for the *Name* enter **Temp**, as shown in Figure 5–35. Clear the **Automatic surface creation** option and click **OK**.

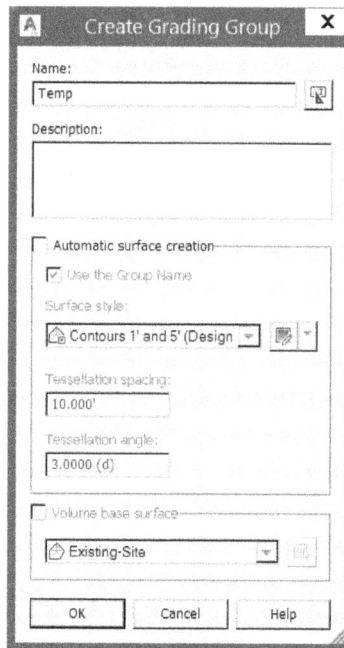

Figure 5–35

Establish a feature line with a **1:1** slope to an elevation of **180' using the following steps**.

6. In the Grading Creation Tools toolbar, set the *Criteria* as **Grade to Elevation** and click ✏ (Create Grading), as shown in Figure 5–36.

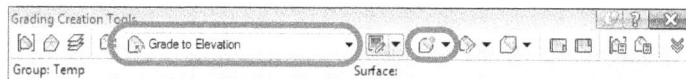

Figure 5–36

7. When prompted to select a feature, select the green pond boundary feature line that defines the perimeter pond site, as shown in Figure 5–37. If prompted to weed the feature line, select **Continue grading without feature line weeding**.

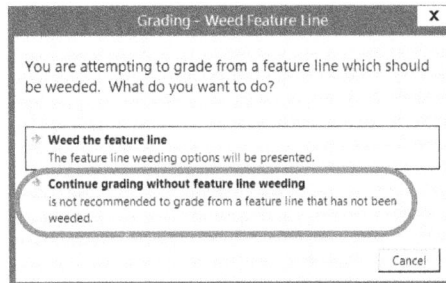

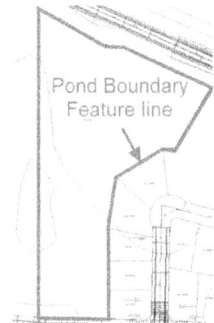

Figure 5–37

8. When prompted for the side to grade, select a point inside of the pond.

9. Select **No** when prompted to *Apply to the entire length*.

10. When prompted for the start point, select the center of the green circle located on the west feature line and press <Enter> to accept <20+09.87'> for the station.

11. When prompted for the end point or length, select the center of the green circle located on the south feature line and press <Enter> to accept <23+77.50'> for the station.

12. When prompted for the elevation, type **180** and press <Enter>.

13. When prompted for the cut format, select **Slope**. Type **1** and press <Enter> to indicate a cut slope of 1:1.

14. When prompted for the fill format, select **Slope**. Type **1** and press <Enter> to indicate a fill slope of 1:1.

15. This defines the 1:1 slope from the road as shown in Figure 5–38.

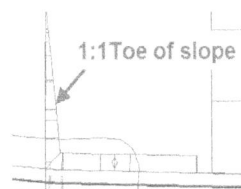

Figure 5–38

Next you will determine where the 3:1 slope from the parcels to the east intersects the 1:1 slope of the pond.

At any time, if you accidentally closed the **Grading** *command, you just need to click* (Create Grading).

16. When prompted to select a feature line, select the pond boundary feature line, which is the green line that defines the outer perimeter of the pond site.

17. When prompted for the grading side, select a point inside the pond.

18. When prompted for the start point, select the center of the southern-most cyan circle located on the east feature line and press <Enter> to accept <0+14.89'> for the station.

19. When prompted for the endpoint or length, select the center of the northern-most cyan circle located on the east feature line and press <Enter> to accept <0+69.25'> for the station, as shown in Figure 5–39.

Figure 5–39

20. When prompted for the elevation, type **165** and press <Enter>.

21. When prompted for the cut format, select **Slope**. Type **3** and press <Enter> for a cut slope of 3:1.

22. When prompted for the fill format, select **Slope**. Type **3** and press <Enter> for a fill slope of 3:1.

This establishes the toe of slope where the 1:1 slope intersects the 3:1 slope.

23. Press <Esc> to end the feature line selection and select the **X** in the Grading Creation Tools toolbar to close the toolbar.

To use the toe of slope for further grading, the feature line that represents the toe of slope must be extracted from the grading object.

24. In Model Space, select the toe of slope feature line, right-click, and select **Move to Site...**, as shown in Figure 5–40.

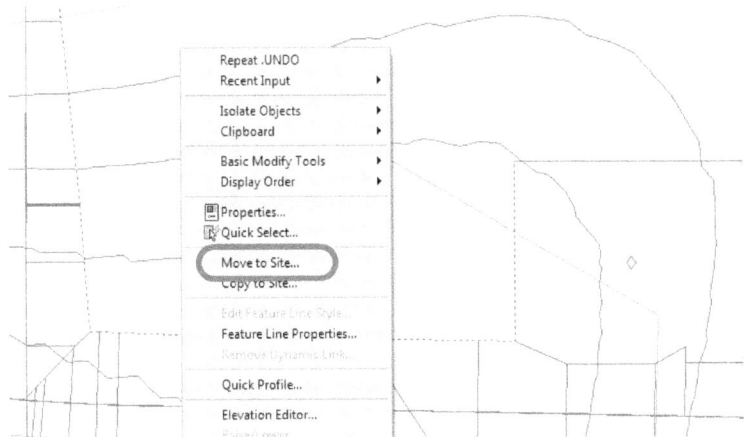

Figure 5–40

25. In the Move to Site dialog box, click **OK** to accept the default site, as shown in Figure 5–41.

It does not matter which site you place it in. By moving the feature line to a different site, the grading object is deleted, leaving just the toe of slope.

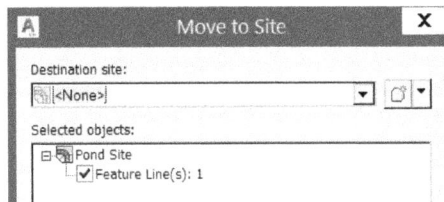

Figure 5–41

26. Select the feature line again and move it back to the **Pond Site**, as shown in Figure 5–42.

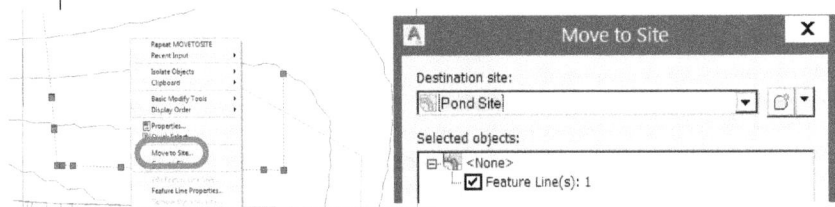

Figure 5–42

27. In Model Space, select the feature line. In the *Feature Line contextual tab*>Modify panel, click ⬚⌐ (Feature Line Properties).

28. In the Feature Line Properties dialog box, select the **Name** option and type **Toe of slope** in the *Name* field, as shown in Figure 5–43. Click **OK**.

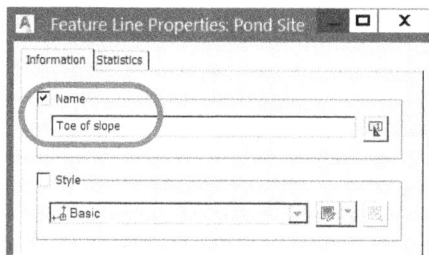

Figure 5–43

29. In Model Space, select the toe of slope feature line. In the *Feature Line contextual tab*>Modify panel, click 🖼 (Edit Elevations). In the Edit Elevations panel, click 🖼 (Elevation Editor).

In the Grading Elevation Editor vista, the elevation shown for station 2+84.74' is 172.50', as shown in Figure 5–44. The correct elevation is 180'.

⚠	1+56.15	180.000'	2.549'	-0.00%	0.00%
⚠	1+68.70	180.000'	0.004'	0.00%	0.00%
⚠	1+68.71	180.000'	5.575'	0.00%	0.00%
⚠	1+74.28	180.000'	25.002'	0.00%	0.00%
⚠	1+99.28	180.000'	17.561'	-0.00%	0.00%
⚠	2+16.84	180.000'	7.439'	0.00%	-0.00%
⚠	2+24.28	180.000'	10.040'	-0.00%	0.00%
⚠	2+34.32	180.000'	14.960'	0.00%	0.00%
⚠	2+49.28	180.000'	25.001'	0.00%	-0.00%
⚠	2+74.28	180.000'	10.454'	-71.74%	71.74%
⚠	2+84.74	180	48.266'	-15.54%	15.54%
⚠	3+33.01	165.000'			

Figure 5–44

30. Select the elevation field for station 2+84.74, type **180**, and press <Enter>.

31. Click ☑ to close the Elevation Editor vista.

32. To join the toe of slope feature line to the east pond boundary, select the toe of slope feature line and select the east feature line to display all of the grips.

33. Select the last grip on the toe of slope feature line and drag it to the intermediate point on the east feature line, as shown in Figure 5–45.

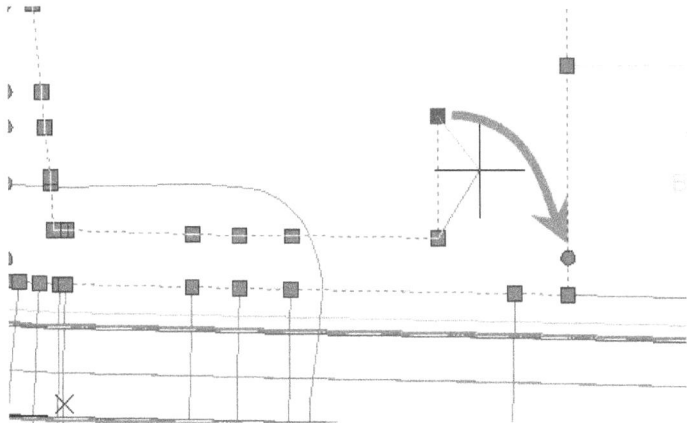

Figure 5–45

34. You have now defined the south pond feature line.

35. Save the drawing.

Task 2 - Establish control feature lines (north end).

In this task you will define the north pond feature line by determining the location of the Pond maintenance access road, based on a 3:1 grade from the existing boundary.

1. Continue working with the drawing from the previous task or open **POND-C2-Grading.dwg**.

2. In the *View* tab>Views panel, select the preset view **Storm Pond**.

3. In the *Home* tab>Create Design panel, expand the Grading drop-down list and click ⬚ (Grading Creation Tools).

4. In the Grading Creation Tools dialog box, set the *Grading Group* name to **Temp** (if not already set) and ensure that the grading criteria is set to **Grade to Elevation**.

5. Click ⬚ (Create Grading) as shown in Figure 5–46, and select the Pond boundary feature line, which is the green line that represents the perimeter of the pond site.

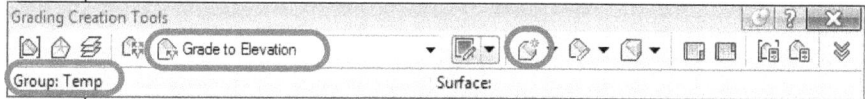

Figure 5–46

6. When prompted to weed the feature line, select **Continue grading without feature line weeding**.

7. When prompted for the side to grade, select a point inside the pond. Select **No** when prompted to *Apply to the entire length*.

8. When prompted for the start point, select the center of the magenta circle located on the northeast corner of the feature line, as shown in Figure 5–47. Press <Enter> to accept <7+88.94'> for the station.

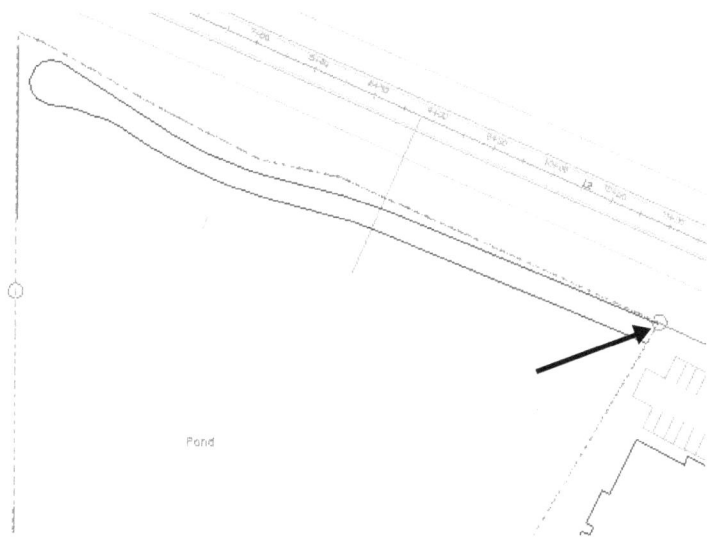

Figure 5–47

9. When prompted for the endpoint or length, select the center of the magenta circle located on the northern part of the west feature line, as shown in Figure 5–48. Press <Enter> to accept <15+31.82'> for the station.

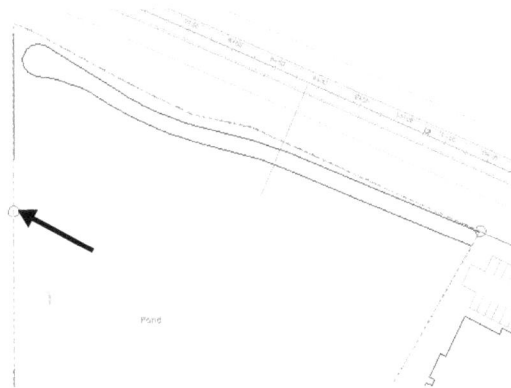

Figure 5–48

10. When prompted for the elevation, type **165.0** and press <Enter>.

11. When prompted for the cut format, select **Slope**. Type **3** and press <Enter> for a cut slope of 3:1.

12. When prompted for the fill format, select **Slope**. Type **3** and press <Enter> for a fill slope of 3:1.

13. Press <Esc> to exit the feature line selection. Select the **X** in the Grading Creation Tools toolbar to close the toolbar.

This grading object defines a 3:1 slope from the existing boundary and establishes the approximate location of the maintenance road. To save time, the access road has already been designed, as shown in Figure 5–49.

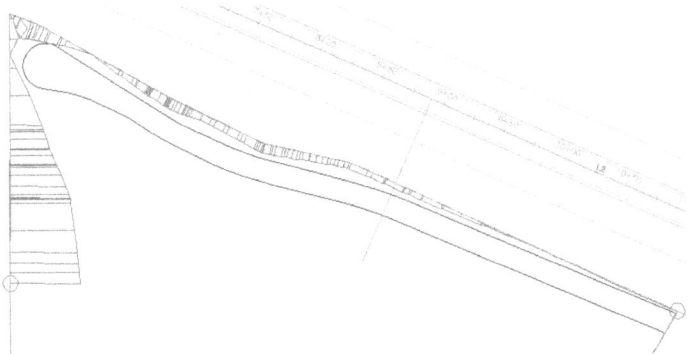

Figure 5–49

Based on the 3:1 cut and fill slope to an elevation of 164.4', you now have a feature line representing the access road. This access road has a maximum side slope of 3:1 to existing ground on the north side of the road. On the south side of the road, you continue to grade based on the design criteria for the pond.

14. You can erase the grading 3:1 maximum slope because it is no longer needed. In Model Space, select the grading object.

    In the *Grading* contextual tab>Modify panel, click ⬚ (Delete Grading).

15. Save the drawing.

Task 3 - Create the pond's outside rim feature line.

1. Continue working with the drawing from the previous task or open **POND-C3-Grading.dwg**.

2. In the *View* tab>Views panel, select the preset view **Storm Pond**.

This list displays the names of the feature lines, style, layer, and 2D length.

3. In the *Prospector* tab, expand the *Sites>Pond Site* collection. Select **Feature lines** and note the grid view that is usually at the bottom of the pane.

The AutoCAD Civil 3D software highlights the appropriate feature line.

4. Select **Toe of slope** from the list, right-click and select **Select**, as shown in Figure 5–50.

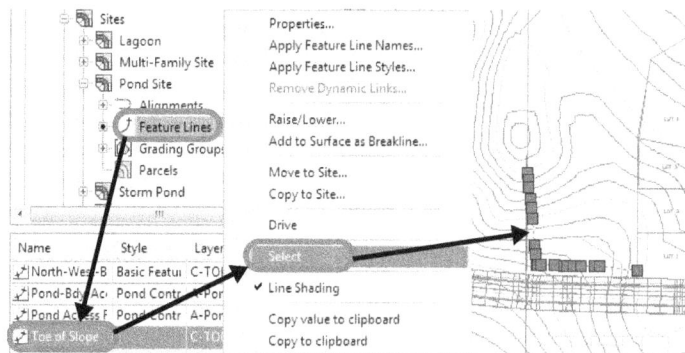

Figure 5–50

5. In the *Feature Line* contextual tab>Modify panel, click ⬚ (Feature Line Properties).

6. In the Feature Line Properties dialog box, complete the following, as shown in Figure 5–51:
   - Change the *Name* to **Pond-Bdy-Control**.
   - Set the *Style* to **Pond Control Feature Line**.
   - Click **OK**.

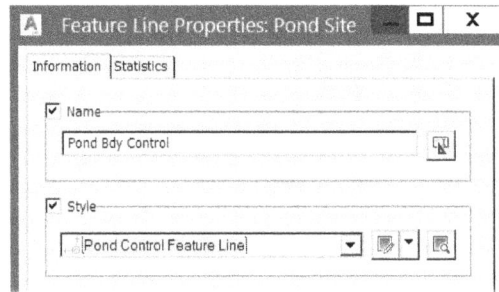

Figure 5–51

7. Press <Esc> to release the feature line.

8. Zoom in on the south end of the pond.

9. Select the feature line named **North-West-Boundary** that surrounds the pond.

10. In the *Feature Line* contextual tab>Modify panel, click
    ▣ (Edit Geometry) if it is not already displayed. In the Edit
    Geometry panel, click ↵ (Break), as shown in Figure 5–52.

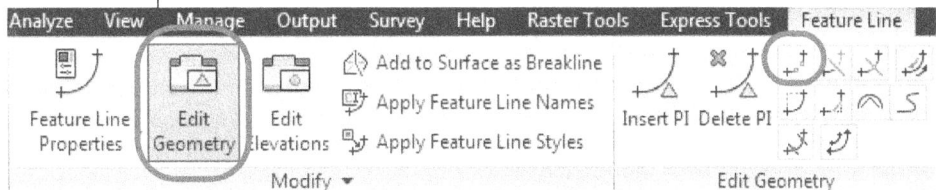

Figure 5–52

11. Select the **North-West-Boundary** feature line again. Type **F** at the Command Line so that you can select the first and second point of the break. Pick a point south of the cyan circle to the south of the control feature line for the first point. Then pick the endpoint of the control line using Osnaps, as shown in Figure 5–53.

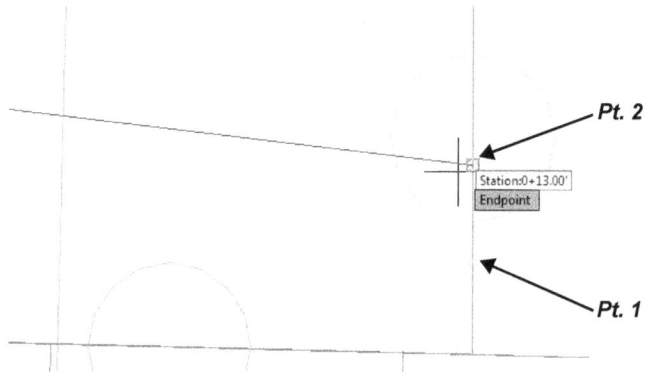

Station:0+13.00'
Endpoint

Pt. 2

Pt. 1

Figure 5–53

12. Select the **North-West-Boundary** feature line. In the *Feature Line* contextual tab>Modify panel, click ⬜ (Edit Geometry) if it is not already visible. In the Edit Geometry panel, click ⬜ (Break).

13. Select the **North-West-Boundary** feature line again. Type **F** at the Command Line so that you can select the first and second point of the break.

14. Pick a point inside the green circle to the south of the control feature line for the first point. Then pick the endpoint of the control line using Osnaps, as shown in Figure 5–54.

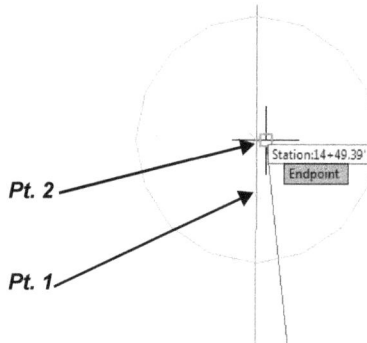

Station:14+49.39'
Endpoint

Pt. 2

Pt. 1

Figure 5–54

15. In the *View* tab>Views panel, select the **Storm Pond** view. Zoom into the north-east corner of the pond.

16. Select the **North-West-Boundary** feature line. In the *Feature Line* contextual tab>Modify panel, click ⬜ (Edit Geometry) if it is not already displayed. In the Edit Geometry panel, click ⬜ (Break).

17. Select the **North-West-Boundary** feature line again just north of the south line of the maintenance road (this is also the first point), as shown in Figure 5–55. Pick the endpoint of the south line of the maintenance road using Osnaps for the second point.

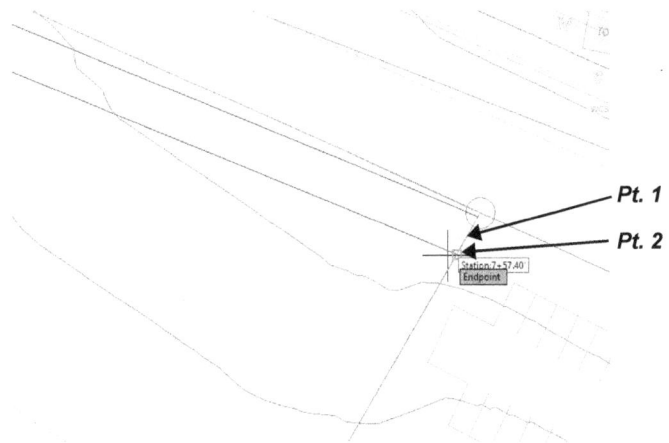

Pt. 1

Pt. 2

Station 7+57.40
Endpoint

Figure 5–55

18. In the *View* tab>Views panel, select the **Storm Pond** view. Zoom into the north-west corner of the pond.

19. Select the **North-West-Boundary** feature line. In the *Feature Line* contextual tab>Modify panel, click ⬜ (Edit Geometry) if it is not already displayed. In the Edit Geometry panel, click ⬜ (Break).

20. Select the **North-West-Boundary** feature line again near the north-western corner of the pond (this is also the first point), as shown in Figure 5–56. Then pick the endpoint near station 5+98.05' (using Osnap) for the second point.

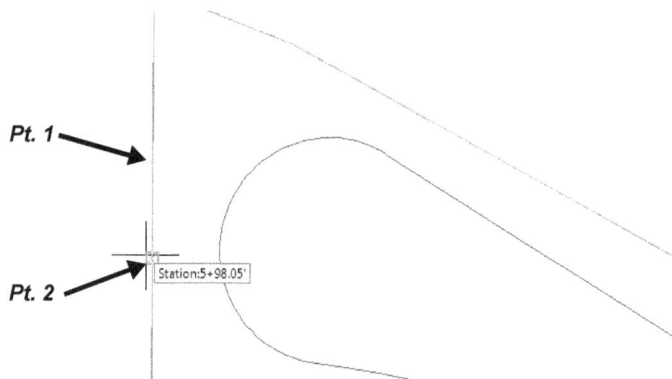

Figure 5–56

21. Select the west feature line. In the *Feature Line* contextual tab>Modify panel, click 🖾 (Edit Elevations). In the Edit Elevations panel, click 🖿 (Elevation Editor).

22. In the Elevation Editor vista, note that an elevation point is located at station 0+20.17 with an elevation of 170', as shown in Figure 5–57. You turn this into a regular vertex.

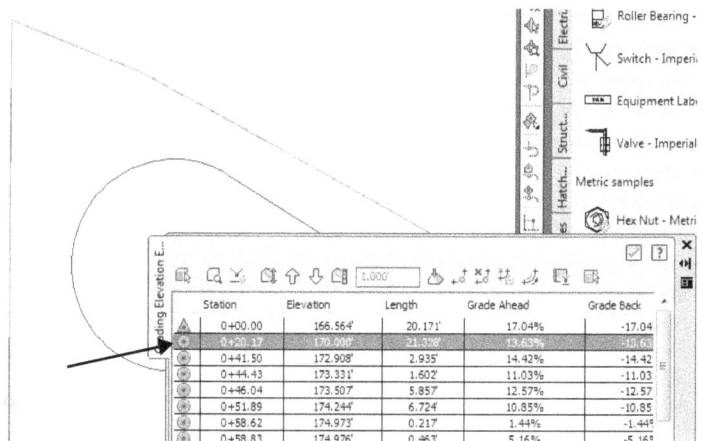

Figure 5–57

23. Select the feature line again. In the *Feature Line* contextual tab>Modify panel, click 🖾 (Edit Geometry). In the Edit Geometry panel, click ⤴ (Insert PI).

24. At the Command Line, for *Distance* type **D** and press <Enter>. For the *Distance* value type **20.17** and press <Enter>. For the *Elevation* type **170** and press <Enter>. Press <Esc> to end the command.

25. Click ☑ to close the Elevation Editor vista.

26. Select the feature line. Using grips, move the first vertex to the endpoint of the southern boundary line of the maintenance road using Osnaps, as shown in Figure 5–58.

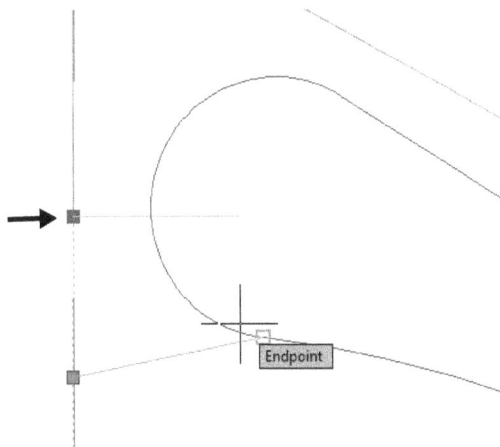

Figure 5–58

27. In the *View* tab>Views panel, select **Storm Pond** to restore the view.

28. To join all of the feature lines, select the feature line **Pond-Bdy-Control**. In the *Feature Line* contextual tab>Modify panel, click ▣ (Edit Geometry). In the Edit Geometry panel, click ⤵ (Join), as shown in Figure 5–59.

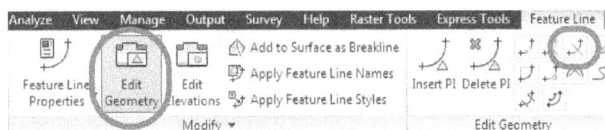

Figure 5–59

29. When prompted to select the connecting feature lines, select the feature line **Pond-Bdy-East** (2), **Pond-Bdy-North** (3), and **Pond-Bdy-West** (4), as shown in Figure 5–60. If you receive an error that they cannot be joined, you might need to grip edit the feature lines to snap them end to end.

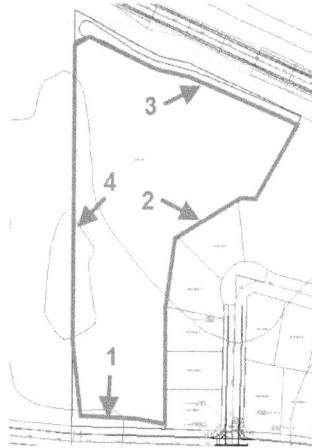

Figure 5–60

30. Press <Esc> to exit the feature line selection.

31. Select the feature line that runs along the Jeffries Ranch Road corridor to the south.

32. In the *Feature Line contextual tab*>Modify tab, click ⊞ (Feature Line Properties).

33. In the Feature Line Properties, for the *Name* type **Pond-Bdy-South**. Click **OK**.

34. Select the feature line that runs along the north of the pond.

35. In the *Feature Line contextual tab*>Modify panel, click ⊞ (Feature Line Properties).

36. In the Feature Line Properties, for the *Name* type **Pond-Bdy-North**. Click **OK**.

37. Save the drawing.

Practice 5d

Pond Grading II - Grading Object (Grading the Proposed Pond)

Practice Objective

Estimated time for completion: 20 minutes

- Create a complex grading group by grading one grading object from another.

In this practice you will create a stormwater detention pond with feature lines and grading tools. With the control feature lines created, you can continue to grade the storm pond.

Task 1 - Create pond grading.

With the pond boundary established, the rest of the pond can now be graded as specified in the cross-section.

1. Continue working with the drawing from the previous practice or open **POND-D1-Grading.dwg** from the *C:\Civil3D-Grading\Pond* folder.

2. In the *Home* tab>Create Design panel, expand the Grading drop-down list and click (Grading Creation Tools), as shown in Figure 5–61.

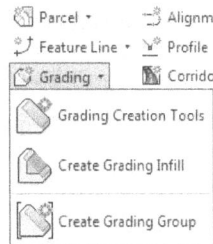

Figure 5–61

3. In the Grading Creation Tools toolbar, click as shown in Figure 5–62.

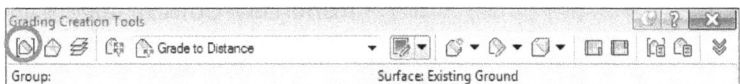

Figure 5–62

4. In the Select Grading Group dialog box, set the *Site name* to **Pond Site**, as shown on the left in Figure 5–63. To create a new group, click ⬚ (Create a Grading Group). In the Create Grading Group dialog box, for the *Name* type **Pond** and clear the **Automatic surface creation** option, as shown on the right in Figure 5–63. Click **OK**.

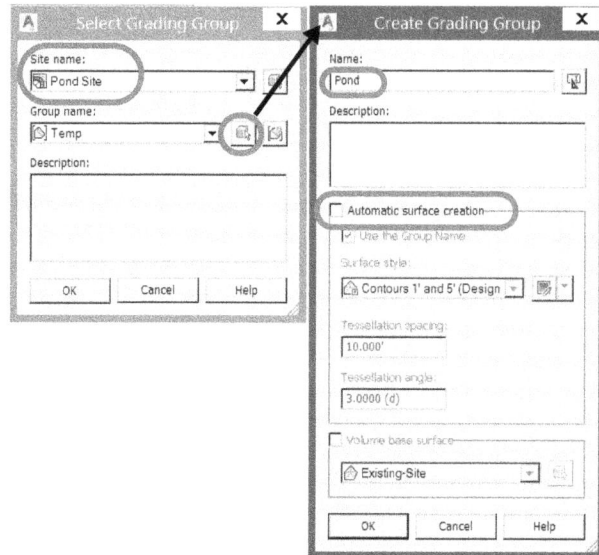

Figure 5–63

5. In the Select Grading Group dialog box, click **OK**.

6. In the Grading Creation Tools toolbar, set the grading criteria to **Grade to Elevation** and click ⬚ (Create Grading), as shown in Figure 5–64. The first step is to grade to the Permanent water level of 160.76 at a slope of 3:1.

Figure 5–64

7. When prompted to select the feature line, select the **Pond-Bdy-Control** feature line. This feature line defines the inside rim of the pond.

8. When prompted to weed the feature line, select **Continue grading without weeding**.

9. When prompted to select the side to grade, select the inside of the pond. Type **Yes** when prompted to *Apply to entire length*.

10. Type **160.76** for the elevation.

11. When prompted for the Cut format, type **Slope** and press <Enter>. For the *Slope* value, type **3** and press <Enter> to signify a 3:1 slope.

12. When prompted for the Fill format, type **Slope** and press <Enter>. For the *Slope* value, type **3** and press <Enter> to signify a 3:1 slope.

13. You now need to grade to the bottom of the pond, which is 13' deep at a slope of 2:1. In the Grading Creation Tools toolbar, change the criteria to **Grade to Relative Elevation**, as shown in Figure 5–65.

Figure 5–65

14. When prompted to select the feature line, select the inside of the pond feature line created by the last grading object, as shown in Figure 5–66. Type **Yes** when prompted to *Apply to entire length*.

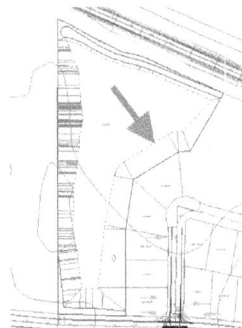

Figure 5–66

15. If prompted to select the side to grade, select the inside of the pond.

16. When prompted for the relative elevation, type **-13** and press <Enter>.

17. When prompted for the format, type **Slope** and press <Enter>. For the *Slope* value, type **2** and press <Enter> to signify a 2:1 slope.

18. In the Grading Creation Tools toolbar, expand the Create Grading drop-down list and click 🐾 (Create Infill).

19. When prompted to select an area to infill, select the center of the pond, and press <Esc> to exit the command.

20. Select the diamond at the center of the infill that you just created.

21. In the *Grading* contextual tab>Modify panel, click 🏠 (Grading Group Properties).

22. In the Grading Group Properties dialog box, select the **Automatic Surface Creation** option to automatically create the surface, as shown in Figure 5–67.

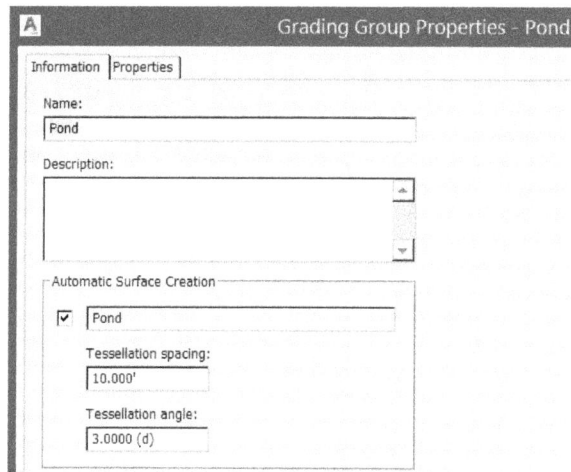

Figure 5–67

23. Click **OK** to close the dialog box. Click **OK** in the Create Surface dialog box. (If the Event vista displays, close it.)

24. To view the pond grading in 3D, select the surface in Model Space, right-click and select **Object Viewer**, as shown in Figure 5–68.

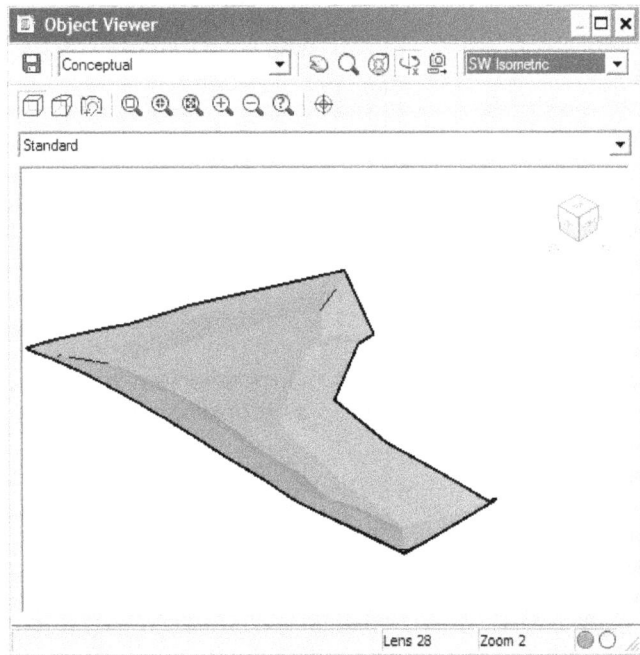

Figure 5–68

25. Select **X** to close the object viewer and save the drawing.

Task 2 - Supplement the surface with feature lines.

Add feature lines to represent critical grade breaks and other important elevation breaklines on the surface. These lines accentuate the geometry and make the surface more accurate. In this task you will add feature lines at the north and south ends of the site.

1. Continue working with the drawing from the previous task or open **POND-D2-Grading.dwg**.

2. In the *View* tab>Views panel, select the preset view **Storm Pond**.

3. In the *Prospector* tab, expand the *Sites* collection, expand the site *Pond Site* collection, and select **Feature Lines**. In the grid view at the bottom, select the three feature lines **Pond-Bdy-North**, **Pond-Bdy-South**, and **Pond-Access Rd-North** using <Ctrl>. Right-click and select **Select**, as shown in Figure 5–69.

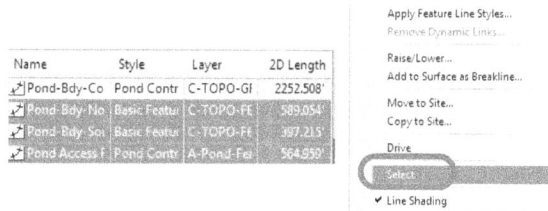

Figure 5–69

4. Once selected, the feature lines can be added to the surface as breaklines. In the *Feature Line contextual tab*>Modify

   panel, click ⟨⟩ (Add to Surface as Breaklines), as shown in Figure 5–70.

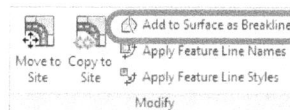

Figure 5–70

5. In the Select Surface dialog box, select the pond surface, as shown in Figure 5–71. Click **OK**.

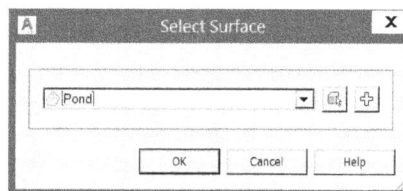

Figure 5–71

6. In the Add Breaklines dialog box, accept all of the defaults and click **OK**.

7. Press <Esc> to end the selection.

8. You now have a pond surface that matches the proposed design of the parcels on the east side and Jeffries Ranch Road on the south side. The north and west sides of the pond have been graded to match the existing ground.

9. Save the drawing.

Chapter Review Questions

1. Which icon in the *Feature Line contextual tab*>Modify panel enables you to edit feature line geometry?

   a.

   b.

   c.

   d.

2. Which icon in the *Feature Line contextual tab*>Modify panel enables you to edit feature line elevations?

   a.

   b.

   c.

   d.

3. Which icon in the *Feature Line contextual tab*>Edit Geometry panel enables you to trim a feature line at selected cutting edges?

   a.

   b.

   c.

   d.

4. Which icon in the *Feature Line contextual tab*>Edit Elevations panel enables you to insert a high/low elevation point?

a.

b.

c.

d.

5. Feature lines can be extracted from corridor models.

a. True

b. False

Command Summary

Button	Command	Location
	Add to Surface as Breakline	• **Ribbon**: *Feature Line* contextual tab> Modify panel • **Command Prompt:** FeatureAddAsBreakline
	Break	• **Ribbon**: *Feature Line* contextual tab> Edit Geometry panel • **Command Prompt:** BreakFeatures
	Create Feature Line from Corridor	• **Ribbon**: *Home* tab>Create Design panel, expanded Feature Line drop-down list • **Command Prompt:** FeatureLinesFromCorridor
	Delete Elevation Point	• **Ribbon**: *Feature Line* contextual tab> Modify panel, click Edit Elevations to display the Edit Elevations panel • **Toolbar**: *Elevation Editor* (*contextual*) • **Command Prompt:** DeleteElevPoint
	Feature Line Properties	• **Ribbon**: *Feature Line* contextual tab> Modify panel
	Insert Elevation Point	• **Ribbon**: *Feature Line* contextual tab> Modify panel, click Edit Elevations to display the Edit Elevations panel • **Toolbar**: *Elevation Editor* (*contextual*) • **Command Prompt:** InsertElevPoint
	Insert PI	• **Ribbon**: *Feature Line* contextual tab> Edit Geometry panel • **Command Prompt:** InsertFeaturePI
	Join	• **Ribbon**: *Feature Line* contextual tab> Edit Geometry panel • **Command Prompt:** JoinFeatures
	Trim	• **Ribbon**: *Feature Line* contextual tab> Edit Geometry panel • **Command Prompt:** TrimFeatures

Grading with Corridor Models

The AutoCAD® Civil 3D® software provides tools that create multiple design scenarios in compressed time. Another benefit is the ease of making changes to a design. You can easily create a finished ground surface using parcel lines, feature lines, and grading objects. Unfortunately, they do not provide the level of flexibility that many projects require. As an alternative to the grading tools, this chapter explores using an AutoCAD Civil 3D corridor as a grading design tool. The corridor and its tools provide easy design and editing capabilities. This is a non-standard approach to grading in the AutoCAD Civil 3D software. Corridor subassemblies provide more daylighting options and the ability to add conditional grades to a finished ground surface. In this chapter, you use the corridor and its tools to redesign a pond area to include a two chamber lagoon.

Learning Objectives in this Chapter

- Create corridor baselines that can be used for a grading solution rather than a road design.
- Create profiles to be used in grading solutions.
- Determine the best subassembly to use for the type of grading being created.
- Create multiple baselines and regions in a corridor model to include multiple alignments, profiles, and assemblies in the grading solution.
- Modify a grading solution by changing the alignments, profiles, assemblies, target surface, or corridor parameters.
- Add feature lines to the corridor surface for additional grading control.

6.1 Corridor Baselines

Corridors can be used to create more than just roads. Using corridors provides greater flexibility and ease in making design changes than grading objects. Additionally, corridors provide more options for materials. For example, a parking lot graded using a corridor model enables you to apply asphalt to the parking surface, concrete for the curbs and gutters, and grass or some other material inside the islands. Not only does this help with visualizations, it can also help create quantity take offs much faster.

Baselines can be either alignments or feature lines. The purpose of a baseline is to apply an assembly to a corridor. As the assembly is applied, it stays perpendicular to the baseline. A great example of this is in an intersection model: edge of pavement baselines can be used to apply a curb return assembly perpendicular to the curb, as shown in Figure 6–1.

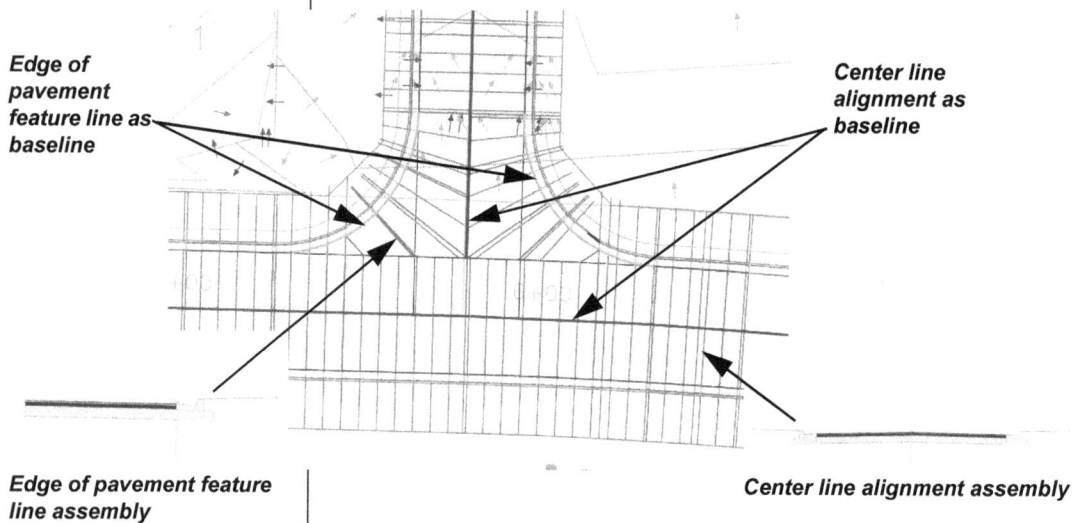

Edge of pavement feature line as baseline

Center line alignment as baseline

Edge of pavement feature line assembly

Center line alignment assembly

Figure 6–1

Feature Line Baselines

New in 2017

Using a feature line for a corridor baseline enables you to quickly set both the horizontal and vertical location for a grading model. If the feature line needs to reference another entity for either the horizontal or vertical location, two options are available. To find them, in the *Home* tab>Create Design panel, expand the Feature Line drop-down list, as shown in Figure 6–2.

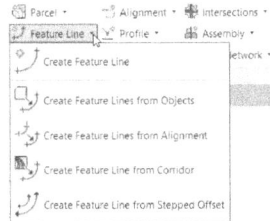

Figure 6–2

Selecting the **Create Feature Lines from Alignment** option enables you to set the following, as shown in Figure 6–3:

*   Select the site in which to place the new feature line so that it interacts with other feature lines and grading objects.

*   Name the feature line.

*   Select a profile to use to assign elevations to vertices.

*   Select a style.

*   Determine if you want the feature line to update each time the alignment changes.

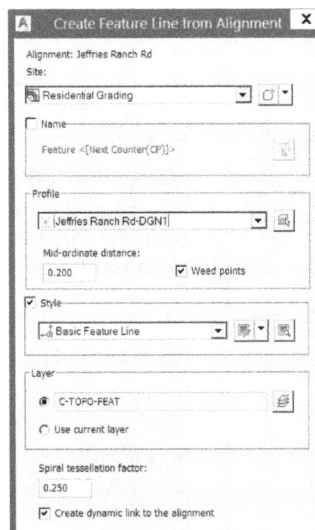

Figure 6–3

Selecting the **Create Feature Lines from Corridor** option enables you to set the following:

- Select which corridor feature lines are extracted, as shown in Figure 6–4. The options include:
  - All feature lines
  - Only those in a select region(s)
  - Only those within a select polygon

- Determine which settings to use, as shown in Figure 6–4:
  - Create a dynamic link to the corridor
  - Smooth the feature line
  - Name the feature line
  - Select a code set style

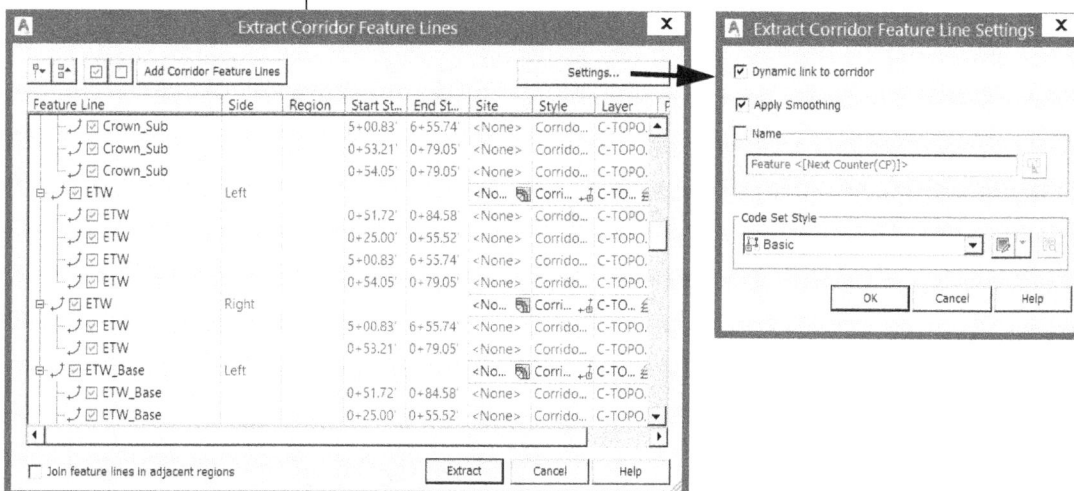

Figure 6–4

Alignment Baselines

Even though you can use feature lines as baselines for corridors, alignments can still add more control during the editing process. For example, alignments are able to keep arcs tangent to straight segments if the right type of curve is added for the corner treatment.

Grading solutions with alignments and corridor models do not have to be linear entities. The solutions can also include enclosed areas, such as parking lots, ponds, or lagoons. When grading an enclosed area, ensure that you begin and end the alignment along a straight segment that does not contain any odd transitions, as shown in Figure 6–5. This ensures that the corridor model built from the alignment correctly projects the grading slopes from their beginning and ending points.

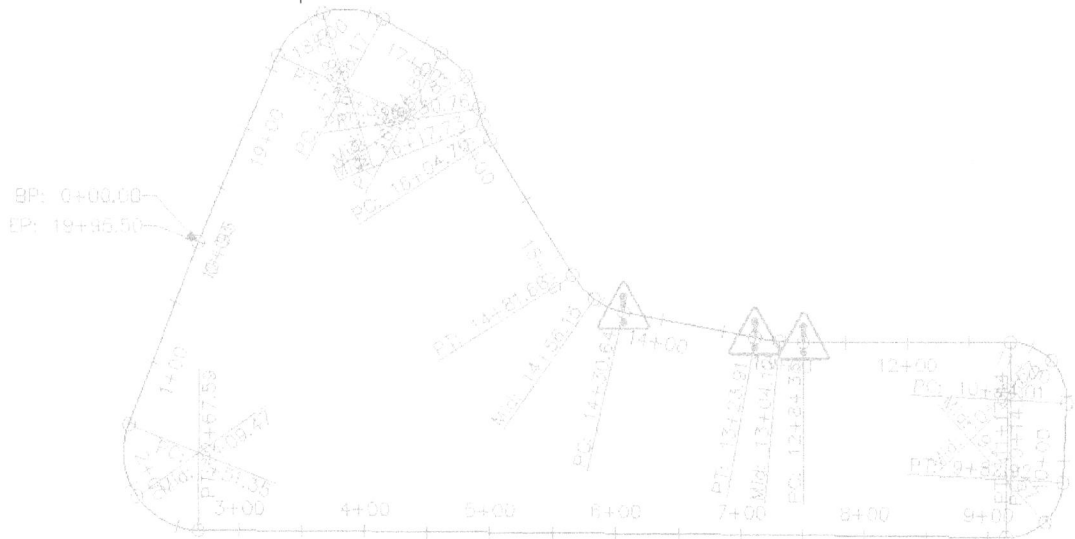

Figure 6–5

Depending on the corner treatment that is required for a project, it is recommended that you include horizontal curves between tangents. Curves enable the corridor models to make smooth transitions between tangents rather than cut the corner off at an angle, as shown in Figure 6–6.

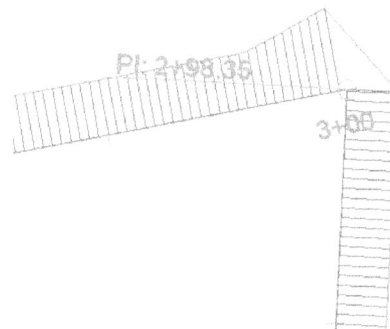

Figure 6–6

How To: Create an Alignment for an Enclosed Grading Solution

1. In the *Home* tab>Create Design panel, expand the Alignment drop-down list and click ⤵ (Alignment Creation Tools)
2. Create the tangents and curves ensuring that the alignment begins and ends at the same location along a straight segment.

   - To ensure that the beginning and ending of the alignment follow the same bearing, use the **Bearing and Distance** transparent command.
   - Alternatively, you can create a line that spans one side of the area to grade. Begin the alignment at the midpoint of the line using Osnaps. Use the endpoint of the line to pick the second point. Loop the alignment around and use the other endpoint to begin the last segment. Use the **Midpoint** Osnap again to pick the last station of the alignment, as shown in Figure 6–7.

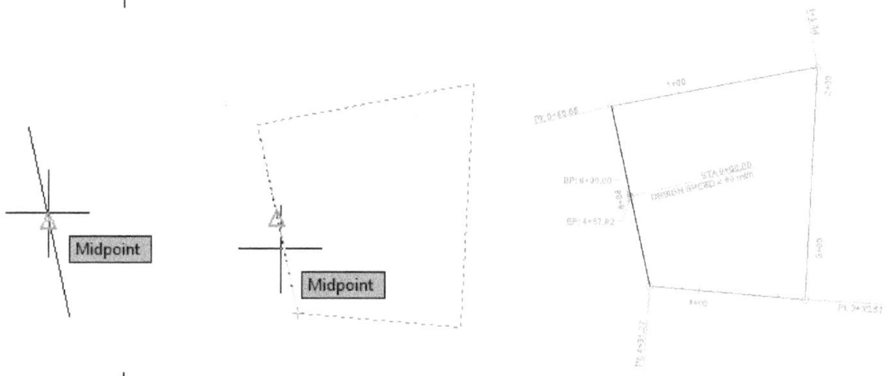

Figure 6–7

Practice 6a

Create Grading Baselines

Practice Objective

Estimated time for completion: 15 minutes

- Create alignments representing the rim of the pond.

In this practice you will use the workflow of creating alignments for the pond's rim, using polylines that are already in the drawing.

Task 1 - Create alignments from objects.

In this task, you will create two alignments that represent the pond's rim. One alignment closes on itself to create an enclosed area and acts as the pond's outer rim. The second alignment is in the pond's interior rim and represents the north bay. It is open because feature lines are used to grade a weir between the two bays. When selecting the polylines, it is important to pick them at the suggested location so that you end up with the same starting and ending points for each alignment.

1. Open **LAGOON-A1-Grading.dwg** from the *C:\Civil3D-Grading\Lagoon* folder.

2. In the *Home* tab>Create Design panel, expand the Alignment drop-down list and click ⤳ (Create Alignment from Objects).

3. In the drawing, select the closed polyline representing the outer rim of the pond, as shown in Figure 6–8. Press <Enter>.

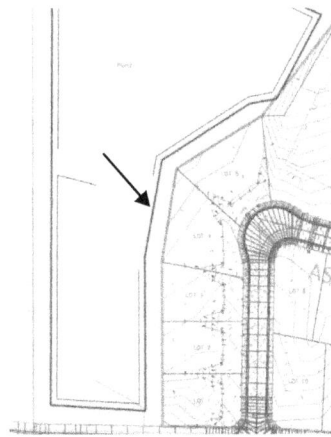

Figure 6–8

4. Press <Enter> to accept the default direction.

5. In the Create Alignment from Objects dialog box, set the following, as shown in Figure 6–9:

- For the *Name*, type **Pond Outer Rim**.
- For the *Type*, select **Miscellaneous**.
- For the *Alignment style*, select **Proposed**.
- Select both options in the *Conversion options* area.
- Set the *Default radius* to **60**'.
- Click OK.

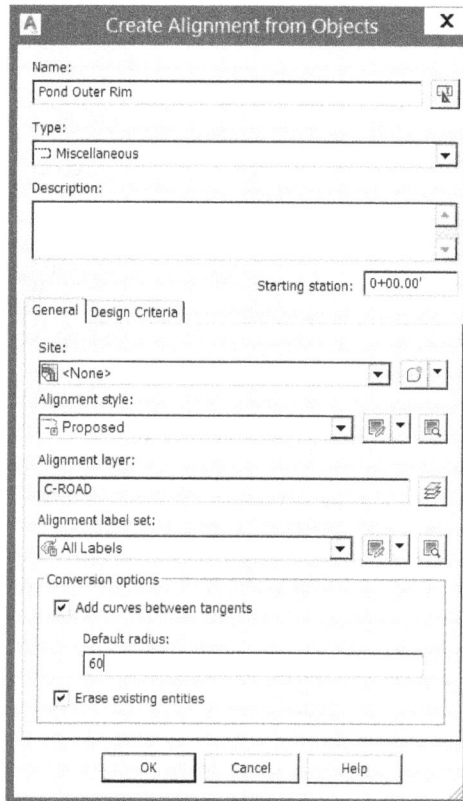

Figure 6–9

6. In the *Home* tab>Create Design panel, expand the Alignment drop-down list and click ⟶ (Create Alignment from Objects).

7. In the drawing, select the northern polyline representing the interior rim of the pond's north bay, as shown in Figure 6–10. Press <Enter>.

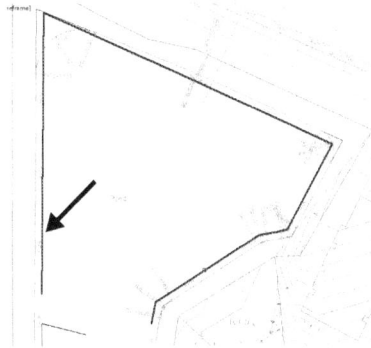

Figure 6–10

8. Press <Enter> to accept the default direction.

9. In the Create Alignment from Objects dialog box, complete the following, as shown in Figure 6–11:

   - For the *Name*, type **Pond North Bay**.
   - For the *Type*, select **Miscellaneous**
   - For the *Alignment style*, select **Proposed**.
   - Select both options in the *Conversion options* area.
   - Set the *Default radius* to **75**'.
   - Click OK

Figure 6–11

Task 2 - Create a feature line to use as a baseline.

1. Continue working in the same drawing as the last task. Alternatively, open **LAGOON-A2-Grading.dwg** from the *C:\Civil3D-Grading\Lagoon* folder.

2. In the *Home* tab>Create Design panel, expand the Feature Line drop-down list and click (Create Feature Lines from Objects).

3. In the drawing, select the southern polyline representing the interior rim of the pond's south bay, as shown in Figure 6–12. Press <Enter>.

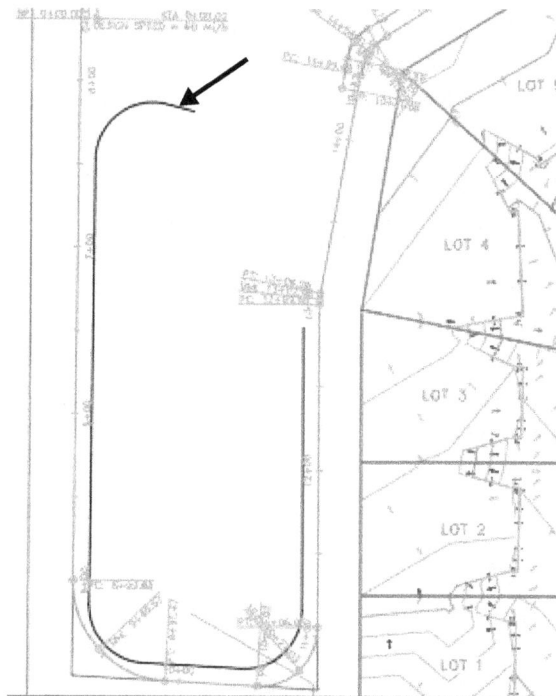

Figure 6–12

4. In the Create Feature Lines dialog box, set the following, as shown in Figure 6–13:

- For the *Site*, select **Pond Site**.
- For the *Name*, type **Pond South Bay**.
- For the *Style*, select **Pond**.
- In the *Conversion options* area, select **Erase existing entities** and **Assign elevations**.
- Click **OK**.

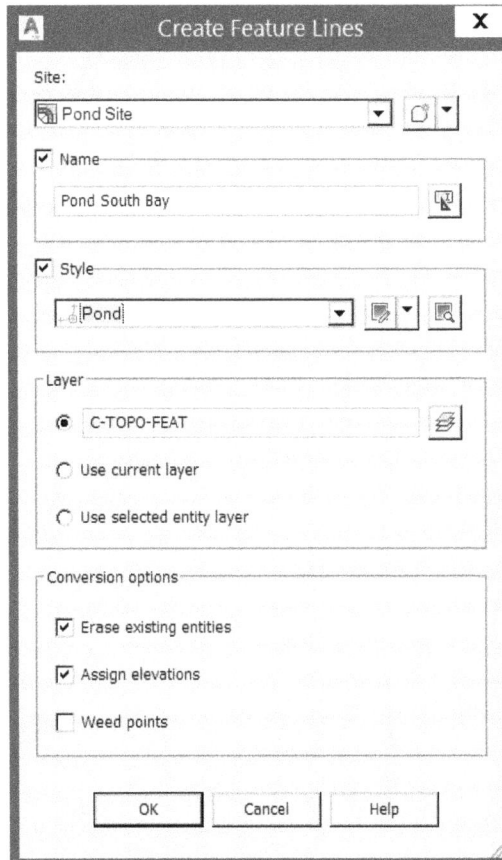

Figure 6–13

5. In the Assign Elevations dialog box, select **Elevation** and set the value to **179**.

6. Click **OK**.

7. Save the drawing

Task 3 - Modify the curves and clean up the drawing.

In this task, you will clean up the alignments by editing their curves to ensure that each has the proper design radius. You will then remove the alignment labels and line extensions that are not required for the design documentation.

1. Continue working in the same drawing as the last task. Alternatively, open **LAGOON-A3-Grading.dwg** from the *C:\Civil3D-Grading\Lagoon* folder.

2. In the drawing, select the **Pond Outer Rim** alignment, as shown in Figure 6–14.

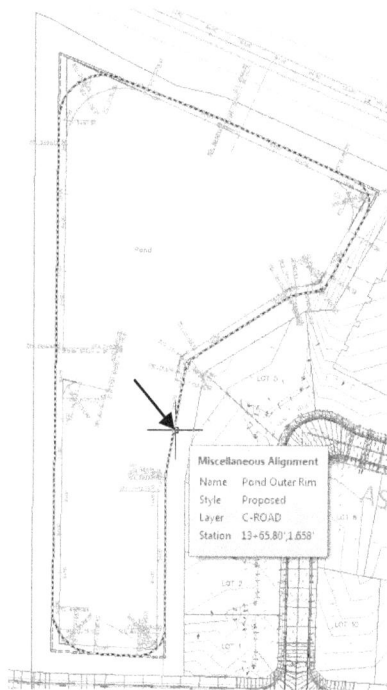

Figure 6–14

3. In the *Alignment* contextual tab>Modify panel, click ✎ (Geometry Editor).

4. In the Alignment Layout Tools toolbar, click ▦ (Alignment Grid View).

5. Set the curve radius values according to those shown in Figure 6–15.

No.	Type	Tangency Constraint	Parameter Constrai...	Parameter C...	Length	Radius
1	Line	Not Constrained (Fixed)	🔒	Two points	151.348'	
2	Curve	Constrained on Both Sides (Free)	🔒	Radius	116.240'	60.000'
3	Line	Not Constrained (Fixed)	🔒	Two points	646.636'	
4	Curve	Constrained on Both Sides (Free)	🔒	Radius	68.693'	45.000'
5	Line	Not Constrained (Fixed)	🔒	Two points	61.087'	
6	Curve	Constrained on Both Sides (Free)	🔒	Radius	73.136'	45.000'
7	Line	Not Constrained (Fixed)	🔒	Two points	157.191'	
8	Curve	Constrained on Both Sides (Free)	🔒	Radius	39.723'	215.000'
9	Line	Not Constrained (Fixed)	🔒	Two points	103.711'	
10	Curve	Constrained on Both Sides (Free)	🔒	Radius	53.954'	65.000'
11	Line	Not Constrained (Fixed)	🔒	Two points	122.949'	
12	Curve	Constrained on Both Sides (Free)	🔒	Radius	25.189'	65.000'
13	Line	Not Constrained (Fixed)	🔒	Two points	1.699'	
14	Curve	Constrained on Both Sides (Free)	🔒	Radius	53.312'	60.000'
15	Line	Not Constrained (Fixed)	🔒	Two points	53.268'	
16	Curve	Constrained on Both Sides (Free)	🔒	Radius	100.119'	60.000'
17	Line	Not Constrained (Fixed)	🔒	Two points	157.209'	

Figure 6–15

6. Close the Alignment Grid View vista.

7. Without closing the Alignment Tools toolbar, select the **Pond North Bay** alignment in the drawing.

8. In the Alignment Layout Tools toolbar, click 🖽 (Alignment Grid View).

9. Set the curve radius values according to those shown in Figure 6–16.

No.	Type	Tangency Constraint	Parameter Constrai...	Parameter C...	Length	Radius
1	Line	Not Constrained (Fixed)	🔒	Two points	264.166'	
2	Curve	Constrained on Both Sides (Free)	🔒	Radius	148.245'	75.000'
3	Line	Not Constrained (Fixed)	🔒	Two points	243.092'	
4	Curve	Constrained on Both Sides (Free)	🔒	Radius	125.149'	75.000'
5	Line	Not Constrained (Fixed)	🔒	Two points	25.693'	
6	Curve	Constrained on Both Sides (Free)	🔒	Radius	44.427'	50.000'
7	Line	Not Constrained (Fixed)	🔒	Two points	2.582'	
8	Curve	Constrained on Both Sides (Free)	🔒	Radius	27.320'	70.500'
9	Line	Not Constrained (Fixed)	🔒	Two points	134.847'	
10	Curve	Constrained on Both Sides (Free)	🔒	Radius	41.503'	50.000'
11	Line	Not Constrained (Fixed)	🔒	Two points	7.921'	

Figure 6–16

10. Close the Alignment Grid View vista.

11. Close the Alignment Tools toolbar.

12. Select the **Pond South Bay** feature line in the drawing.

13. In the contextual *Feature Line* tab>Edit Geometry panel, click ⤶ (Edit Curve).

14. Select the curve shown in Figure 6–17.

Figure 6–17

15. In the Edit Feature Line Curve dialog box, set *Radius* to **43**.

16. Click **OK**.

17. In the drawing, select the **Pond Outer Rim** alignment, right-click and select **Edit Alignment Labels**, as shown in Figure 6–18.

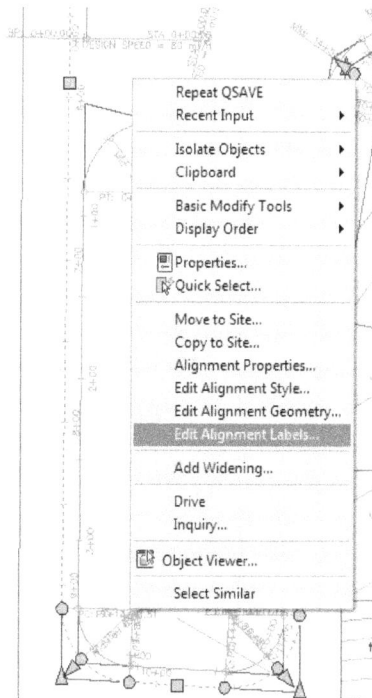

Figure 6–18

18. In the Alignment Labels dialog box, select **Import Label Set**. In the Select Label Set dialog box, select **_No Labels**, as shown in Figure 6–19. Click **OK** twice to close the dialog boxes and remove the labels from the alignment.

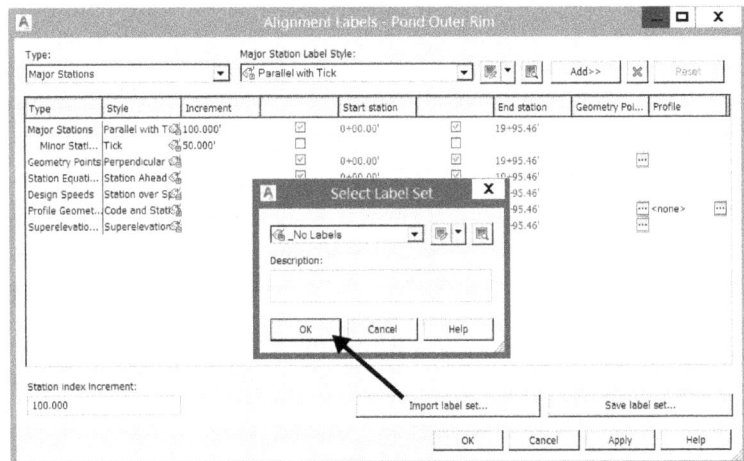

Figure 6–19

19. Press <Esc> to clear the previously selected object.

20. Repeat Steps 16 to 18 for the North Bay pond alignment.

21. In the drawing, select one of the pond alignments. In the *Alignment* contextual tab>Modify panel, expand the Alignment Properties drop-down list and click ⬚ (Edit Alignment Style) as shown in Figure 6–20.

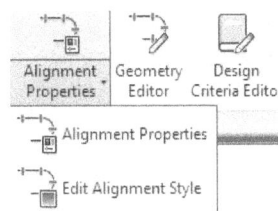

Figure 6–20

22. In the *Markers* tab, change the *Point of Intersection* marker style to **<None>**, as shown in Figure 6–21.

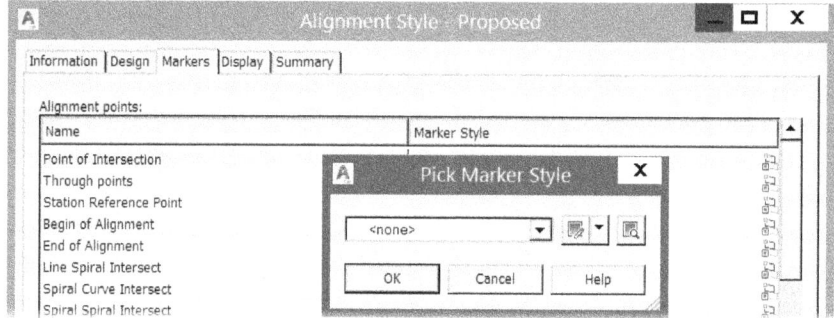

Figure 6–21

23. In the *Display* tab, turn off the light bulb next to **Line Extensions**, as shown in Figure 6–22.

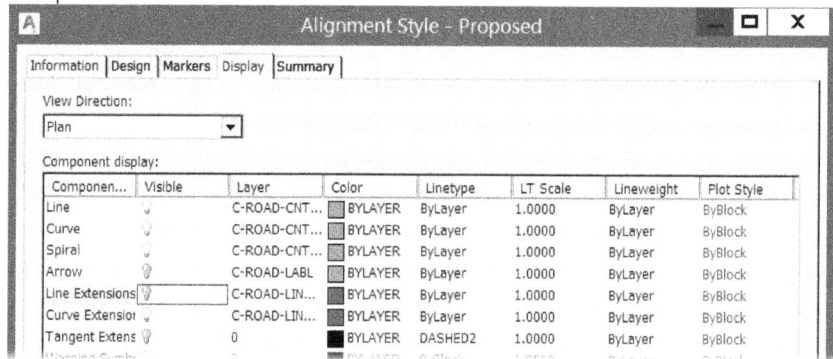

Figure 6–22

24. Click **OK** to close the dialog box.

25. Save the drawing.

6.2 Profiles

The process of creating a grading profile is similar to creating a profile for a road design. The same tools are used but different precautions are needed. First, as you make adjustments to the alignment, the stationing might change. This causes the alignment to become longer than its originally designed profile. Therefore, it is recommended that you extend the designed profile a approximately 200 feet beyond the existing surface profile, as shown in Figure 6–23. This ensures that the corridor model does not jump to elevation zero if the alignment is lengthened. The gap in the vertical design creates spikes in the finished ground surface that extend to elevation zero.

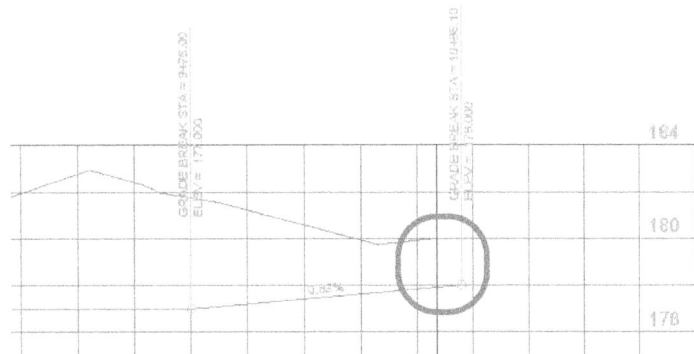

Figure 6–23

In a road design, you would not create a profile without vertical curves. When using corridor models to design grading projects, vertical curves are optional because having smooth transitions between grades is not as critical. Second, when grading enclosed areas with corridors, the beginning and ending elevations must match.

How To: Create Profiles for Grading Solutions

1. Create a surface profile of the alignment and any required offsets. In the *Home* tab>Create Design panel, expand the Profile drop-down list and click ⌇ (Create Profile from surface).
2. In the Create Profile From Surface dialog box, select the alignment. Select the surface(s) in the surface area and select **Add**. Select **Draw in profile view**.
3. In the Create Profile View dialog box, select **Create Profile View**. In the drawing, select a point for the insertion point.

4. In the *Home* tab>Create Design panel, expand the Profile drop-down list and click ⋎ (Profile Creation Tools). In the drawing, select the profile view.

5. In the Create Profile dialog box, type a *Name* and select the *Profile style* and *Profile label set*, as shown in Figure 6–24. Click **OK** to close the dialog box.

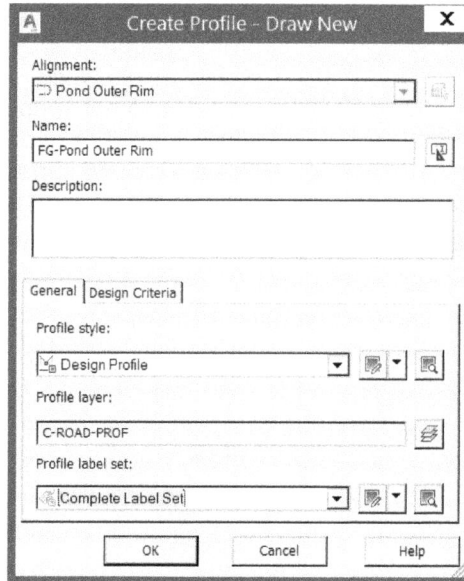

Create Profile – Draw New

Alignment:
Pond Outer Rim

Name:
FG-Pond Outer Rim

Description:

General | Design Criteria

Profile style:
Design Profile

Profile layer:
C-ROAD-PROF

Profile label set:
Complete Label Set

OK   Cancel   Help

Figure 6–24

6. In the Profile Layout Tools toolbar, click ⋎ (Draw Tangents).

7. In the Transparent Tools toolbar, click ⌐⌐ (Profile Station Elevation).

8. In the drawing, select the appropriate profile view.

9. In the Command Line, enter the stations and elevations for the beginning and ending of the profile along with any intermediate PVIs. Verify that the alignment closes on itself, and that the beginning and ending elevations match.

Practice 6b

Estimated time for completion: 10 minutes

Create Grading Profiles

Practice Objective

• Create profiles representing the rim of the pond.

In this practice you will create profiles for the pond's rim.

Task 1 - Create a profile for the outer rim of the pond.

In this task, you will create a profile that represents the outer rim of the pond. The alignment for the outer rim closes on itself to create an enclosed area and requires the beginning and ending elevations to be the same.

1. Open **LAGOON-B1-Grading.dwg** from the *C:\Civil3D-Grading\Lagoon* folder.

2. In the *Home* tab>Create Design panel, expand the Profile drop-down list and click — (Create Surface Profile).

3. In the Create Profile from Surface dialog box, for the *Alignment* select **Pond Outer Rim**. In the *Surface* area select **Existing Ground** and click **Add>>**.

4. With the Pond Outer Rim alignment still selected, complete the following, as shown in Figure 6–25:

    • Select **Sample offsets** and type **30** for the *Offset value*.

    • Select **Residential Surface** in the *Surface* area and click **Add>>**.

    • In the *Profile list* area, select **Residential Profile** and change the *Style* to **Right Sample Profile**.

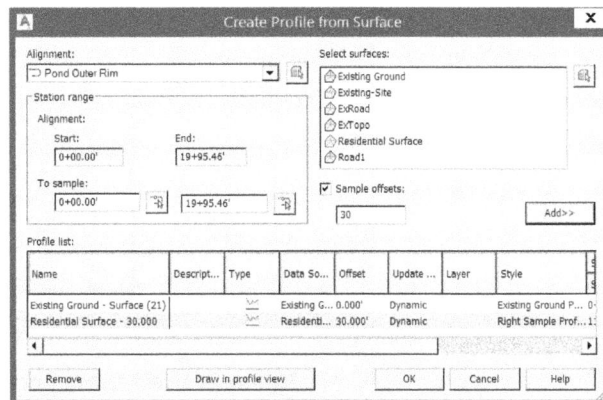

Figure 6–25

5. Select **Draw in profile view**.

6. In the Create Profile View dialog box, click **Create Profile View**.

7. In the drawing, select a point above Mission Ave as the insertion point, as shown in Figure 6–26.

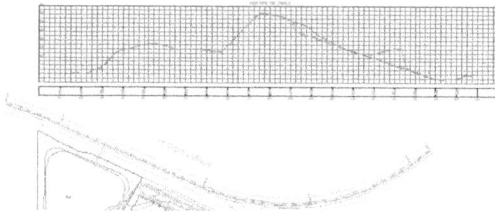

Figure 6–26

8. In the *Home* tab>Create Design panel, expand the Profile drop-down list and click ⬐ (Profile Creation Tools).

9. In the drawing, select the Pond Outer Rim profile view.

10. In the Create Profile dialog box, complete the following, as shown in Figure 6–27:

   • For the *Name*, type **FG-Pond Outer Rim**
   • For the *Style*, select **Design Profile**
   • For the *Profile label set*, select **Complete Label set**.
   • Click **OK** to close the dialog box.

Figure 6–27

11. In the Profile Layout Tools toolbar, click ⬐ (Draw Tangents).

12. In the Transparent Tools toolbar, click 📐 (Profile Station Elevation).

13. In the drawing, select the **Pond Outer Rim** profile view.

14. In the Command Line, for the *Station* type **0** and press <Enter>. For the elevation type **177** and press <Enter>. Use the following table to set the remaining stations and elevations.

Note that you are going past the ending station. This ensures that if a curve changes (causing the alignment to lengthen or shorten), the corridor does not apply itself to elevation zero.

Station	Elevation
5+00.0'	177'
7+00.0'	180'
13+23.91'	180'
15+00.0'	177'
20+25.0'	177'

15. Press <Esc> to end the **Transparent** command. Press <Esc> again to end the command.

16. Save the drawing.

Task 2 - Create the Pond North Bay profile.

In this task, you will create a profile that represents the interior rim of the pond's north bay.

1. Open **LAGOON-B2-Grading.dwg** from the *C:\Civil3D-Grading\Lagoon* folder.

2. In the *Home* tab>Create Design panel, expand the Profile drop-down list and click ⁓ (Create Profile from surface).

3. In the Create Profile From Surface dialog box, complete the following:
   - For the *Alignment*, select **Pond North Bay**.
   - In the *Surface* area, select **Existing Ground** and click **Add>>**.
   - Click **Draw in profile view**.

4. In the Create Profile View dialog box, click **Create Profile view**.

5. In the drawing, select a point above the Pond Outer Rim profile view as the insertion point.

6. In the *Home* tab>Create Design panel, expand the Profile drop-down list and click ⤋ (Profile Creation Tools). In the drawing, select the **Pond North Bay** profile view.

7. In the Create Profile dialog box, complete the following, as shown in Figure 6–28:
   - For the *Name*, type **FG-Pond North Bay**.
   - For the *Style*, select **Design Profile**.
   - For the *Profile Label, set* select **Complete Label set**.
   - Click **OK** to close the dialog box.

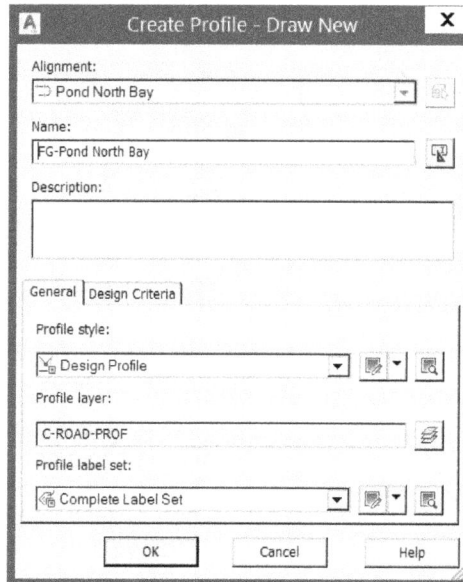

Figure 6–28

8. In the Profile Layout Tools toolbar, click ⩔ (Draw Tangents).

9. In the Transparent Tools toolbar, click ⌐⌐ (Profile Station Elevation).

10. In the drawing, select the **Pond North Bay** profile view.

11. In the Command Line, for the *Station* type **0** and press <Enter>. For the *Elevation* type **178** and press <Enter>.

12. Use the table below to set the remaining stations and elevations.

Station	Elevation
1+25.0'	177'
9+75.0'	177'
10+64.95'	178'
11+00.0'	178'

13. Press <Esc> to end the **Transparent** command. Press <Esc> again to end the command.

14. Save the drawing.

6.3 Create Grading Assemblies

Three subassemblies are available that accomplish the same results as grading criteria would in a grading group. The three subassemblies and their grading criteria equivalent are as follows:

1. Link Width and Slope = Grade to Distance
2. Link Slope to Surface = Grade to Surface
3. Link Slopes to Elevations = Grade to Elevation or Grade to Relative Elevation.

These subassemblies are accessed in the *Generic* tab in the Tool Palettes, as shown in Figure 6–29.

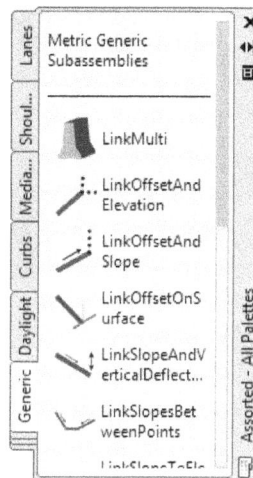

Figure 6–29

The Tool Palettes contains numerous subassemblies that act like grading scenarios. You need to determine when and how to use them. Most of the time, grading projects use the link and daylight subassemblies. However, they might also include curb, sidewalk, and other subassemblies that include structures, especially if the grading project is a parking lot.

Link Subassemblies

The *Generic* tab in the Tool Palettes contains 14 subassemblies that create surface links between the grading alignment/profile and other objects in the drawing. The other objects might include offsets, elevations, alignments, profiles, surfaces, etc. When using any of the link subassemblies, only a top or datum surface can be created from the points assigned to the subassembly because they do not include Point, Link, or Shape codes. For more information on the link subassembly's parameters, right-click on the subassembly in the Tool Palette and select **Help**.

Link Width and Slope

The Link Width and Slope subassembly adds a surface link by specifying its width and slope. The inside edge of the link is the attachment point. It is programmed for the left or right side and can override a fixed width by targeting an alignment. It can also override a fixed slope using a profile. The target types include profiles, 3D polylines, feature lines, or survey figures. An example is shown in Figure 6–30.

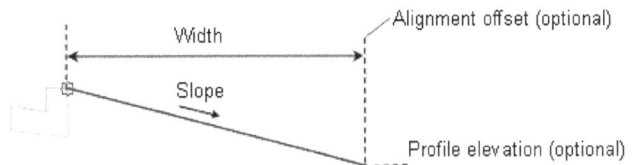

Figure 6–30

Link Slope to Surface

The Link Slope to Surface subassembly adds a surface link by specifying its slope and target surface. The inside edge of the link is the attachment point. It is programmed for the left or right side and can override a fixed width by targeting an alignment. The target types include alignments, 3D polylines, feature lines, or survey figures. An example is shown in Figure 6–31.

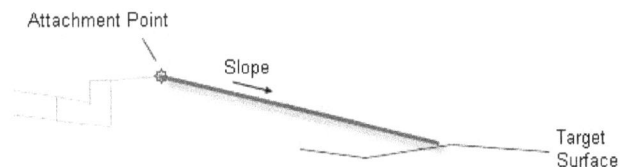

Figure 6–31

Link Slopes to Elevation

The Link Slopes to Elevation subassembly adds a surface link by specifying its slope and target elevation. The inside edge of the link is the attachment point. It is programmed for the left or right side and targets a specified elevation or target profile. An example is shown in Figure 6–32.

Slope

Target Elevatoin

Figure 6–32

Link Offset on Surface

The Link Offset on Surface subassembly adds a surface link by specifying an offset location and target surface. The beginning of the link is the attachment point. It is programmed to permit positive or negative offsets and can override a fixed width by targeting an alignment. An example is shown in Figure 6–33.

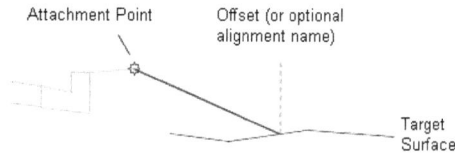

Attachment Point

Offset (or optional alignment name)

Target Surface

Figure 6–33

Link to Marked Point

The Link to Marked Point subassembly enables you to connect a link from the attached point to a previously named marked point. The beginning of the link is the attachment point and it can go in any direction. The direction is determined by the location of the named marked point, which can be on an adjacent corridor model. An example is shown in Figure 6–34.

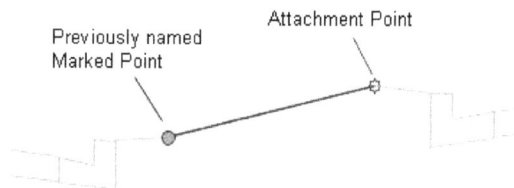

Attachment Point

Previously named Marked Point

Figure 6–34

Link to Marked Point 2

The Link to Marked Point 2 subassembly enables you to connect a link from the attached point to a previously named marked point. The beginning of the link is the attachment point and it can go in any direction. The direction is determined by the location of the named marked point, which can be on an adjacent corridor model. The difference between the Link to Marked Point and the Link to Marked Point 2 subassemblies is that the marked point is on a different assembly baseline compared to the link and the baselines do not need to be parallel. An example is shown in Figure 6–35.

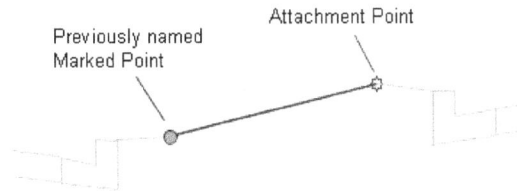

Figure 6–35

Daylight Subassemblies

The *Daylight* tab in the Tool Palettes contains 17 subassemblies that create surface links between the grading alignment/profile and other objects in the drawing. In addition to creating links, materials can be assigned to the links to help with quantity calculations and visualization of the grading model. For more information on each daylight subassembly's parameters, right-click on the subassembly in the Tool Palette and select **Help**.

Daylight General

The Daylight General subassembly is a generalized solution to create cut and fill slopes from the edge of the grading design out to a target surface. This is the most commonly used daylight subassembly. However, it is seldom used to its full potential because many people do not realize the variety of cut and fill slope conditions it contains.

By default, the Daylight General subassembly attempts to create a cut first according to the parameter settings. The parameters can include up to eight different cut slopes, each with their own assigned material, before reaching the Cut Hinge Point, as shown in Figure 6–36. You do not have to use all eight cut parameters. If only one slope is required, you can leave all of the other Cut Slope Width and Slope parameters set to zero. The slope after the Hinge Point can be set to define the final slope out to the target surface. It can vary according to the Max Cut Height settings. Therefore, the Flat Cut Slope (6:1 by default) is used if the height of the cut is less than the Flat Cut Height (5' by default). If the height of the cut from the Hinge Point to the surface is greater than the Flat Cut Height, but less than the Max Cut Height, the Medium Cut conditions are used automatically. The Medium Cut Slope enables the slope to be slightly more steep (4:1) than the Flat Cut Slope up to the Medium Cut Max Height (10'). If the cut is greater than the Medium Cut Max Height, the Steep Cut Slope (2:1) is used. The Steep Cut Slope does not have a maximum height parameter.

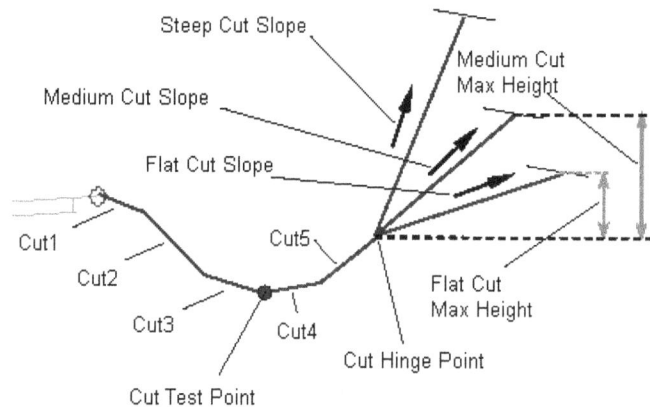

Figure 6–36

If a cut condition is not found, a fill condition is used. Multiple fill conditions can be set similar to setting a cut condition, except that only three Fill Slopes can be set before the Fill Hinge Point. As with cut conditions, the fill conditions can include a Flat Fill Slope (6:1 by default) for a Maximum Height (5' by default), a Medium Fill Slope (4:1 by default) for a Maximum Height (10' by default), and a Steep Fill Slope (2:1) with no height restrictions as shown in Figure 6–37.

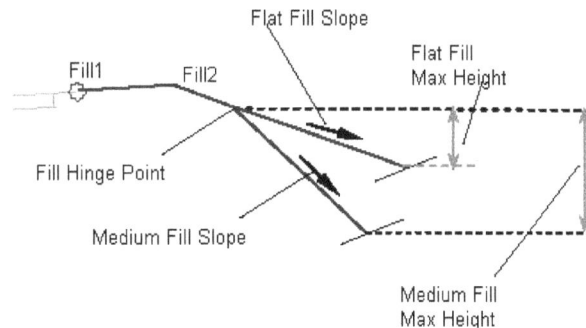

Figure 6–37

If the Steep Slope is used in a cut situation, a guardrail can be incorporated into the design automatically by setting the guardrail parameter to **Include** and setting the slope, width and post position parameters, as shown in Figure 6–38.

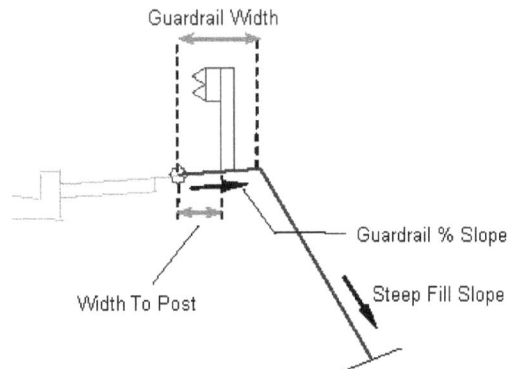

Figure 6–38

Daylight Max Width

The Daylight Max Width subassembly creates a link that daylights to a target surface. The slope used is determined by the Maximum Width permitted. If the daylight link can touch the target surface within the Maximum Width parameter set, the slope is defined by the Slope parameter entered. If the daylight link cannot touch the target surface within the Maximum Width parameter set, the Slope parameter is ignored and the slope is defined by the Width parameter and the difference in elevation from the Hinge Point and the Target Surface at the Maximum Width permitted, as shown in Figure 6–39.

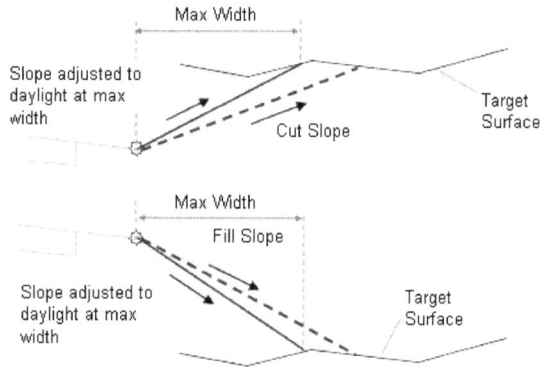

Figure 6–39

Daylight to Offset

The Daylight to Offset subassembly creates a daylight link from the attachment point to a set offset from the baseline. This offset can be parallel to the baseline or target an alignment, polyline, feature line, or survey figure. Different materials can be assigned to the link according to the slope range in which it falls, as shown in Figure 6–40.

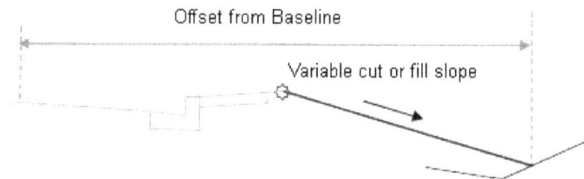

Figure 6–40

Daylight Bench

The Daylight Bench subassembly creates repeating benches as needed at specified heights, widths, and slopes until it finds daylight on a target surface. The cut benches can have different parameters than fill benches if required, as shown in Figure 6–41.

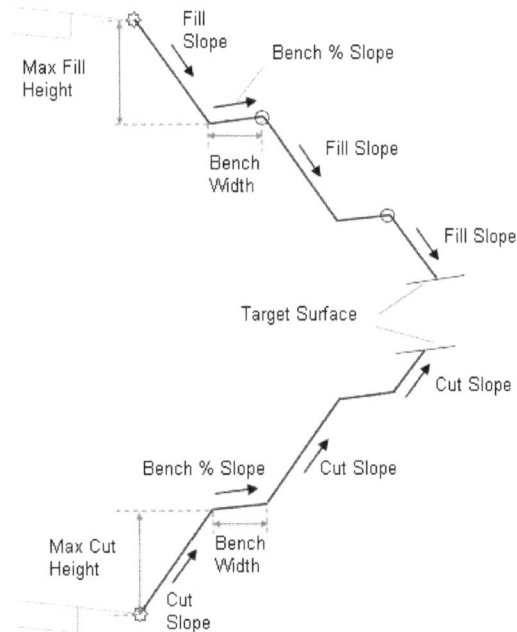

Figure 6–41

How To: Create an Assembly for a Grading Solution

1. In the *Home* tab>Create Design panel, expand the Assembly drop-down list and click ⬚ (Create Assembly).
2. In the Create Assembly dialog box, type a name. Set the *Assembly Type* to **Other**. Click **OK** to accept all of the other defaults and close the dialog box.
3. In the drawing, select a point as the insertion point.
4. In the *Home* tab>Create Design panel, click ⬚ (Tool Palettes).
5. Select the required subassembly.

6. In the Properties palette, set the parameters in the *Advanced* area, as shown in Figure 6–42.

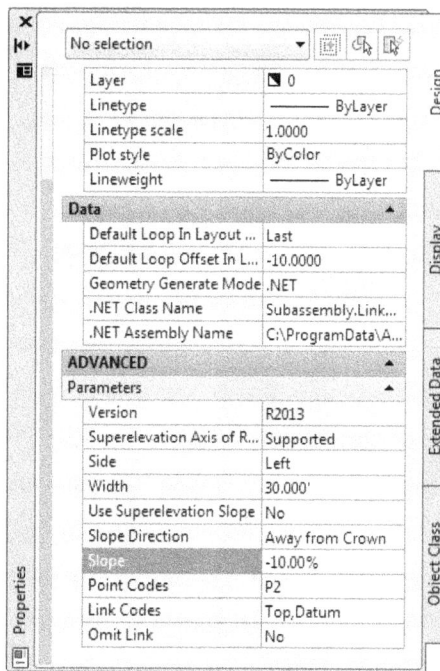

Figure 6–42

7. In the drawing, select the assembly marker to which to connect the subassembly. Press <Enter> to end the command.
8. In the Tool Palettes, select another required subassembly.
9. In the Properties palette, set the parameters in the *Advanced* area.
10. In the drawing, select the required connection point, as shown in Figure 6–43. Press <Enter> to end the command.

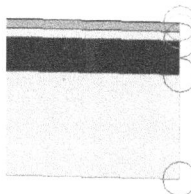

Figure 6–43

11. Continue adding additional subassemblies as required.

Practice 6c

Create Grading Assemblies

Practice Objective

- Create typical cross-sections of the grading corridor using assemblies and selecting the best subassemblies for the design specifications.

In this practice you will create multiple assemblies for the pond grading.

Estimated time for completion: 15 minutes

Task 1 - Create assemblies for the outer rim of the pond.

In this task, you will create an assembly that represents the outer rim of the pond and daylights to the existing ground surface.

1. Continue working in the drawing from the last practice or open **LAGOON-C1-Grading.dwg** from the *C:\Civil3D-Grading\Lagoon* folder.

2. In the *Home* tab>Create Design panel, expand the Assembly drop-down list and click (Create Assembly).

3. In the Create Assembly dialog box, complete the following:
    - For the *Name*, type **Pond Outer Rim**.
    - Set the *Assembly Type* to **Other**.
    - Click **OK** to accept all of the other defaults and close the dialog box.

The AutoCAD Civil 3D software automatically zooms in on the assembly marker.

4. In the drawing, select a point near the Pond Outer Rim Profile view as the insertion point to remember which profile it goes with.

5. In the *Home* tab>Create Design panel, click (Tool Palettes) to display the Tool Palettes.

6. In the *Daylight* tab in the Tool Palettes, select **Daylight Max Width** to display the Properties palette.

7. In the Properties palette, set the parameters according to those shown in Figure 6–44.
   - **Side:** Right
   - **Max Width:** 25'
   - **Rounding Parameter:** 3'
   - **Material 1 Thickness:** 1'
   - **Material 2 Thickness:** 0.5'
   - **Material 3 Thickness:** 0.33'

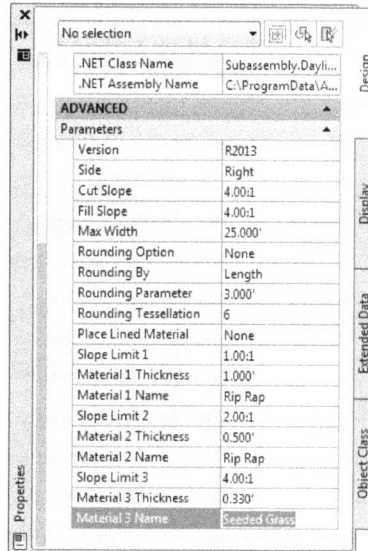

No selection		
.NET Class Name	Subassembly.Dayli...	
.NET Assembly Name	C:\ProgramData\A...	
ADVANCED		
Parameters		
Version	R2013	
Side	Right	
Cut Slope	4.00:1	
Fill Slope	4.00:1	
Max Width	25.000'	
Rounding Option	None	
Rounding By	Length	
Rounding Parameter	3.000'	
Rounding Tessellation	6	
Place Lined Material	None	
Slope Limit 1	1.00:1	
Material 1 Thickness	1.000'	
Material 1 Name	Rip Rap	
Slope Limit 2	2.00:1	
Material 2 Thickness	0.500'	
Material 2 Name	Rip Rap	
Slope Limit 3	4.00:1	
Material 3 Thickness	0.330'	
Material 3 Name	Seeded Grass	

Figure 6–44

8. In the drawing, select the **Pond Outer Rim** assembly marker to which to connect the subassembly. Press <Enter> to end the command.

9. Save the drawing

Task 2 - Create the north bay assemblies.

In this task, you will create three assemblies that represent the interior of the pond's north bay rim and daylights to the existing ground surface.

1. Open **LAGOON-C2-Grading.dwg** from the *C:\Civil3D-Grading\Lagoon* folder.

2. In the *Home* tab>Create Design panel, expand the Assembly drop-down list and click 🗒 (Create Assembly).

3. In the Create Assembly dialog box, complete the following:
   - For the *Name*, type **Pond North Bay 33 percent**.
   - Set the *Assembly Type* to **Other**.
   - Click **OK** to accept all of the other defaults and close the dialog box.

4. In the drawing, select a point near the **Pond North Bay** profile view as the insertion point.

5. If the Tool Palettes is not already displayed, in the *Home* tab> Create Design panel, click ⬚ (Tool Palettes).

6. In the *Generic* tab in the Tool Palettes, select **Link Slope To Elevation**.

7. In the Properties palette, set the parameters according to those shown in Figure 6–45.
   - Side**: Right**
   - Slope: **-33**
   - Target Elevation: **165'**

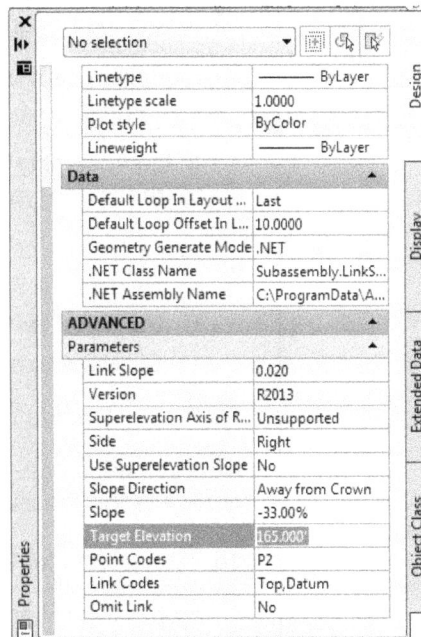

Figure 6–45

Now you will create a copy of the assembly and change the slope for part of the north interior rim grading.

8. In the drawing, select the **Pond Outer Rim** assembly marker to which to connect the subassembly. Press <Enter> to end the command.

9. In the *Home* tab>Modify panel, click ⌖ (Copy).

10. In the drawing, select the **North Bay 33 Percent** assembly marker and press <Enter> to end the selection process.

11. In the drawing, pick two points of displacement to copy the assembly below the original, as shown in Figure 6–46.

Figure 6–46

12. Select the bottom assembly marker, in the *Assembly* contextual tab>Modify panel and click ⊞ (Assembly Properties).

13. In the Assembly Properties dialog box, in the *Information* tab, for the *Name* type **North Bay 40 percent**.

14. In the *Construction* tab, complete the following:
    • Select **LinkSlopeToElevation**.
    • For *Input values*, for the *Slope Value,* type **-40**.
    • Click **OK** to close the dialog box.

15. Press <Esc> to release the selection.

Now you will create an assembly with two links for part of the north interior rim grading.

16. In the *Home* tab>Create Design panel, expand the Assembly drop-down list and click ⊞ (Create Assembly).

17. In the Create Assembly dialog box, complete the following:
    • For the *Name,* type **Pond North Bay double slope**.
    • Set the *Assembly Type* to **Other**.
    • Click **OK** to accept all of the other defaults and close the dialog box.

If the Tool Palettes is not already displayed, in the Home tab> Create Design panel,

click ⬚ (Tool Palettes).

18. In the drawing, select a point below the other two north bay assemblies as the insertion point.

19. In the *Generic* tab in the Tool Palettes, select **Link Width & Slope**.

20. In the Properties palette, set the parameters according to those shown in Figure 6–47.
    - **Side:** Right
    - **Width:** 30'
    - **Slope:** -10

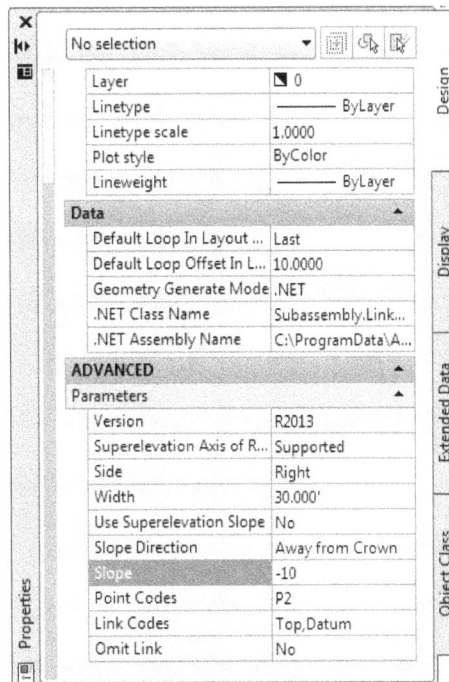

Figure 6–47

21. In the drawing, select the **Pond North Bay** double slope assembly marker to which to connect the subassembly. Press <Enter> to end the command.

22. In the *Generic* tab in the Tool Palettes, select **Link Slope to Elevation**.

23. In the Properties palette, set the parameters according to those shown in Figure 6–48.

- **Side:** Right
- **Slope:** -50
- **Target Elevation:** 165'

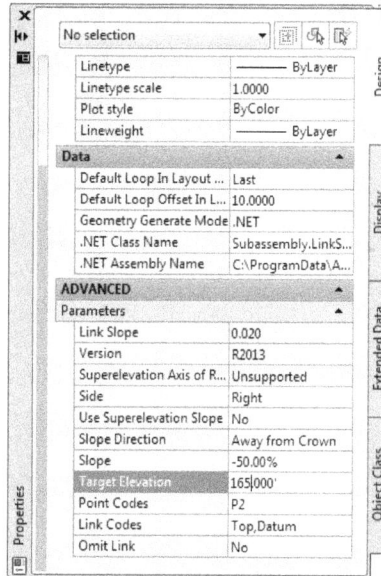

Figure 6–48

24. In the drawing, select the **Pond North Bay** double slope assembly's Link Width & Slope subassembly to which to connect the new subassembly. Press <Enter> to end the command.

25. Save the drawing.

Task 3 - Create the south bay assemblies.

In this task, you will create four assemblies that represent the interior rim of the pond's south bay and daylights to a temporary surface.

1. Open **LAGOON-C3-Grading.dwg** from the *C:\Civil3D-Grading\Lagoon* folder.

2. In the *Home* tab>Create Design panel, expand the Assembly drop-down list and click (Create Assembly).

3. In the Create Assembly dialog box, complete the following:
   - For the *Name,* type **Pond South Bay Bench**.
   - Set the *Assembly Type* to **Other**.
   - Click **OK** to accept all of the other defaults and close the dialog box.

4. In the drawing, select a point to the left of the Pond North Bay assemblies as the insertion point.

If the Tool Palettes is not already displayed, in the Home tab> Create Design panel, click ⬚ (Tool Palettes).

5. In the *Daylight* tab in the Tool Palettes, select **Daylight Bench**.

6. In the Properties palette, set the parameters according to those shown in Figure 6–49.
   - **Side:** Left
   - **Cut Slope:** 3:1
   - **Max Cut Height:** 4'
   - **Bench Width:** 2'
   - **Bench Slope:** -5%
   - **Rounding Parameter:** 1.5'
   - **Material 1 Thickness:** 1'
   - **Material 3 Thickness:** 0.33'

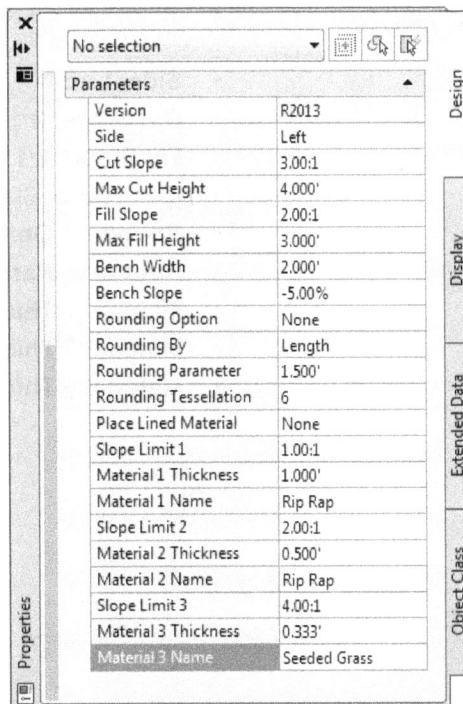

Parameters	
Version	R2013
Side	Left
Cut Slope	3.00:1
Max Cut Height	4.000'
Fill Slope	2.00:1
Max Fill Height	3.000'
Bench Width	2.000'
Bench Slope	-5.00%
Rounding Option	None
Rounding By	Length
Rounding Parameter	1.500'
Rounding Tessellation	6
Place Lined Material	None
Slope Limit 1	1.00:1
Material 1 Thickness	1.000'
Material 1 Name	Rip Rap
Slope Limit 2	2.00:1
Material 2 Thickness	0.500'
Material 2 Name	Rip Rap
Slope Limit 3	4.00:1
Material 3 Thickness	0.333'
Material 3 Name	Seeded Grass

Figure 6–49

7. In the drawing, select the **Pond South Bay Bench** assembly marker to which to connect the subassembly. Press <Enter> to end the command.

Now you will create the last three assemblies for the south bay. The first uses the Daylight Max Width subassembly and the other two are copies of the assembly with different slopes for part of the south interior rim grading.

8. In the *Home* tab>Create Design panel, expand the Assembly drop-down list and click 🏛 (Create Assembly).

9. In the Create Assembly dialog box, complete the following:
    • For the *Name,* type **Pond South 2 percent**.
    • Set the *Assembly Type* to **Other**.
    • Click **OK** to accept all of the other defaults and close the dialog box.

10. In the drawing, select a point below the first Pond South Bay assembly as the insertion point.

If the Tool Palettes is not already displayed, in the Home tab> Create Design panel,

click 🗔 (Tool Palettes).

11. In the *Daylight* tab in the Tool Palettes, select **Daylight Max Width**.

12. In the Properties palette, set the parameters according to those shown in Figure 6–50.
    • **Side: Left**
    • **Cut Slope:** 2:1
    • **Fill Slope:** 2:1
    • **Max Width:** 30'
    • **Rounding Option:** Parabolic
    • **Rounding Parameter:** 6'
    • **Material 1 Thickness:** 1'
    • **Material 2 Thickness:** 0.5'
    • **Material 3 Thickness:** 0.33'

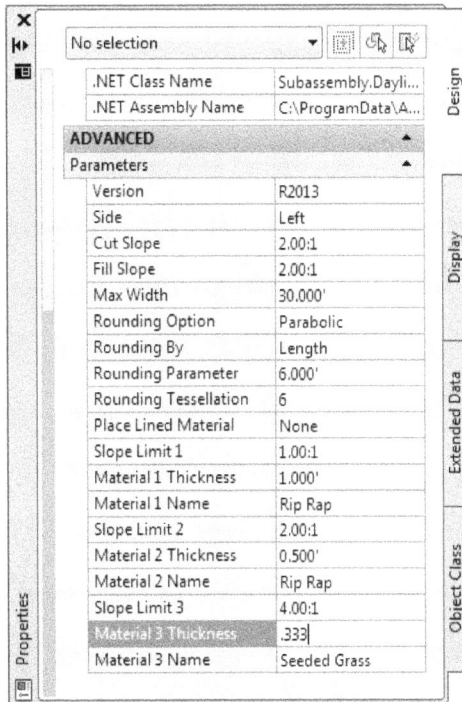

Figure 6–50

13. In the drawing, select the **Pond South Bay 2** percent assembly marker to which to connect the subassembly. Press <Enter> to end the command.

14. In the *Home* tab>Modify panel, click ⬡ (Copy).

15. In the drawing, select the **South Bay 2** percent assembly marker, press <Enter> to end the selection process.

16. In the drawing, pick three points of displacement to make two copies of the assembly below the original, as shown in Figure 6–51.

Figure 6–51

17. Select the middle assembly marker. In the *Assembly* contextual tab>Modify panel, click ⬚ (Assembly Properties).

18. In the Assembly Properties dialog box, complete the following:
    - In the *Information* tab, for the *Name* type **South Bay 3.33 percent**.
    - In the *Construction* tab, select **DaylightMaxWidth**.
    - In *Input values*, for the *Cut Slope* and *Fill Slope Values* type **3.33**.
    - Click **OK** to close the dialog box.

19. Press <Esc> to release the selection.

20. Select the bottom assembly marker, in the *Assembly* contextual tab>Modify panel, click ⬚ (Assembly Properties).

21. In the Assembly Properties dialog box, complete the following:
    - In the *Information* tab, for the *Name* type **South Bay 4 percent**.
    - In the *Construction* tab, select **DaylightMaxWidth**.
    - In *Input values*, for the *Cut Slope* and *Fill Slope Values* type **4**.
    - Click **OK** to close the dialog box.

22. Press <Esc> to release the selection.

23. Save the drawing.

6.4 Creating Complex Corridors

You can create a simple corridor model, set targets for the assembly, and create intersections using the Intersection Wizard. It automatically includes multiple baselines and regions in the corridor model to accommodate the many transitions that need to take place in intersections. Complex grading projects also use baselines and regions to permit multiple grading slopes and non-parallel paths.

Baselines

Baselines represent the path of a corridor model and are based on alignments or feature lines for the horizontal control and profiles for the vertical control. Multiple baselines can be included in one corridor to permit multiple assemblies in the same area or to change the distance between lanes or slopes in the corridor model.

How To: Add Baselines to a Corridor

1. In the *Home* tab>Create Design panel, click ▨ (Corridor).
2. In the Create Corridor dialog box, do the following, as shown in Figure 6–52:
   - Type a *Name*.
   - Select the *Baseline type*.
   - Select the *Alignment* or *Feature line*.
   - Select the *Profile* (if an alignment baseline was selected).
   - Select the *Assembly*.
   - Select the *Target Surface*.
   - Select the **Set baseline and region parameters** option.
   - Click **OK** close the dialog box.

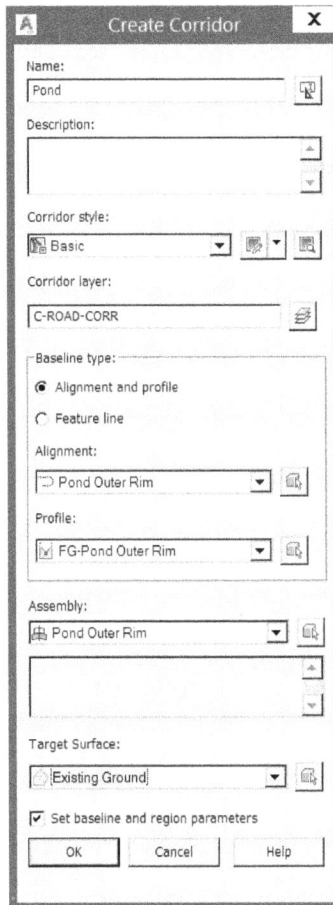
Figure 6–52

3. In the Baseline and Region Parameters dialog box, click **Add Baseline**, select the alignment, and click **OK**.
4. In the Create Corridor Baseline dialog box, type a *Name* and select a *Horizontal alignment*, as shown in Figure 6–53. Click **OK** close the dialog box.

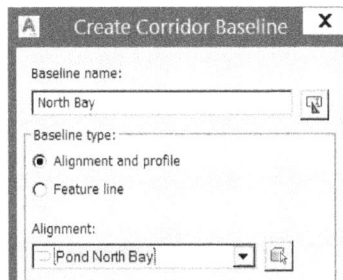
Figure 6–53

5. In the Baseline and Region Parameters dialog box, in the *Profile* value of the baseline, select **<Click here>**, as shown in Figure 6–54.

Figure 6–54

6. In the Select a Profile dialog box, select a design profile as shown in Figure 6–55. Click **OK** close the dialog box.

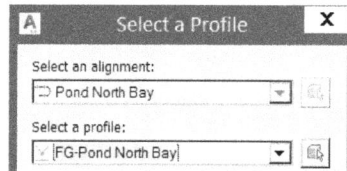

Figure 6–55

Regions

Baselines consist of one or more regions. Each region is assigned its own assembly and provides a way to transition from one typical cross-section to another along the baseline. In addition, each region can target a different design element.

How To: Add Regions to a Corridor

1. In the drawing, select the corridor. In the *Corridor* contextual tab>Modify Region panel, click 🖳 (Add Regions).
2. In the drawing, select the baseline alignment, as shown in Figure 6–56.

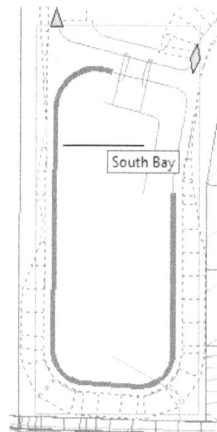

Figure 6–56

3. In the drawing, select a point or type a station number and press <Enter> for the beginning station. Then select a point or type a station number and press <Enter> for the ending station.

4. In the Create Corridor Region dialog box, type a *Region name* and select an *Assembly*, as shown in Figure 6–57.

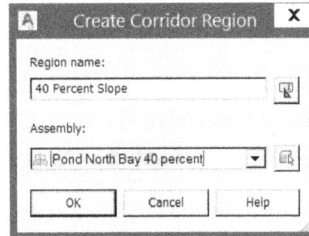

Figure 6–57

5. In the Target Mapping dialog box, set the required targets, as shown in Figure 6–58. Click **OK**.

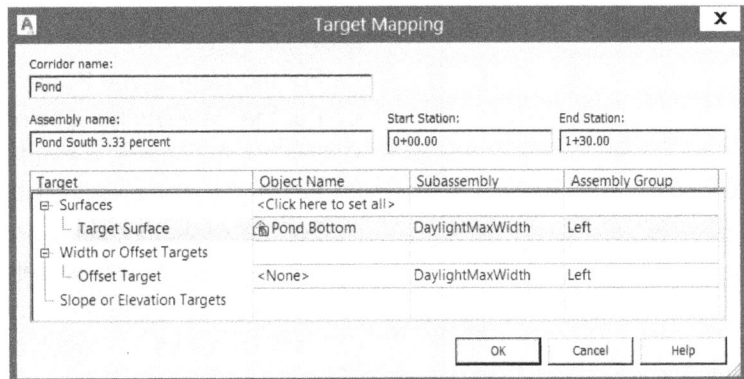

Figure 6–58

Practice 6d

Estimated time for completion: 20 minutes

Create Complex Corridors

Practice Objective

- Create a corridor model with multiple baselines and regions in the grading solution.

In this practice you will create a corridor model with multiple baselines and regions and edit it to include multiple alignments, profiles, a feature line, and assemblies to model the pond area.

Task 1 - Create a corridor with multiple baselines.

1. Continue working in the drawing from the last practice or open **LAGOON-D1-Grading.dwg** from the *C:\Civil3D-Grading\Lagoon* folder.

2. In the *Home* tab>Create Design panel, click 🖾 (Corridor).

3. In the Create Corridor dialog box, complete the following, as shown in Figure 6–59:
   - For the *Name*, type **Pond**.
   - For the *Baseline type*, select **Alignment and profile**.
   - For the *Alignment*, select **Pond Outer Rim**.
   - For the *Profile*, select **FG-Pond Outer Rim**.
   - For the *Assembly*, select **Pond Outer Rim**.
   - For the *Target Surface*, select **Existing Ground**.
   - Check the **Set baseline and region parameters** option.
   - Click **OK** close the dialog box.

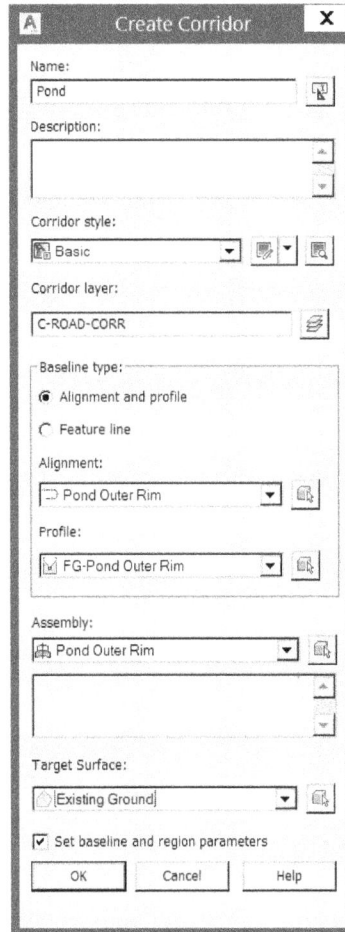

Figure 6–59

4. In the Baseline and Region Parameters dialog box, click **Add Baseline**.

5. In the Create Corridor Baseline dialog box, complete the following, as shown in Figure 6–60:
   - For the *Name* type **North Bay**.
   - For the *Baseline type*, select **Alignment and profile**.
   - For the *Alignment*, select **Pond North Bay**.
   - Click **OK** close the dialog box.

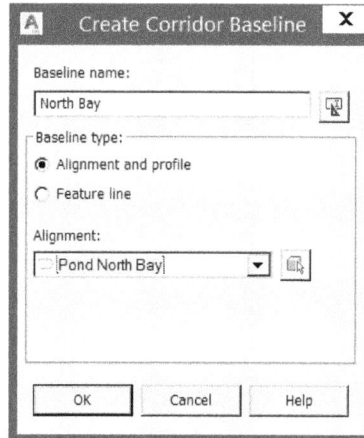

Figure 6–60

6. In the Baseline and Region Parameters dialog box, in the Profile value of the North Bay baseline select **<Click here>**, as shown in Figure 6–61.

Figure 6–61

7. In the Select a Profile dialog box, for the *Profile* select **FG-Pond North Bay**, as shown in Figure 6–62. Click **OK** close the dialog box.

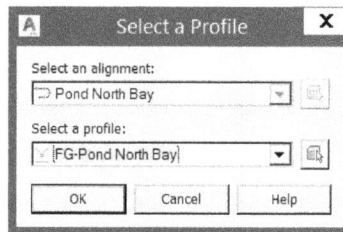

Figure 6–62

8. In the Baseline and Region Parameters dialog box, click **Add Baseline**.

9. In the Create Corridor Baseline dialog box, complete the following, as shown in Figure 6–63:

    • For the *Name*, type **South Bay**.

    • For the *Baseline, type* select **Feature line**.

    • For the *Site*, select **Pond Site**.

    • For the *Feature line*, select **Pond South Bay**.

    • Click **OK** to close the dialog box.

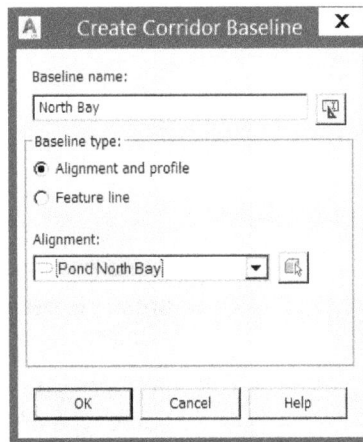

Figure 6–63

10. Click **OK** close the dialog box and create the corridor model.

11. In the Corridor Properties - Rebuild dialog box, click **Rebuild the corridor**.

12. Save the drawing.

Task 2 - Add regions to the corridor to accommodate varying slopes around the north bay of the pond.

---

1. Continue working in the drawing from the previous task or open **LAGOON-D2-Grading.dwg** from the *C:\Civil3D-Grading\Lagoon* folder.

2. In the drawing, select the **Pond** corridor. In the *Corridor* contextual tab>Modify Region panel, click 🔲 (Add Regions).

3. In the drawing, select the **North Bay** baseline, as shown in Figure 6–64.

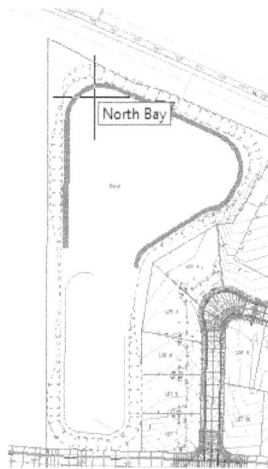

Figure 6–64

4. In the Command Line, for the *Beginning Station* type **0** and press <Enter>. For the *Ending Station* type **420** and press <Enter>.

5. In the Create Corridor Region dialog box, for the *Region name* type **40 Percent Slope** and for the *Assembly* select **Pond North bay 40 percent** as shown in Figure 6–65. Click **OK**.

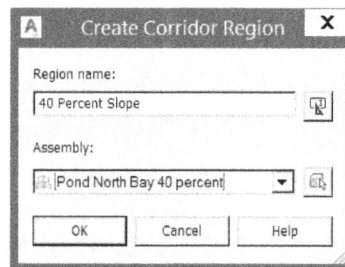

Figure 6–65

6. Click **OK** to ignore the Target dialog box because the target elevation was already set when the assembly was created.

7. In the Command Line, for the *Beginning Station* type **440** and press <Enter>. For the *Ending Station* type **630** and press <Enter>.

8. In the Create Corridor Region dialog box, for the *Region name* type **Double Slope** and for the *Assembly* select **Pond North bay double slope**. Click **OK**.

9. Click **OK** to ignore the Target dialog box because the target was already set when the assembly was created.

10. In the Command Line, for the *Beginning Station* type **650** and press <Enter>. Use the **Endpoint** Osnap to snap to the ending station in the drawing.

11. In the Create Corridor Region dialog box, for the *Region name* type **33 Percent Slope** and for the *Assembly* select **Pond North bay 33 percent**. Click **OK**.

12. Click **OK** to ignore the Target dialog box because the target was already set when the assembly was created.

13. Press <Esc> to end the command.

Task 3 - Create a surface to set the pond bottom slope in the south bay.

In this task, you will create a target surface for the south bay of the pond to set the correct slope of the pond bottom. A number of feature lines in the pond area have already been drawn to speed up the design process.

1. Continue working in the drawing from the previous task or open **LAGOON-D3-Grading.dwg** from the *C:\Civil3D-Grading\Lagoon* folder.

2. In the *Home* tab>Layers panel, expand the layers and scroll down to the layer **C-TOPO-FEAT**. Select the light bulb to turn on the layer, as shown in Figure 6–66.

You may have to enter RE in the command line to regenerate the drawing in order for all of the feature lines to appear.

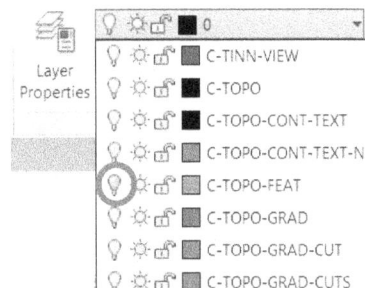

			░	0
Layer Properties				C-TINN-VIEW
				C-TOPO
				C-TOPO-CONT-TEXT
				C-TOPO-CONT-TEXT-N
				C-TOPO-FEAT
				C-TOPO-GRAD
				C-TOPO-GRAD-CUT
				C-TOPO-GRAD-CUTS

Figure 6–66

3. In the *Home* tab>Create Ground Data panel, expand the Surfaces drop-down list and click 🗗 (Create Surface).

4. In the Create Surface dialog box, for the *Name* type **Pond Bottom** and for the *Style* select **Border Only**. Click **OK** to close the dialog box.

5. In the drawing, zoom in on the south bay of the pond.

6. In the *Prospector* tab, expand **Sites>Lagoon**, and select **Feature Lines**. In the preview window below, select **Feature1** and **Feature2**, right-click and select **Select**.

7. In the *Feature Lines* contextual tab>Modify panel, click

   ⬙ (Add to Surface as Breakline).

8. In the Select Surface dialog box, select the **Pond Bottom** surface and click **OK**.

9. In the Create Breaklines dialog box, click **OK** to accept all of the defaults. A surface is created that you can control by modifying the two feature lines.

10. Save the drawing.

Task 4 - Add regions to the corridor to accommodate varying slopes around the south bay of the pond.

---

1. Continue working in the drawing from the previous task or open **LAGOON-D4-Grading.dwg** from the C:\Civil3D-Grading\Lagoon folder.

2. In the drawing, select the **Pond** corridor. In the *Corridor* contextual tab>Modify Region panel, click 🔲 (Add Regions).

3. In the drawing, select the **South Bay** baseline, as shown in Figure 6–67.

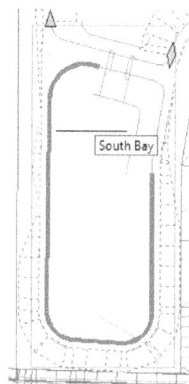

Figure 6–67

4. In the Command Line, for the *Beginning Station* type **0** and press <Enter>. For the *Ending Station*, type **130** and press <Enter>.

---

5. In the Create Corridor Region dialog box, for the *Region name* type **3 Percent Slope** and for the *Assembly* select **Pond South bay 3.33 percent**, as shown in Figure 6–68.

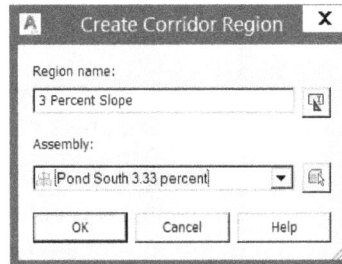

Figure 6–68

6. In the Target Mapping dialog box, set the **Pond Bottom** as the *Target Surface*, as shown in Figure 6–69. Click **OK**.

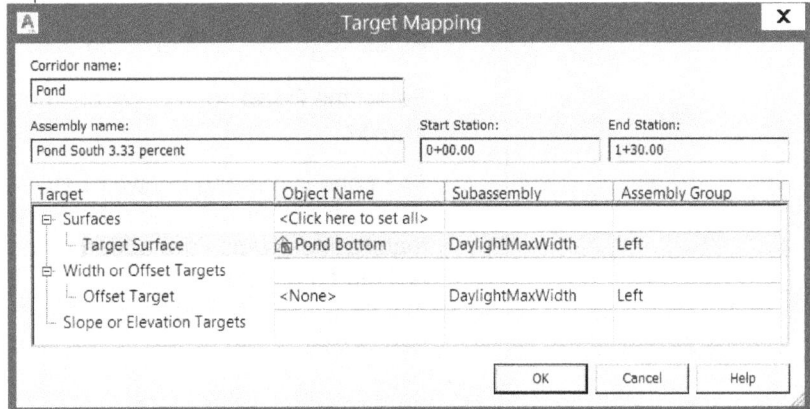

Figure 6–69

7. In the Command Line, for the *Beginning Station* type **150** and press <Enter>. For the *Ending Station* type **310** and press <Enter>.

8. In the Create Corridor Region dialog box, for the *Region name* type **Benched** and for the *Assembly* select **Pond South bay Bench**. Click **OK**.

9. In the Target Mapping dialog box, set the **Pond Bottom** as the *Target Surface*. Click **OK**.

10. In the Command Line, for the *Beginning Station* type **320** and press <Enter>. For the *Ending Station* type **550** and press <Enter>.

11. In the Create Corridor Region dialog box, for the *Region name* type **2 Percent Slope** and for the *Assembly* select **Pond South bay 2 percent**. Click **OK**.

12. In the Target Mapping dialog box, set the **Pond Bottom** as the *Target Surface*. Click **OK**.

13. In the Command Line, for the *Beginning Station*, type **560** and press <Enter>. For the *Ending Station*, use the Endpoint Osnap and select the endpoint of the feature line.

14. In the Create Corridor Region dialog box:
    - For the *Region name,* type **4 Percent Slope**.
    - For the *Assembly*, select **Pond South 4 percent**.
    - Click **OK**.

15. In the Target Mapping dialog box, set **Pond Bottom** as the *Target Surface*. Click **OK**.

16. Press <Esc> to end the command.

17. Select the **Pond** corridor model, right-click and select **Object Viewer**.

    The pond is missing the weir between the two ponds, as shown in Figure 6–70. The weir has been designed using feature lines, which are added to the surface in the following task as breaklines.

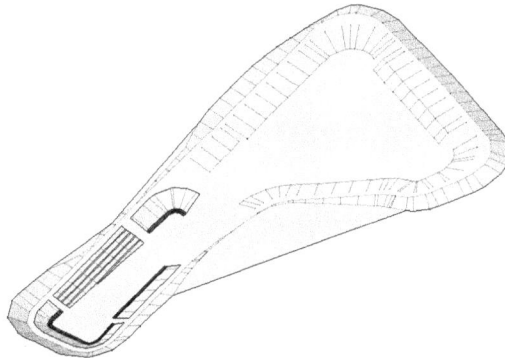

Figure 6–70

18. Close the object viewer.

19. Save the drawing.

Task 5 - Create a surface from the corridor and add weir feature lines.

1. Continue working in the drawing from the previous task or open **LAGOON-D5-Grading.dwg** from the *C:\Civil3D-Grading\Lagoon* folder.

2. In the drawing, select the **Pond** corridor. In the *Corridor* contextual tab>Modify Corridor panel, click 🔲 (Corridor Surfaces).

3. In the Corridor Surfaces dialog box>*Surfaces* tab, click 🔲 (Create Corridor Surface).

4. In the Corridor Surfaces dialog box, select the **Pond** surface. Set the *Data type* to **Links** and the *Specify code* to **Top**. Click ⊕ (Add surface item) to add the top codes to the surface, as shown in Figure 6–71.

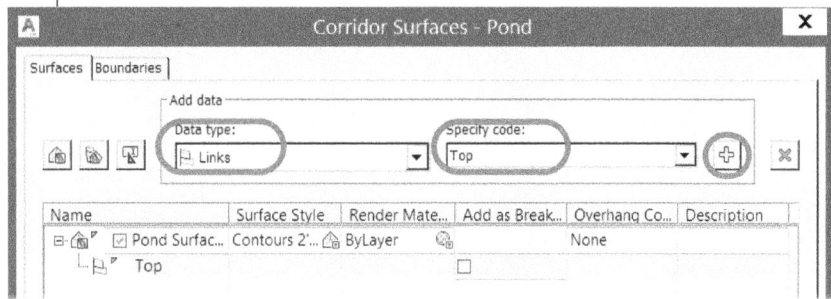

Figure 6–71

5. In the Corridor Surfaces dialog box>*Boundaries* tab, right-click on the Pond surface, and select **Corridor extents as outer boundary**, as shown in Figure 6–72.

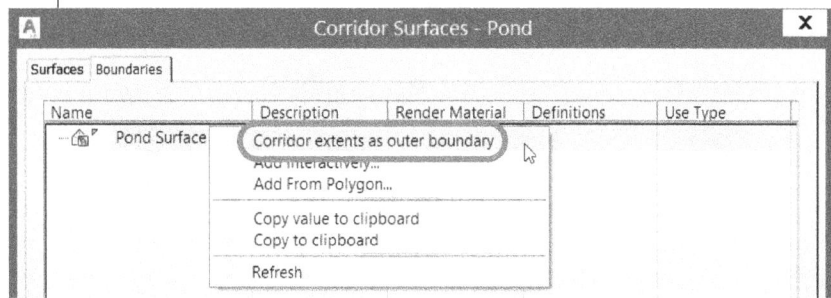

Figure 6–72

6. Click **OK** to close the dialog box and create the surface.

7. Click **Rebuild Corridor Model**.

8. In the *Prospector* tab, expand **Sites>Lagoon**, and select **Feature Lines**. In the preview window, select **Feature3**, hold down <Shift> and select **South bay bottom**, and right-click and select **Select**.

9. In the *Feature Lines* contextual tab>Modify panel, click

   ⌂ (Add to Surface as Breakline).

10. In the Select Surface dialog box, select the **Pond** surface and click **OK**.

11. In the Create Breaklines dialog box, click **OK** to accept all of the defaults. A surface is created that you control by modifying the two feature lines.

12. Select the **Pond** surface, right-click and select **Object Viewer**. **Zoom** and **Orbit** around the pond, as shown in Figure 6–73.

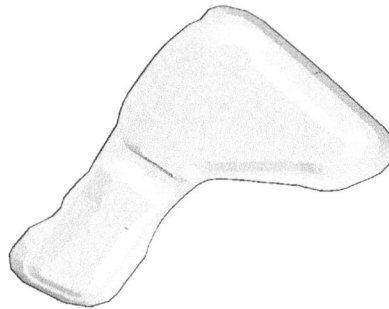

Figure 6–73

13. Close the object viewer.

14. Save the drawing.

6.5 Modify Corridor Grading

Change occurs in any project. Using corridor models for grading projects speeds up the change process and makes it easier to add slope changes. There are a number of ways in which you can make changes to a grading solution.

Grip Editing

Grips can be used to edit a corridor model quickly. ▷ (Triangle Grip) is located at the beginning and ending of regions that

enable you to adjust the regions stations. ◁▷ (Diamond Grip) is located between two regions that enable you to adjust both regions at the same time while the triangle grips enable you to modify one region separate from the other.

Modify Regions

The Modify Region panel in the *Corridors* contextual tab provides all of the required tools for making changes to corridor regions, as shown in Figure 6–74. The following table describes each command.

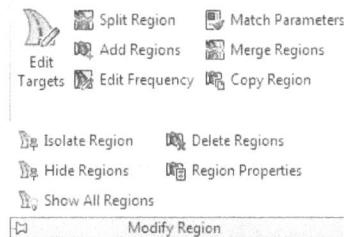

Figure 6–74

Icon	Command	Description
	Edit Targets	Sets the targets for the assembly along the specific region only.
	Split Region	Splits a corridor region into multiple regions enabling different assemblies to be applied to a corridor.
	Add Regions	Enables an assembly to be applied to a gap on a corridor.
	Edit Frequency	Changes the frequency that an assembly is applied to a corridor within a region.
	Match Parameters	Match the assembly, target, and/or frequency of selected corridor regions.

	Merge Regions	Merges corridor regions along the same baseline.
	Copy Region	Copies regions along the same baseline.
	Isolate Region	Sets the visibility of all regions except the selected one to off.
	Hide Region	Sets the visibility of the selected region to off.
	Show All Regions	Sets the visibility of all regions to on.
	Delete Region	Removes a region from a corridor.
	Region Properties	Edits the assembly, beginning and ending stations, frequency, targets, and station overrides of a selected region.

Modify Corridor

The Modify Corridor panel in the *Corridors* contextual tab provides all of the tools required to make changes to the entire corridor at the same time, as shown in Figure 6–75. The table below lists each command and describes what they do.

Figure 6–75

Icon	Command	Description
	Corridor Properties	Edits corridor properties including *Name, Description, Object style,* Baselines, Regions, Targets, *Frequencies, Code sets, Feature lines, Surfaces, Boundaries,* and *Slope patterns.*
	Rebuild Corridor	Applies changes to a corridor that is out of date.
	Corridor Surface	Creates and manages surfaces built from links and codes assigned to assemblies used in the corridor.

	Add Baseline	Attaches alignments to a corridor to accommodate widening and non-parallel designs in road and grading projects.
	Edit Code Set Styles	Edits code set styles assigned to points, links, and shapes within subassemblies used in the corridor.
	Feature Lines	Edits feature line connections by indicating the point codes that are connected.
	Slope Patterns	Edits the patterns that are applied between any two feature lines.

Modify Corridor Sections

The Modify Corridor Sections panel in the *Corridors* contextual tab provides all of the tools required to make changes to the entire corridor at the same time, as shown in Figure 6–76. The following table describes each command.

Figure 6–76

Icon	Command	Description
	Section Editor	Applies overrides to assembly parameters at specific stations.
	Add Section	Adds a section to the corridor at a defined location.
	Delete Section	Removes a selected section from a corridor.

Practice 6e

Modify Corridor Grading

Practice Objective

- Modify the corridor using grips and corridor parameters.

In this practice you will create an assembly for the outer rim of the pond, modify the corridor, and modify the frequency of the corridor and edit the corridor sections.

Estimated time for completion: 20 minutes

Task 1 - Create an assembly for the outer rim of the pond.

In this task, you will create an assembly that represents the outer rim of the pond and daylights to the Residential Grading surface.

1. Continue working in the drawing from the previous practice or open **LAGOON-E1-Grading.dwg** from the *C:\Civil3D-Grading\Lagoon* folder.

2. In the *Home* tab>Create Design panel, expand the Assembly drop-down list and click (Create Assembly).

3. In the Create Assembly dialog box, for the *Name* type **Pond Outer Rim-Tie to Residential Surface**. Set the *Assembly Type* to **Other**. Click **OK** to accept all of the other defaults and close the dialog box.

The AutoCAD Civil 3D software automatically zooms in on the assembly marker.

4. In the drawing, select a point near the Pond Outer Rim Profile view as the insertion point to remember which profile it goes with.

5. In the *Home* tab>Create Design panel, click (Tool Palettes) to display the Tool Palettes.

6. In the *Daylight* tab in the Tool Palettes, select **Daylight to Offset** to display the Properties palette.

7. In the Properties palette, set *Rounding Option* to **Circular**. Leave all of the other parameters as their default value, as shown in Figure 6–77.

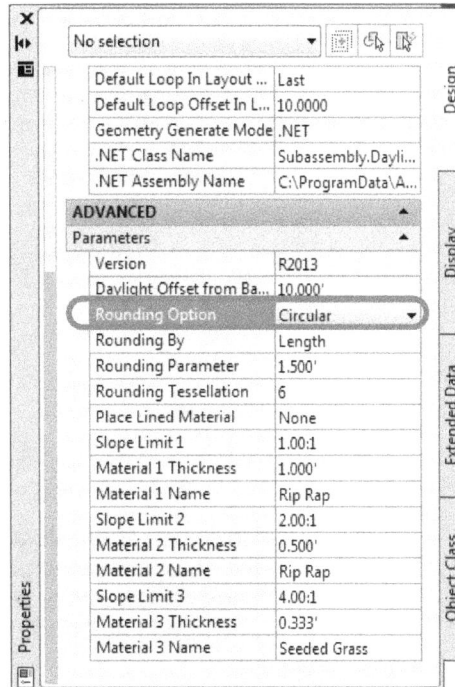

Figure 6–77

8. In the drawing, select the **Pond Outer Rim-Tie to Residential Surface** assembly marker to which to connect the subassembly. Press <Enter> to end the command.

9. Save the drawing

Task 2 - Modify the corridor.

In this task, you will adjust the corridor using grips. You will then create a polyline 6" inside the residential parcels to target and add the Pond Outer Rim-Tie to Residential Surface assembly to the corridor.

1. Continue working in the drawing from the previous practice or open **LAGOON-E2-Grading.dwg** from the *C:\Civil3D-Grading\Lagoon* folder.

2. In the drawing, zoom in on the weir that divides the pond into two bays. Select the pond corridor model.

3. On the east side of the north bay, the corridor encroaches on the feature lines that create the weir. Select the region grip at the endpoint of the North Bay baseline. Using the **Midpoint** Osnap, move the grip to the midpoint of the curve, as shown in Figure 6–78.

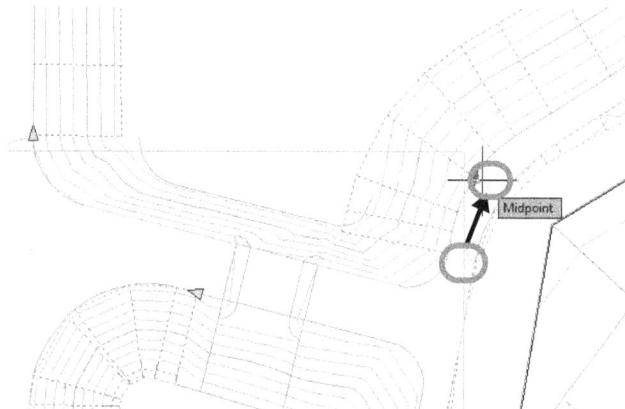

Figure 6–78

Now you will create a polyline that is used to target an offset for the outer rim of the pond. To do so, you will offset the pond parcel segments and trim them at the northern boundaries of Lot 1 and Lot 5 leaving a polyline between lots 2 to 5.

4. In the *Home* tab>Modify panel, click ⌐ (Offset). In the Command Line, for the *Offset value* type **.5**.

5. In the drawing, select the **Pond** parcel segments, as shown in Figure 6–79.

Figure 6–79

6. In the drawing, pick a point outside the parcel as the side to which to offset.

7. In the *Home* tab>Modify panel, click ⌐┄ (Trim).

8. In the drawing, for the cutting edges, select the parcel segments for **Lot 1** and **Lot 5**, as shown in Figure 6–80. Press <Enter>.

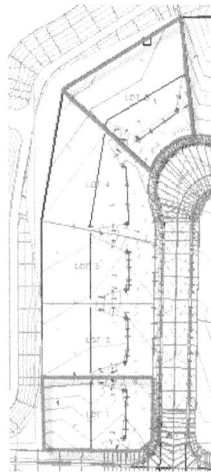

Figure 6–80

9. In the drawing, select a point to the north of Lot 5 for the first object to trim and pick a point inside Lot 1 for the second object to trim, as shown in Figure 6–81. Press <Enter>.

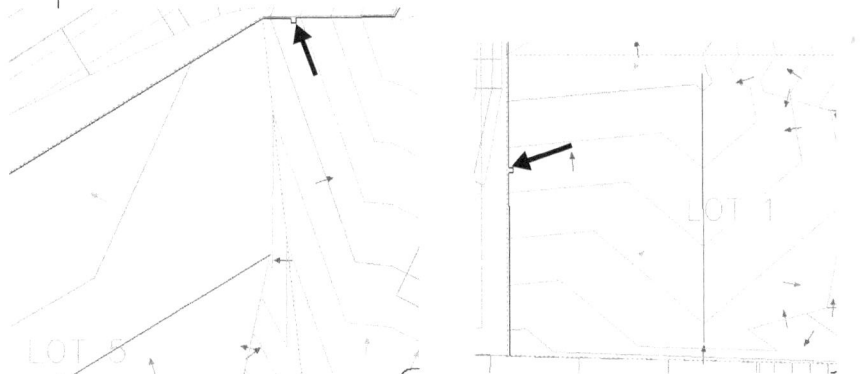

Figure 6–81

In the drawing a polyline remains, which represents the target offset for the assembly that was created in task 1, as shown in Figure 6–82.

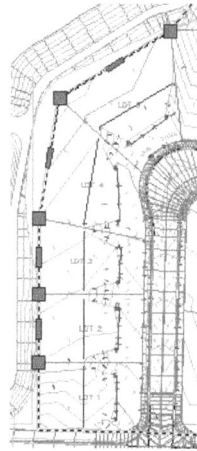

Figure 6–82

10. In the drawing, select the **Pond** corridor. In the *Corridor* contextual tab>Modify Region panel, click (Split Region).

11. In the drawing, select the **Outer Rim** region, as shown in Figure 6–83.

Figure 6–83

12. In the drawing line, use **Endpoint** Osnap to split at the northern boundary of Lot 1, as shown in Figure 6–84.

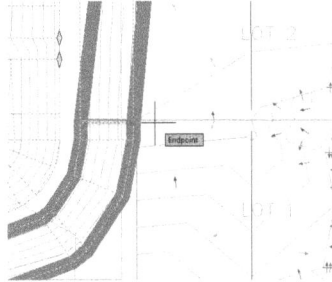

Figure 6–84

13. With the corridor still selected, in the *Corridor* contextual tab> Modify Region panel, click (Split Region).

14. In the drawing, select the eastern region of the **Outer Rim**, as shown in Figure 6–85.

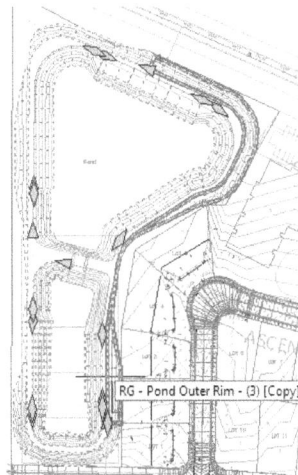

Figure 6–85

15. In the drawing line, use **Endpoint** Osnap to split at the northern boundary of Lot 5, as shown in Figure 6–86.

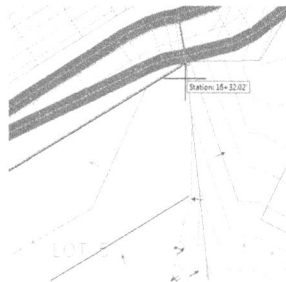

Figure 6–86

16. Press <Esc> to end the **Split** command.

17. In the drawing, select the **Pond** corridor. In the *Corridor* contextual tab, expand the Modify Region panel, and click (Region Properties), as shown in Figure 6–87.

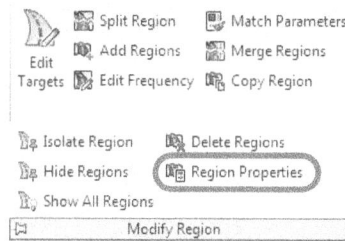

Figure 6–87

18. In the model, click the Outer Rim Region on the east side of the pond, as shown in Figure 6–88.

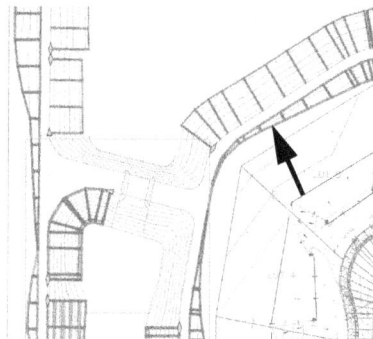

Figure 6–88

19. In the Corridor Region Properties dialog box, in the *Assembly value* field, click ⋯ to open the Edit Corridor Region dialog box.

20. In the Edit Corridor Region dialog box, for the *Region name* type **Residential Daylight** and for the *Assembly* select **Pond Outer Tim-Tie to Residential Surface**, as shown in Figure 6–89. Click **OK**.

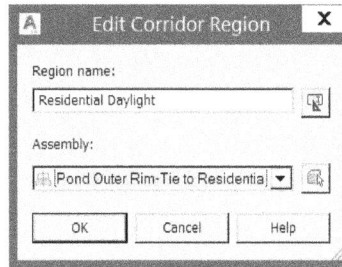

Figure 6–89

21. In the Corridor Region Properties dialog box, in the *Target value* field, click ⋯ to open the Target Mapping dialog box.

22. In the Target Mapping dialog box, for the *Target Surface* set the **Residential Surface**. Select the *Object Name* field next to *Target Alignment Daylight*, as shown in Figure 6–90.

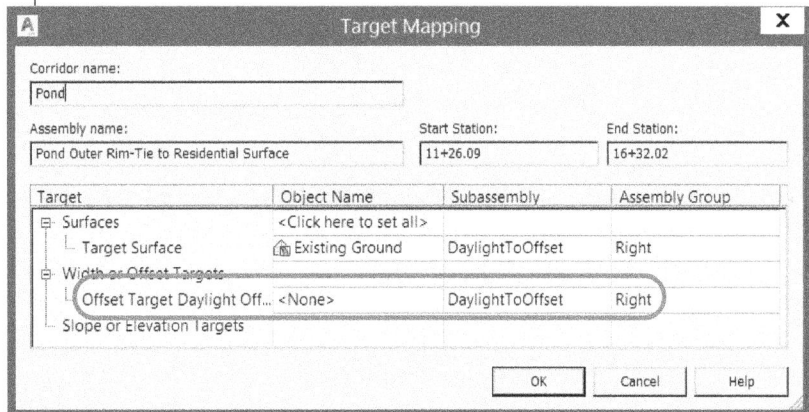

Figure 6–90

23. In the Set Width or Offset Target dialog box, expand the
    Select object type to target drop-down list and select **Feature
    lines, survey figures and polylines**, as shown in
    Figure 6–91. Click **Select from drawing**.

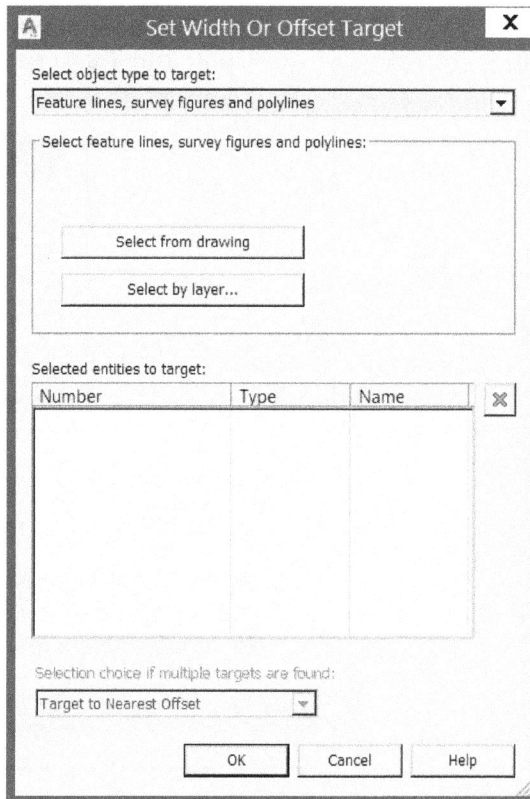

Figure 6–91

24. In the drawing, select the polyline that was created from the
    Pond boundary offset, as shown in Figure 6–92.

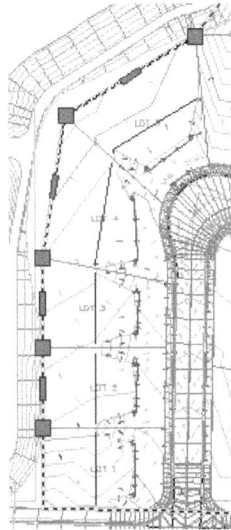

Figure 6–92

25. In the Set Width or Offset Target dialog box, click **OK**.

26. In the Target Mapping dialog box, click **OK**.

27. In the Corridor Region Properties dialog box, click **OK**.

Task 3 - Modify the frequency of the corridor and edit the corridor sections.

In this task, you will change the frequency of the assemblies that are applied to the corridor to smooth transitions around curves. You will also edit the sections to accommodate another design change.

1. Continue working in the drawing from the previous task or open **LAGOON-E3-Grading.dwg** from the *C:\Civil3D-Grading\Lagoon* folder.

2. In the drawing, select the **Pond** corridor.

3. In the *Corridor* contextual tab>Modify Corridor panel, click

    (Corridor Properties).

4. In the *Parameters* tab or the Corridor Properties dialog box, click **Set all Frequencies**.

5. In the Frequencies to Apply Assemblies dialog box (as shown in Figure 6–93):

- Set *Along tangents* to **10**.
- Set *Curve increment* to **3**.
- Click **OK** twice.
- When prompted, rebuild the corridor.

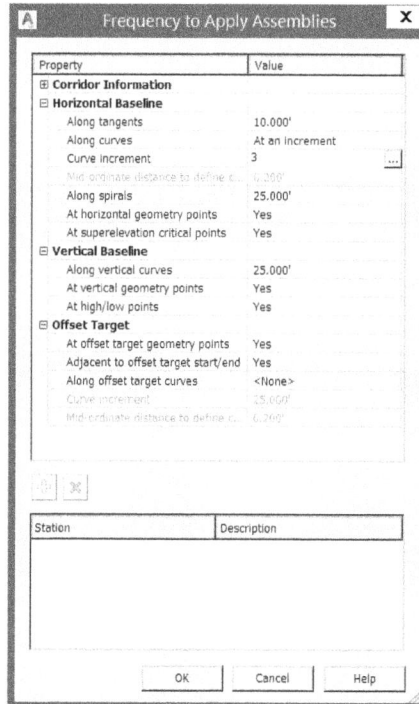

Figure 6–93

Now you will edit a small section of the pond to extend the grade into the pond with less slope.

6. In the drawing, select the **Pond** corridor. In the *Corridor* contextual tab, click 📐 (Section Editor). This splits the drawing area into three viewports.

7. In the *Section Editor* contextual tab, in the Baselines & Offsets panel, complete the following, as shown in Figure 6–94:

- For the *Baseline,* select **North Bay**.
- In the Station Selection panel, for the *Station,* select **5+00.00'**.
- In the Corridor Edit Tools panel, click 🗔 (Parameter Editor).

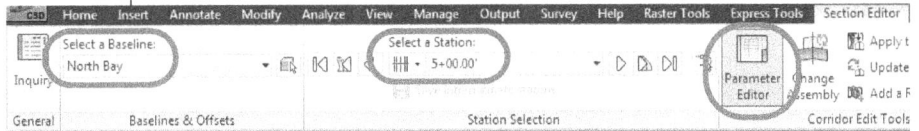

Figure 6–94

8. In the Parameter Editor vista, expand the subassemblies. Under the Link Width and Slope subassembly, change the *Slope value* to **-3%** and the *Width value* to **50.00'**, as shown in Figure 6–95.

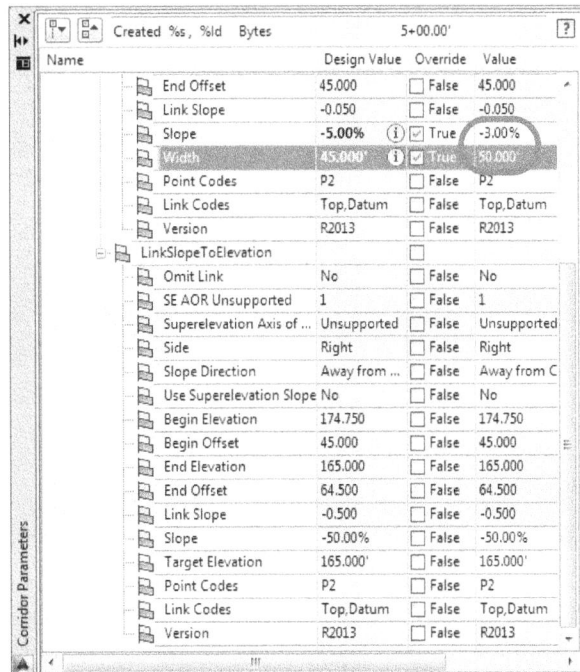

Figure 6–95

9. In the *Section Editor* contextual tab>Corridor Edit Tools panel, click 🖼 (Apply to a Station Range).

10. In the Apply to a Range of Stations dialog box, for the *End station* value type **530**, as shown in Figure 6–96. Click **OK**.

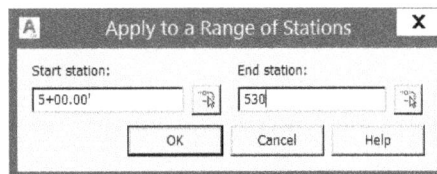

Figure 6–96

11. In the *Section Editor* contextual tab, click the **X** icon to close the Section editor.

12. In the drawing, select the **Pond** surface, right-click and select **Object Viewer**. **Zoom** and **Orbit** around the pond, as shown in Figure 6–97.

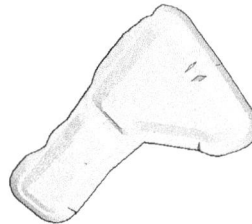

Figure 6–97

13. Close the object viewer.

14. Save the drawing.

Chapter Review Questions

1. Which of the following is important to remember when grading an enclosed area with a corridor model?

    a. You cannot grade enclosed areas with corridor models.

    b. Begin and end the alignment for the corridor at a corner.

    c. Begin and end the alignment or feature line for the corridor along a straight segment.

    d. Begin and end the alignment for the corridor along a curve.

2. Which of the following is important when creating a profile for an enclosed area grading corridor model? (Select all that apply.)

    a. Begin and end the profile at the same elevation.

    b. Extend the design profile approximately 200 feet beyond the alignment to accommodate changes in length.

    c. End the profile with a tangent rather than a vertical curve.

    d. You cannot grade enclosed areas with corridor models.

3. Which subassembly does the same thing as the Grade to Distance grading criteria?

    a. Daylight General

    b. Link Width and Slope

    c. Daylight to Offset

    d. Link to Surface

4. If you need to have a corridor model follow multiple alignments or feature lines, which would you do?

    a. Add Baselines.

    b. Add Regions.

    c. Create a second corridor model.

    d. Split Regions.

5. What is assigned to a corridor region?

    a. Alignment

    b. Profile

    c. Subassembly

    d. Assembly

6. Which tool would you use to add a corridor region to a corridor to which an assembly has already been applied to its entire length?

   a.

   b.

   c.

   d.

Command Summary

Button	Command	Location
	Add Baseline	• **Ribbon:** *Corridor* contextual tab> Modify Corridor panel • **Command Prompt:** AddCorrBaseline
	Add Regions	• **Ribbon:** *Corridor* contextual tab> Modify Region panel • **Command Prompt:** AddCorrRegions
	Alignment Creation Tools	• **Ribbon:** *Home* tab>Create Design panel • **Command Prompt:** CreateAlignmentLayout
	Alignment Grid View	• **Toolbar:** Alignment Layout Tools (*contextual*)
	Assembly Properties	• **Ribbon:** *Assembly* contextual tab> Modify panel • **Command Prompt:** EditAssemblyProperties
	Corridor Properties	• **Ribbon:** *Corridor* contextual tab> Modify Corridor panel • **Command Prompt:** EditCorridorProperties
	Create Alignment from Objects	• **Ribbon:** *Home* tab>Create Design panel • **Command Prompt:** CreateAlignmentEntities
	Create Assembly	• **Ribbon:** *Home* tab>Create Design panel • **Command Prompt:** CreateAssembly
	Create Corridor	• **Ribbon:** *Home* tab>Create Design panel • **Command Prompt:** CreateCorridor
	Create Profile From Surface	• **Ribbon:** *Home* tab>Create Design panel • ***Command Prompt:*** CreateProfileFromSurface
	Draw Tangents	• **Toolbar:** Profile Layout Tools (*contextual*)
	Edit Alignment Style	• **Ribbon:** *Alignment* contextual tab> Modify panel>Alignment Properties drop-down list • **Command Prompt:** EditAlignmentStyle
	Geometry Editor	• **Ribbon:** *Alignment* contextual tab> Modify panel • **Command Prompt:** EditAlignment
	Profile Creation Tools	• **Ribbon:** *Home* tab>Create Design panel • **Command Prompt:** CreateProfileLayout
	Profile Station Elevation	• **Toolbar:** Transparent commands • **Command Prompt:** 'PSE

	Region Properties	• **Ribbon:** *Corridor* contextual tab> Modify Region panel
		• **Command Prompt:** EditCorrRegionProp
	Section Editor	• **Ribbon:** *Corridor* contextual tab> Modify Corridor Sections panel
		• **Command Prompt:** ViewEditCorridorSection
	Split Region	• **Ribbon:** *Corridor* contextual tab> Modify Region panel
		• **Command Prompt:** SplitCorrRegion
	Tool Palettes	• **Ribbon:** *Home* tab>Palettes panel
		• **Command Prompt:** ToolPalettes, <Ctrl>+<3>

Combining Surfaces

Grading objects can cause your drawing size to increase and slow down your computer. Therefore, when you are working on grading projects you need to carefully plan the best way to organize your drawings before you start designing. This chapter reviews various ways of organizing your AutoCAD® Civil 3D® projects. You then use data shortcuts to create a final grading plan.

Learning Objectives in this Chapter

- List the three different ways in which AutoCAD Civil 3D project drawings can be organized.
- Share design information with other members of a design team using data shortcuts.

7.1 AutoCAD Civil 3D Projects

There are multiple ways of organizing AutoCAD Civil 3D project drawings. Three of the most common approaches are as follows:

Single-Design Drawing Projects

Since AutoCAD Civil 3D surfaces, alignments, and other AEC objects can be entirely drawing-based, a single drawing file can act as the repository for all of the design data. Realistically, this might only be feasible with the smallest projects and/or those worked on by only one person. The only external data would be survey databases, and possibly drawings containing plotting layouts that XREF the single design drawing.

Multiple Drawings Sharing Data using Shortcuts

This approach permits multiple survey and design drawings to share data. For example, a surface could exist in one drawing and an alignment in another. A third could contain a surface profile based on the alignment and terrain model, and all could be kept in sync with each other using **Data Shortcuts**. This approach is usually preferable to the single-drawing approach, because it permits more than one user to work on the project at the same time (in the different design drawings). It does not create any external project data other than survey databases and XML data files that are used to share data between drawings.

Shortcuts tend to be efficient for projects with a small number of drawings and project team members. Since the XML data files that connect drawings must be managed manually, keeping a large number of drawings and/or people in sync with shortcuts can be cumbersome. It is highly recommended that you establish procedures to ensure that data is not unintentionally deleted or changed. You need to document these procedures very carefully.

Multiple Drawings Sharing Data with Autodesk Vault

The Autodesk® Vault software is a data and document management system (ADMS). It is used in conjunction with other Autodesk® applications in different industries. When working with the Autodesk Vault program, all project drawings, survey databases, and references are managed and stored inside an SQL-managed database. The Autodesk Vault software consists of user-level access permissions, drawing check-in/out, project templates, automated backups, data versioning, etc. These benefits are offset by the additional time required to manage and administer the database, and in some cases for purchasing additional hardware and software. If you work on large projects with multiple design drawings or have many team members (more than 10), you might find that the Autodesk Vault software is the best way to keep those projects organized.

7.2 Data Shortcuts

Data Shortcuts can be used to share design data between drawing files through the use of XML files. Using Data Shortcuts is similar to using the Autodesk Vault software, but it does not provide the protection of your data or the tracking of versions the way the Autodesk Vault software does.

Data Shortcuts are managed using the *Prospector* tab in the Toolspace in the *Data Shortcuts* collection, as shown in Figure 7–1. The shortcuts are stored in XML files within one or more working folders that you create. They can use the same folder structure as the Autodesk Vault software. This method simplifies the transition to using the Autodesk Vault software at a future time.

Figure 7–1

Whether using the Autodesk Vault software or Data Shortcuts, the intelligent AutoCAD Civil 3D object design data can be consumed and used on different levels. However, this referenced data can only be edited in the drawing that contains the original object. As referenced data can be assigned a different style than those in the source drawing, you can separate the design phase (where drawing presentation is not critical) from the drafting phase (where drawing presentation is paramount). Therefore, after the styles have been applied at the drafting phase, any changes to the design have minimal visual impact on the completed drawings.

Changing the name of a drawing file that provides Data Shortcuts or the shortcut XML file itself invalidates the shortcut. Although the Data Shortcuts Editor outside the AutoCAD Civil 3D software permits re-pathing if a source drawing moves, shortcuts might not resolve if the source drawing file name has changed.

Update Notification

If the shortcut objects are modified and the source drawing is saved, any drawings that reference those objects are updated when opened. If the drawings consuming the data referenced in the shortcuts were open at the time of the edit, a message displays to warn you of the changes, as shown in Figure 7–2.

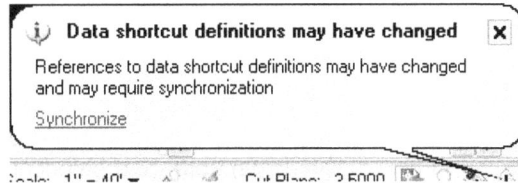

> ⓘ **Data shortcut definitions may have changed** ✕
> References to data shortcut definitions may have changed and may require synchronization
> Synchronize

Figure 7–2

The following modifier icons help you to determine the state of many AutoCAD Civil 3D objects.

▽	The object is referenced by another object. In the *Settings* tab this also indicates that a style is in use in the current drawing.
↗	The object is being referenced from another drawing file (such as through a shortcut or Autodesk Vault reference).
⚠	The object is out of date and needs to be rebuilt, or is violating specified design constraints.
◣	A project object (such as a point or surface) has been modified since it was included in the current drawing.
◢	You have modified a project object in your current drawing and those modifications have not yet been updated to the project.

Figure 7–3 shows how the modifier icons are used with an AutoCAD Civil 3D object as it displays in the *Prospector* tab.

Surfaces
  Existing Ground
    Masks
  Watersheds

Figure 7–3

To update the shortcut data, select **Synchronize** in the balloon message or right-click on the object in the Prospector and select **Synchronize**.

Removing and Promoting Shortcuts

Shortcut data can be removed from the Shortcut tree in the Prospector by right-clicking on it and selecting **Remove**, but this does not remove the data from the drawing. To do so, right-click on the object in the Prospector and select **Delete**. This removes the shortcut data from the current list, so that the item is not included if a Data Shortcut XML file is exported from the current drawing.

You can also promote shortcuts, which converts the referenced shortcut into a local copy without any further connection to the original. You can promote objects by right-clicking on them in the Prospector and selecting **Promote**.

eTransmit Data References

Projects that use Data Shortcuts can be packaged and sent to reviewers, clients, and other consultants using the AutoCAD **eTransmit** command. With this command, all of the related dependent files (such as XML files, XREFs, and text fonts) are automatically included in the package. This reduces the possibility of errors and ensures that the recipient can use the files you send them. A report file can be included in the package explaining what must be done with drawing-dependent files (e.g., XML or XREFs) so that they are usable with the included files. The Create Transmittal dialog box is shown in Figure 7–4.

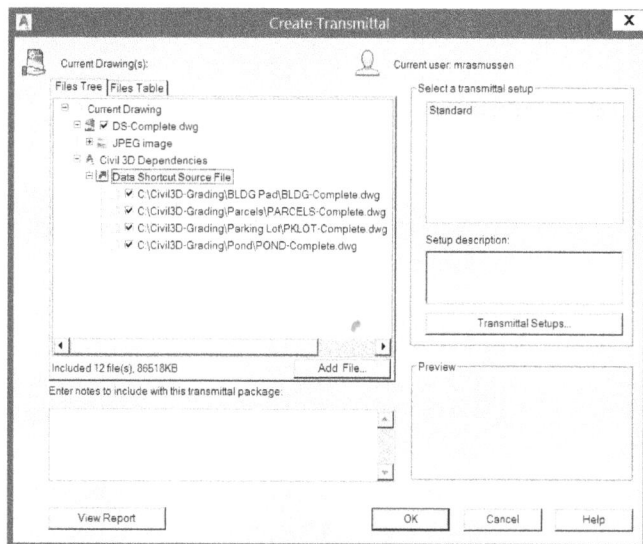

Figure 7–4

Data Shortcut Workflow

1. In the *Prospector* tab, right-click on Data Shortcuts and select **Set the Working Folder...**
2. In the *Prospector* tab, right-click on Data Shortcuts and select **New Data Shortcuts Folder...** to create a new project folder for all of your drawings.
3. Create or import the data that you want to share in the source drawing and save it in the current working folder under the correct project folder.
4. In the *Prospector* tab, right-click on Data Shortcuts and select **Associate Project to Current Drawing**.
5. In the *Prospector* tab, right-click on Data Shortcuts and select **Create Data Shortcuts**.
6. Select all of the items that you want to share, such as surfaces, alignments, or profiles, and click **OK**.
7. Save the source drawing (and close as needed).
8. Open, create, and save the drawing to receive the shortcut data. Expand the *Data Shortcuts* collection and the relevant object trees (*Surfaces, Alignments, Pipe Networks,* or *View Frame Groups*).
9. Highlight an item to be referenced, right-click and select **Create Reference...** Repeat for all of the objects as needed. You are prompted for the styles and other settings that are required to display the object in the current drawing.
10. You might also want to add an XREF to the source drawing if there is additional AutoCAD® line work that you want to display in the downstream drawing.
11. The AutoCAD Civil 3D tools for Data Shortcuts are located in the *Manage* tab (as shown in Figure 7–5), and in the *Prospector* tab.

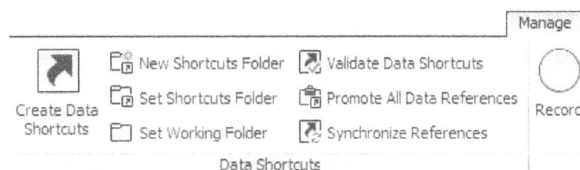

Figure 7–5

Workflow Details

- **Set Working Folder:** Sets a new working folder as the location in which to store the Data Shortcut project. The default working folder for Data Shortcut projects is *C:\Civil 3D Projects*. The default working folder is also used for Autodesk Vault projects and local (non-Vault) Survey projects. If you work with the Autodesk Vault software, local Survey, and Data Shortcut projects, you should have separate working folders for each project type for ease of management.

- **New Shortcuts Folder:** Creates a new folder for storing a set of related project drawings and Data Shortcuts.

- **Create Data Shortcuts:** Creates Data Shortcuts from the active drawing.

Data Shortcuts are stored in the *Shortcuts* folder for the active project and used to create data references to source objects in other drawings. Each Data Shortcut is stored in a separate XML file.

Advantages of Data Shortcuts

- Data Shortcuts provide a simple mechanism for sharing object data, without the added system administration needs of the Autodesk Vault software.

- Data Shortcuts offer access to an object's intelligent data while ensuring that this referenced data can only be changed in the source drawing.

- Referenced objects can have styles and labels that differ from the source drawing.

- When you open a drawing containing revised referenced data, the referenced objects are updated automatically.

- During a drawing session, if the referenced data has been revised, you are notified in the Communication Center and in the *Prospector* tab in Toolspace.

Limitations of Data Shortcuts

- Data Shortcuts cannot provide data versioning.

- Data Shortcuts do not provide security or data integrity controls.

- Unlike the Autodesk Vault software, Data Shortcuts do not provide a secure mechanism for sharing point data or survey data.

- Maintaining links between references and their source objects requires fairly stable names and locations on the shared file system. However, most broken references can easily be repaired using the tools in the AutoCAD Civil 3D software.

Practice 7a

Estimated time for completion: 15 minutes

Data Shortcuts I

Practice Objective

• Create a new data shortcut project with the correct working folder for the project being worked on.

In this practice you will walk through the steps of creating project-based Data Shortcuts folders.

Task 1 - Set the Working folder.

In this task, you will set up a new working folder as the location in which to store Data Shortcut projects. The default working folder for Data Shortcut projects is *C:\Civil 3D Projects*.

1. Start a new drawing from **Grading Template.dwt** from the *C:\Civil3D-Grading\Template* folder.

2. In the *Manage* tab>Data Shortcuts panel, select **Set Working Folder**, as shown in Figure 7–6.

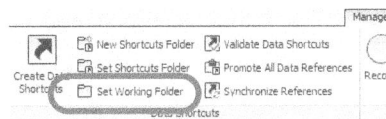

Figure 7–6

3. In the Browse For Folder dialog box, select the *Civil3D-Grading* folder and click **Make New Folder**, as shown on the left in Figure 7–7. Type **Learning Data Shortcuts** as the folder name and click **OK**, as shown on the right in Figure 7–7.

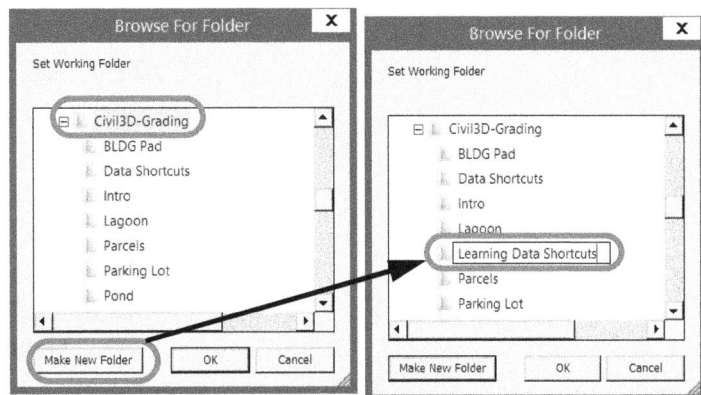

Figure 7–7

Task 2 - Create new Shortcuts folders.

In this task, you will create a new folder for storing a set of related project drawings and Data Shortcuts. Create a folder name that reflects the project name and specify whether or not to use a project template to organize your data.

1. Continue working with the drawing from the previous task.

2. In the *Manage* tab>Data Shortcuts panel, select **New Shortcuts Folder**, as shown in Figure 7–8.

Figure 7–8

3. In the New Data Shortcut Folder dialog box, complete the following, as shown in Figure 7–9:

   • Type **Ascent Phase 1** for the name.
   • Do not select the **Use project template** option.
   • Click **OK** to close the dialog box.

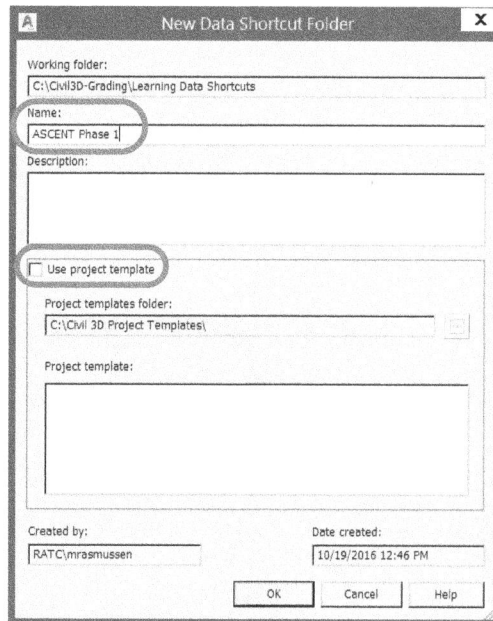

Figure 7–9

In the Prospector tab, a Data Shortcuts folder should be displayed in the C:\Civil3D-Grading\ Learning Data Shortcuts\ Ascent Phase 1 folder.

4. In Windows Explorer, verify that the *Civil 3D* folder structure has been created for this project, as shown in Figure 7–10.

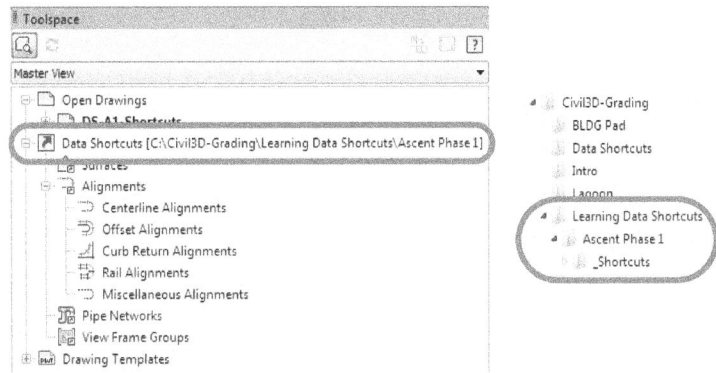

Figure 7–10

Task 3 - Associate the project to the drawings.

Associating drawings to the project is an important step to ensure that the data reference is inserted and an associate between project drawings is created.

1. Continue working with the drawing from the previous task.

2. In the *Prospector* tab, right-click on Data Shortcuts and select **Associate Project to Current Drawing**, as shown in Figure 7–11.

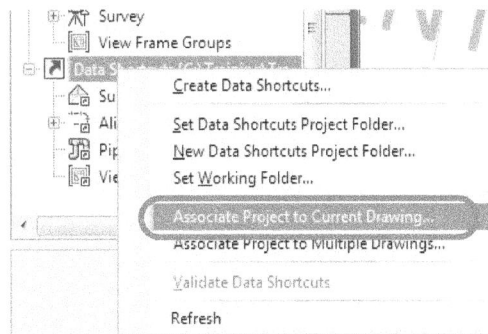

Figure 7–11

3. In the Associate Project to Current Drawing dialog box, click **OK** to accept the default working folder and project, as shown in Figure 7–12.

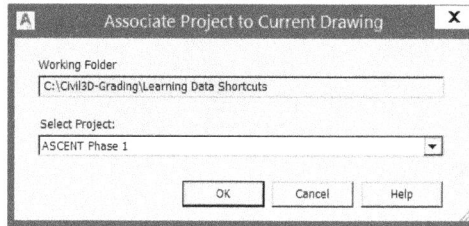

Figure 7–12

4. In the *Prospector* tab, right-click on Data Shortcuts and select **Associate Project to Multiple Drawings**, as shown in Figure 7–13.

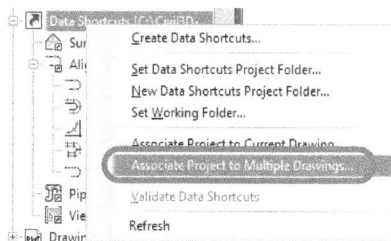

Figure 7–13

5. In the Associate Project to Multiple Drawings dialog box, click **OK** to accept the default working folder and project.

6. In the Browse for Folder dialog box, select *C:\Civil3D-Grading*, as shown in Figure 7–14. Click **OK**.

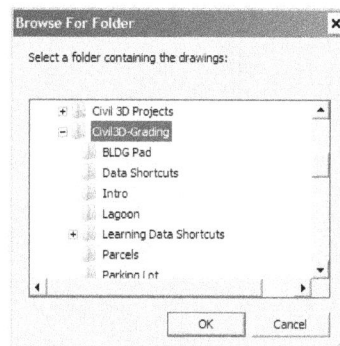

Figure 7–14

7. Close the drawing without saving.

Practice 7b

Data Shortcuts II

Practice Objective

* Create Data Shortcuts from objects in a drawing to share with other team members.

Estimated time for completion: 20 minutes

In this practice you will walk through the steps of creating project-based *Data Shortcuts* folders.

Task 1 - Create data shortcuts.

1. Open **PARCELS-Complete.dwg** from the *C:\Civil3D-Grading\Parcels* folder.

2. In the *Prospector* tab, verify that the Data Shortcuts points to the correct folder, as shown in Figure 7–15.

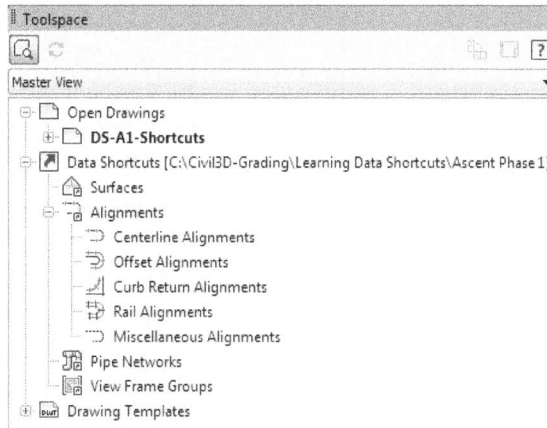

Figure 7–15

This drawing contains some surfaces for which you need to create Data Shortcuts.

3. In the *Manage* tab>Data Shortcuts panel, click (Create Data Shortcuts), as shown in Figure 7–16.

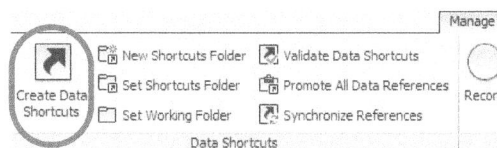

Figure 7–16

4. If you receive a message that the drawing has not yet been saved, click **OK**. Save the drawing and start the **Create Data Shortcuts** command again.

5. In the Create Data Shortcuts dialog box, a list of all of the objects available for use in shortcuts is displayed. Select **Surfaces: Road1**, **Existing Ground**, and **Residential Surface**, as shown in Figure 7–17, and click **OK**.

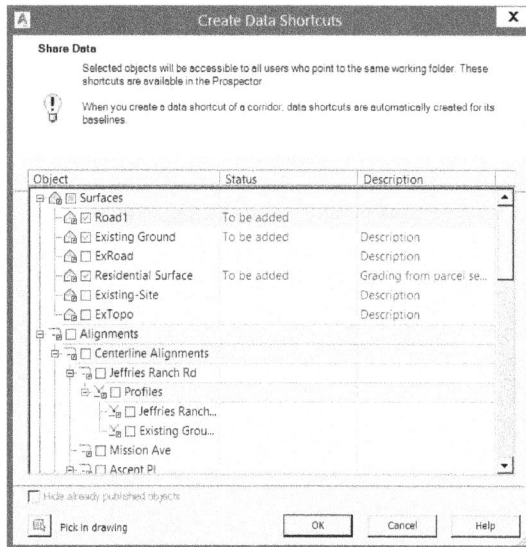

Figure 7–17

6. Open **PKLOT-Complete.dwg** from the *C:\Civil3D-Grading\ Parking Lot* folder.

7. In the *Prospector* tab, verify that the Data Shortcuts points to the correct folder, as shown in Figure 7–18.

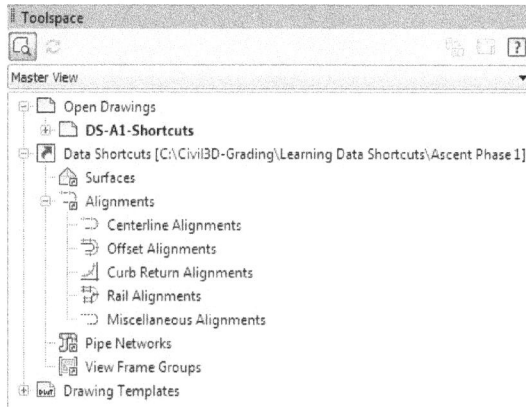

Figure 7–18

8. In the *Manage* tab>Data Shortcuts panel, click (Create Data Shortcuts).

9. If you receive a message that the drawing has not yet been saved, click **OK**. Save the drawing and start the **Create Data Shortcuts** command again.

10. In the Create Data Shortcuts dialog box, select the **Parking Lot** surface as shown in Figure 7–19, and click **OK**.

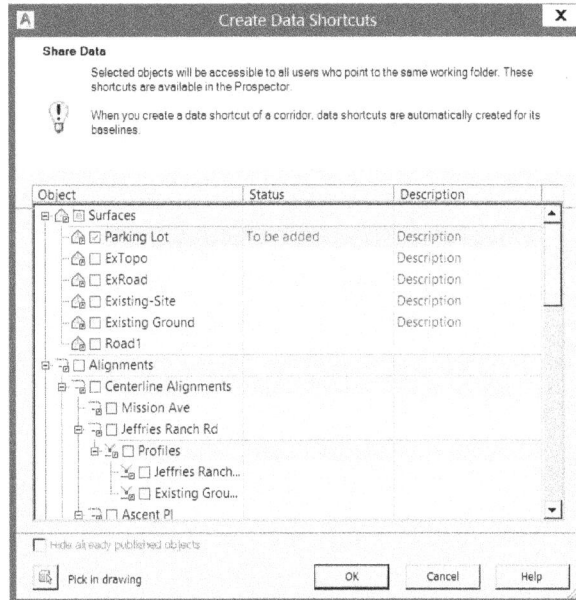

Figure 7–19

11. Open **BLDG-Complete.dwg** from the *C:\Civil3D-Grading\ BLDG Pad* folder.

12. In the *Prospector* tab, verify that the Data Shortcuts points to the correct folder, as shown in Figure 7–20.

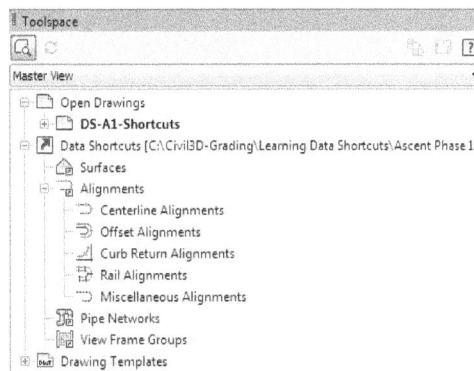

Figure 7–20

13. In the *Manage* tab>Data Shortcuts panel, click ⬈ (Create Data Shortcuts).

14. If you receive a message that the drawing has not yet been saved, click **OK**. Save the drawing and start the **Create Data Shortcuts** command again.

15. In the Create Data Shortcuts dialog box, select the **Building1** surface, as shown in Figure 7–21, and click **OK**.

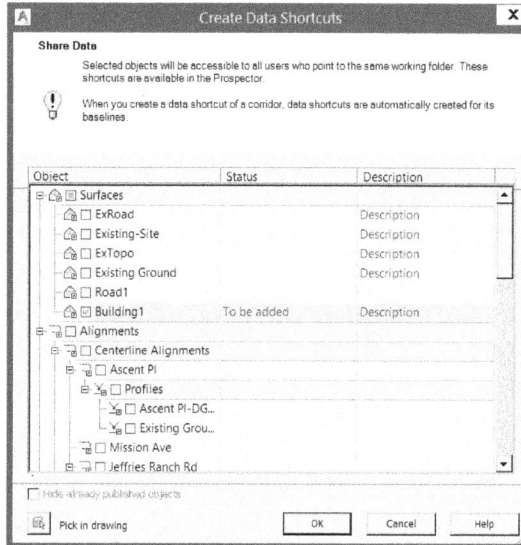

Figure 7–21

16. Open **POND-Complete.dwg** from the *C:\Civil3D-Grading\ Pond* folder.

17. In the *Manage* tab>Data Shortcuts panel, click ⬈ (Create Data Shortcuts).

18. If you receive a message that the drawing has not yet been saved, click **OK**. Save the drawing and start the **Create Data Shortcuts** command again.

19. In the Create Data Shortcuts dialog box, select the **Pond** surface, as shown in Figure 7–22, and click **OK**.

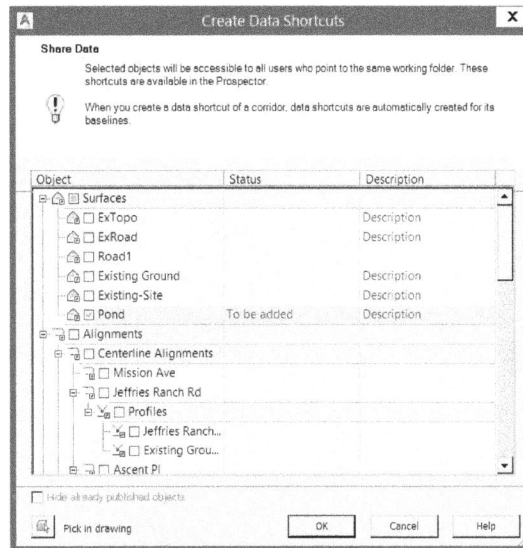

Figure 7–22

You have now created shortcuts for the surfaces. This means that if the shortcuts and drawings are in a shared network folder, anyone on the network has access to these AutoCAD Civil 3D objects.

- Note that in the *Prospector* tab, under the *Data Shortcuts* and *Surfaces* collections, you can now access all of the surfaces. In the list view, the source file name and source path are displayed, as shown in Figure 7–23.

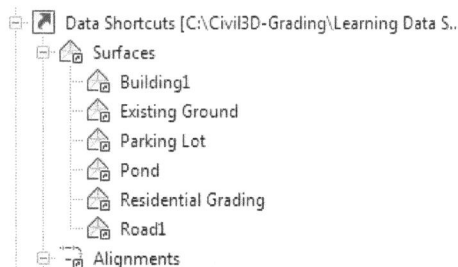

Figure 7–23

20. Save and close the drawings.

Task 2 - Data-reference data shortcuts.

1. Start a new drawing from **Grading Template.dwt** from the *C:\Civil3D-Grading\Template* folder.

2. Save it as **Datashortcuts.dwg** in the *C:\Civil3D-Grading\ Learning Data Shortcuts\Ascent Phase 1* folder.

3. In the *Prospector* tab, ensure that the Data Shortcuts points to the *C:\Civil3D-Grading\Learning Data Shortcuts\ Ascent Phase 1* folder.

4. In the *Prospector* tab, under the *Data Shortcuts* collection, expand the *Surfaces* collection (if not already expanded), as shown in Figure 7–24.

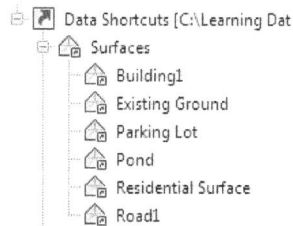

Figure 7–24

5. Under the *Surfaces* collection, right-click on the surface **Existing Ground** and select **Create Reference**, as shown in Figure 7–25.

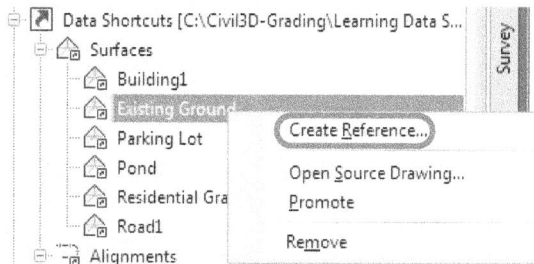

Figure 7–25

You can rename the reference surface and assign a different surface and render style.

6. In the Create Surface Reference dialog box, complete the following, as shown in Figure 7–26:

   • For the *Name,* type **ExSurface**.

   • For the *Description,* type **Data referenced surface.**

   • For the *Style,* select **Contours 5' and 25' (Background)**.

   • Click **OK** to close the dialog box.

   • Type **ZE** and press <Enter> to display the surface reference.

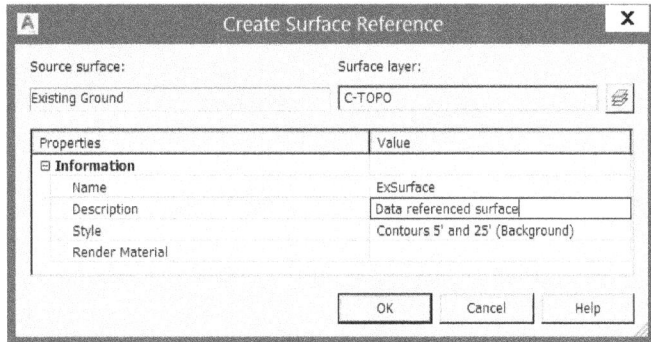

Figure 7–26

7. Repeat Steps 4 to 6 to create references to the other five surfaces in the project but give them the **_No Display** surface style.

8. Save the drawing.

Task 3 - Combine surfaces into one.

1. Continue working in the drawing from the previous task or open **DS-B3-Shortcuts.dwg** from the *C:\Civil3D-Grading\ Data Shortcuts* folder.

2. In the *Home* tab>Create Ground Data panel, expand the Surfaces drop-down list and click ⬦ (Create Surface).

3. In the Create Surface dialog box, complete the following:
   • In the *Name* field, type **Finished Ground with Pond**.
   • For the *Description*, type **Combined finish grading surfaces from references**.
   • For the *Style,* select **Contours 2' and 10' (Design)**.
   • Click **OK** to close the dialog box.

4. In the *Prospector* tab, expand **Surfaces>Finished Ground with Pond>Definition**. Right-click on Edits and select **Paste Surface**.

5. In the Select Surface to Paste dialog box, select the **Building1**, **Parking Lot**, **Pond**, **Residential Surface**, and **Road1** surfaces. Click **OK** to close the dialog box.

6. To ensure that the surfaces were pasted in the proper order, select the surface in the drawing. In the *Tin Surface* contextual tab>Modify panel, click ⬦ (Surface Properties).

7. In the Surface Properties>*Definition* tab, arrange the Operation Type order by selecting a **Paste** operation and moving it up or down with the arrows on the left so that it matches that shown in Figure 7–27. Click **OK** to close the dialog box. Select **Rebuild the Surface**.

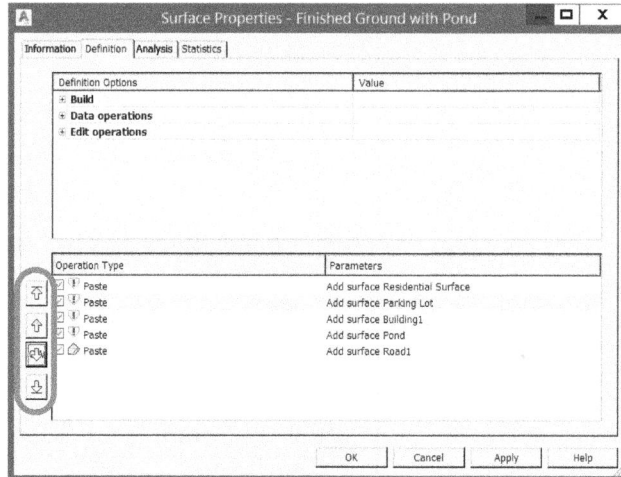

Figure 7–27

8. In the drawing, select the surface, right-click and select **Object Viewer** to verify that the correct paste order was selected. The finished surface should look like that shown in Figure 7–28.

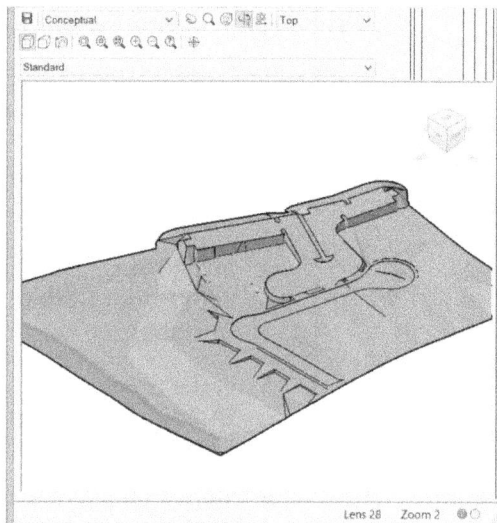

Figure 7–28

9. Save the drawing.

Chapter Review Questions

1. In the AutoCAD Civil 3D workflow, what are the two main methods of project collaboration (or the sharing of intelligent AutoCAD Civil 3D design data)?

   a. Windows Explorer and XREFS.

   b. Data shortcuts and Vault references.

   c. X-refs and Data shortcuts.

   d. Vault references and XREFS.

2. Why would you want to use Vault references over Data Shortcuts?

   a. Added security and version control.

   b. Permit more people to have access.

   c. It works more like the Autodesk® Land Desktop software.

   d. It works better with multiple offices.

3. How can you edit an object referenced through Data Shortcuts?

   a. Open the source drawing.

   b. With grips.

   c. Using the Panorama view.

   d. You cannot do it.

4. What is the file format that Data Shortcuts use to share design data between drawing files?

   a. SHP

   b. DWT

   c. DWG

   d. XML

Command Summary

Button	Command	Location
	Create Data Shortcuts	• **Ribbon:** *Manage* tab>Data Shortcuts panel • **Command Prompt:** CreateDataShortcuts
	New Shortcuts Folder	• **Ribbon:** *Manage* tab>Data Shortcuts panel • **Command Prompt:** NewShortcutsFolder
	Set Shortcuts Folder	• **Ribbon:** *Manage* tab>Data Shortcuts panel • **Command Prompt:** SetShortcutsFolder
	Set Working Folder	• **Ribbon:** *Manage* tab>Data Shortcuts panel • **Command Prompt:** SetWorkingFolder

Visualization

In this chapter you learn how to use the 3D workspace. You practice viewing a 3D model from different angles, shading the model using visual styles, and adding materials to objects. Then you create sun studies and set up lights in preparation for rendering the model using basic tools.

Learning Objectives in this Chapter

- Understand how to access the 3D drawing and viewing tools using the Ribbon through 3D specific workspaces.
- Control how elements are displayed in a view using visual styles.
- Apply materials to AutoCAD Civil 3D objects, by layer, and to objects faces.
- Specify light sources that cast shadows to create realistic views.
- Create a rendered image of a 3D solid model to be used for presentations.

8.1 Introduction to the 3D Modeling Workspace

When you are ready to begin working in 3D, you need special tools and visual clues to help you move from the flat 2D world into the full-featured world of the third dimension. The AutoCAD® Civil® 3D software includes a 3D modeling workspace with easy access to 3D drawing and viewing tools, as shown in Figure 8–1.

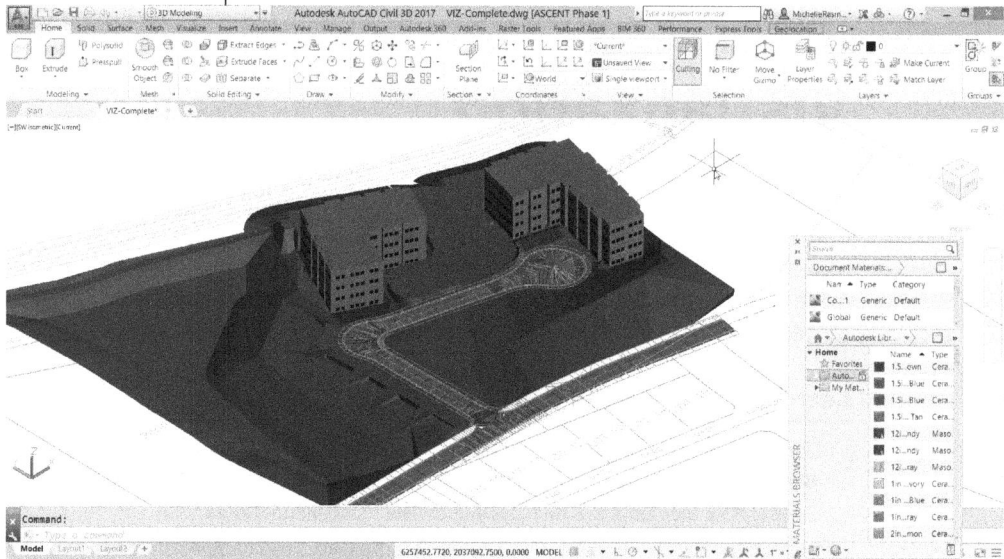

Figure 8–1

- To open the 3D Modeling workspace, expand

  [⚙ Civil 3D ▾] in the Quick Access Toolbar and select **3D Modeling**.

- Use the Ribbon tabs and panels to access the 3D tools.

- Turn the Tool Palettes off or set them to **Auto-Hide** to save space in the drawing window.

3D Ribbon Panels

The 3D Modeling workspace includes Ribbon tabs and panels that contain commonly used 3D tools. The tabs are: *Home*, *Solid*, *Surface*, *Mesh*, *Visualize*, and *View*.

The *Home* tab includes the following panels: Modeling, Mesh, Solid Editing, Draw, Modify, Section, Coordinates, View, Selection, Layers, and Groups, as shown in Figure 8–2.

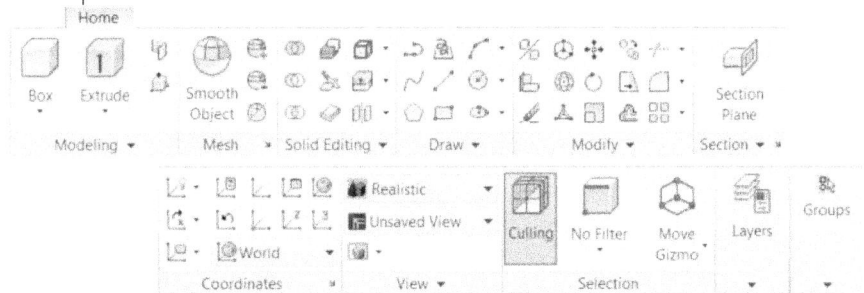

Figure 8–2

The *Solid* tab includes the following panels: Primitives, Solid, Boolean, Solid Editing, Section, and Selection as shown in Figure 8–3.

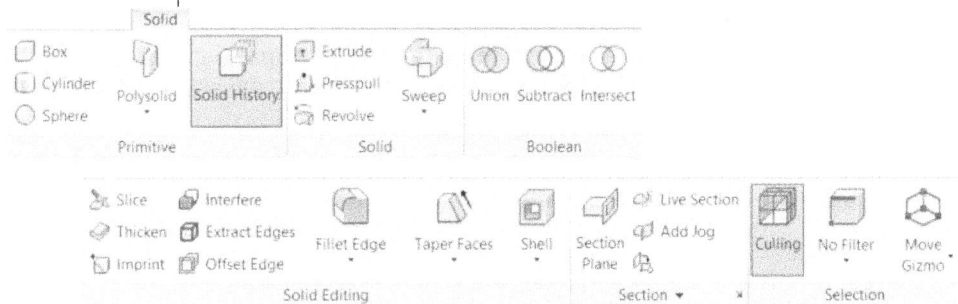

Figure 8–3

The *Surface* tab includes the following panels: Create, Edit, Control Vertices, Curves, Project Geometry, and Analysis as shown in Figure 8–4. (This panel is for object surfaces, not ground surfaces that you are used to working with in the AutoCAD Civil 3D software).

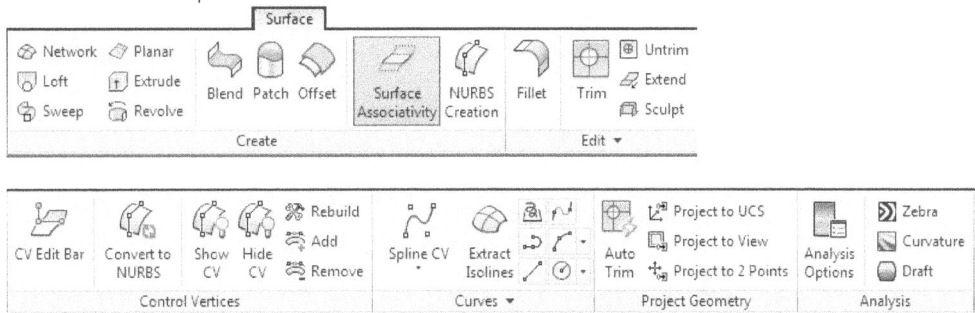

Figure 8–4

The *Mesh* tab includes the following panels: Primitives, Mesh, Mesh Edit, Convert Mesh, Section, and Selection as shown in Figure 8–5.

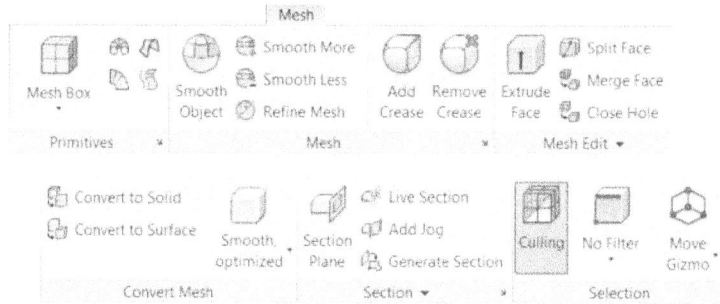

Figure 8–5

The *Visualize* tab includes the following panels: Lights, Sun & Location, Materials, Animations, Camera, Render, Views, Coordinates, Visual Styles, Viewports, and Autodesk 360, as shown in Figure 8–6.

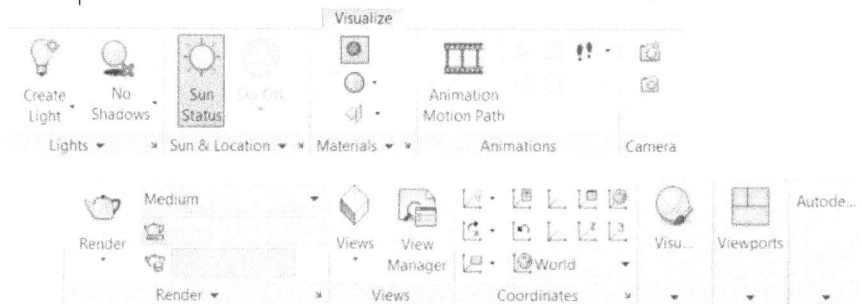

Figure 8–6

The *View* tab includes the following panels: Navigate, Views, Coordinates, Visual Styles, Viewports, Palettes, Interface, Viewport Tools, and Palettes, as shown in Figure 8–7.

Figure 8–7

8.2 Basic 3D Viewing Tools

As you are working in 3D, you need to be able to view objects using different Visual Styles.

Using Visual Styles

While viewing a model, setting a visual style can help you gain a clearer understanding of the model. Visual styles control how elements are displayed in a view. They might display all of the edges of the objects at the same time or just the ones closest to the viewer. Materials associated with the objects might be displayed or only shaded surfaces. You can add and modify objects and orbit in any of the visual styles.

Twelve visual styles come with the AutoCAD Civil 3D software: **2D Wireframe, 3D Hidden, 3D Wireframe, Conceptual, Hidden, Realistic, Shaded, Shaded with Edges, Shades of Gray, Sketchy, Wireframe**, and **X-Ray**. Select a Visual Style by expanding 2D Wireframe in the *View* tab>Visual Styles panel (or *Home* tab>View panel) and then selecting an option as shown on the left in Figure 8–8. Alternatively, you can select the Visual Style at the top left of the drawing window by selecting **2D Wireframe**, as shown on the right in Figure 8–8.

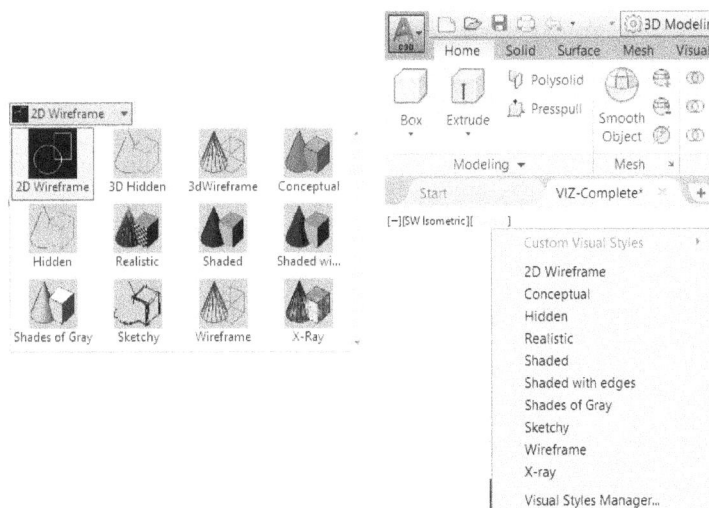

Figure 8–8

- If you are working in an orthographic view, set the *Visual Style* to **2D Wireframe** for the best results.

- In Paper Space, you must be in an active Model Space viewport before applying a visual style.

8.3 Working with Materials

When you look at an object, you do not only see its shape. You also gather information about it by its material. The same is true when you view a 3D drawing, as shown in Figure 8–9. Materials help you to understand the purpose and qualities of the objects. For example, if you see a box made of wood, you would have a different sense of its probable weight and durability than a box made of glass.

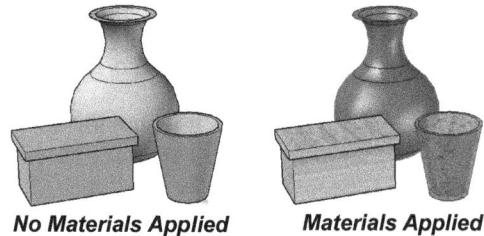

No Materials Applied   **Materials Applied**

Figure 8–9

You can attach materials to objects using the Materials Browser, attaching materials by layer or adding a render material in the object's properties dialog box. Materials are stored in libraries. The Autodesk Library contains a variety of standard materials. You can also create and edit custom libraries and custom materials and textures.

- Most of the materials that are supplied with the AutoCAD Civil 3D software, such as masonry, wood, and flooring, are designed for use in architectural and civil drawings. If you place them on small objects, the materials do not display at the expected scale, as shown in Figure 8–10.

Masonry material on small box

Figure 8–10

Using the Materials Browser

The Materials Browser is the primary way of adding materials to drawings. It is used to view and apply existing materials to your drawing and to create, modify, and manage new and existing materials. You can drag-and-drop materials directly onto objects. In the *Visualize* tab>Material panels or the *View* tab>Palettes panel, click (Materials Browser).

You can use the Materials Browser to manage, search for, sort, select and organize your materials. They can be saved in custom libraries. You can also display all of the available materials or only the ones used in the current drawing. The materials include preview images, to help when selecting them.

The Materials Browser contains the *Document Materials:* area, which displays previews of all of the materials that have been added to the drawing. It also contains the *Libraries:* area, which contains two panels. The panel on the left in Figure 8–11 displays the names of all of the libraries in the drawing. When you expand a library, it displays a list of categories. Select a category to display preview images of its material in the panel shown on the right in Figure 8–11.

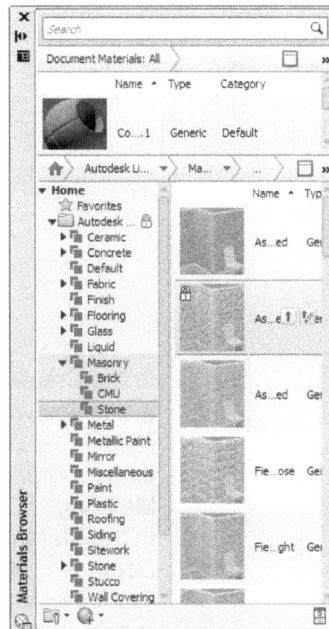

Figure 8–11

- Type a material name in the *Search* field to search for materials with that name in all open libraries. The *Document Materials* and *Libraries* areas display the search results.

Libraries

To add materials to a drawing you need to open the library in which they are located. By default, the standard Autodesk Library is open. To open a custom library, expand ![icon] (Manage Libraries) at the bottom of the Materials Browser and select **Open Existing Library**. In the Add Library dialog box, navigate to the location in which the custom library has been saved, select its name and click **Open**. Library files are saved with an .ADSKLIB file extension.

You can also create custom libraries. These can be useful for organizing commonly used materials, custom materials, job specific materials, etc.

How To: Create a New Custom Library

1. In the Materials Browser, expand ![icon] (Manage Libraries) and select **Create New Library**, as shown in Figure 8–12.

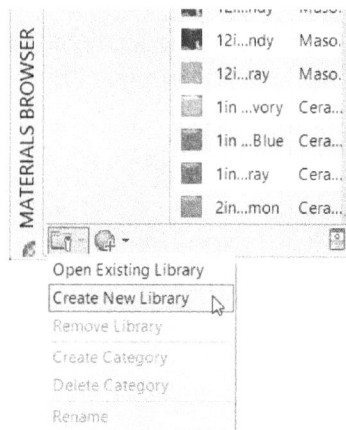

Figure 8–12

2. In the Create Library dialog box, navigate to the location in which you want to store the library, type a name, and click **Save**.
3. In the *Libraries* area, the new library displays below My Materials.
4. In the Materials Browser, drag-and-drop materials from the *Document Materials* area to the new library.
5. Right-click on the library name and select **Create Category** to create categories in the library.
6. Create categories and drag-and-drop materials to them as needed as shown in Figure 8–13.

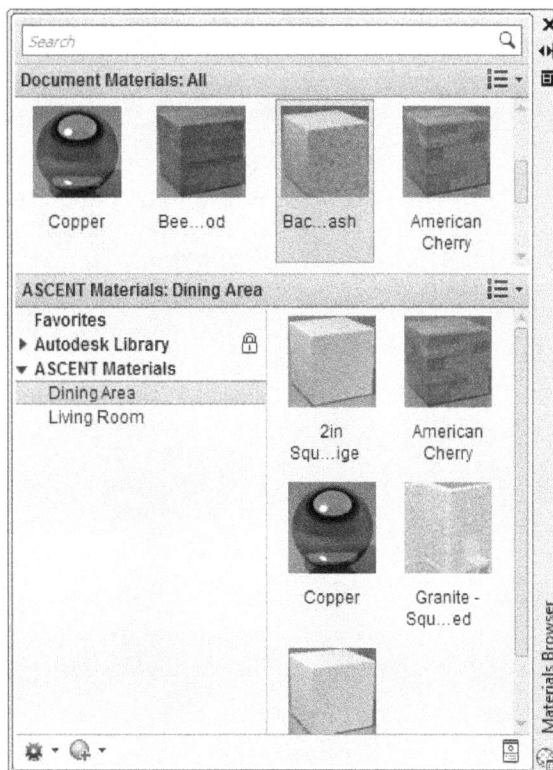

Figure 8–13

- To delete a library, select it in the *Libraries* area, expand Manage and select **Remove Library**. You can also right-click on the library's name and select **Remove Library**.

Adding Materials

Once you have created a library or when you are ready to add materials to objects, you need to load materials into the drawing. This is done by selecting a category in a library, then hovering over the material swatch that you want to add to the drawing, and selecting one of the **Apply** buttons.

How To: Load Materials

1. Open the Materials Browser.
2. In the *Libraries* area, expand a library.
3. In the Library, select a category to display previews of the materials stored in that category.
4. Hover over the material that you want to use and click

   (Apply). It is added to the *Drawing Materials* area and loaded into the drawing.
5. The materials can then be added to objects or layers.

It might be necessary to expand a library category first.

How To: Apply Materials to AutoCAD Civil 3D Objects.

1. Select the AutoCAD Civil 3D object (surface, pipe network, corridor, etc.).
2. Right-click and select the object's properties (Surface Properties).
3. In the *Information* tab, set the Render Material, as shown in Figure 8–14.

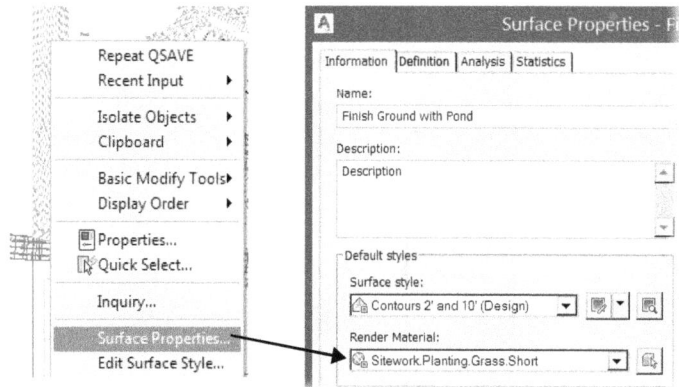

Figure 8–14

How To: Attach Materials from the Materials Browser

1. Open the Materials Browser.
2. In the *Drawing Materials* area, select a material or load one from the library as needed.
3. Drag-and-drop the material onto an object.

• To attach a material to multiple objects, select the objects so that they display their grips, right-click on the material in the *Document Materials* area in the Materials Browser, and select **Assign to Selection**. The material is applied to all of the selected objects.

• To delete materials from an object, click ⊗ (Remove Materials) in the *Visualize* tab>expanded Materials panel. At the *Select objects* prompt, select the objects from which you want to remove the materials.

Applying, Displaying, and Removing Materials

You can apply a material to individual faces. If you only apply materials to visible faces, it saves rendering time later. To attach a material to a single face, hold down <Ctrl> as you drag-and-drop the material.

You can also assign the material to the full solid. In Figure 8–15, the glass material is assigned to the full solid of the object on the left and only to the outside face of the object on the right. The transparency is limited if the entire solid is not selected.

Figure 8–15

You can independently control various display options in the *Document Materials* and *Library* areas by expanding the Display Options drop-down list and selecting an option, as shown in Figure 8–16.

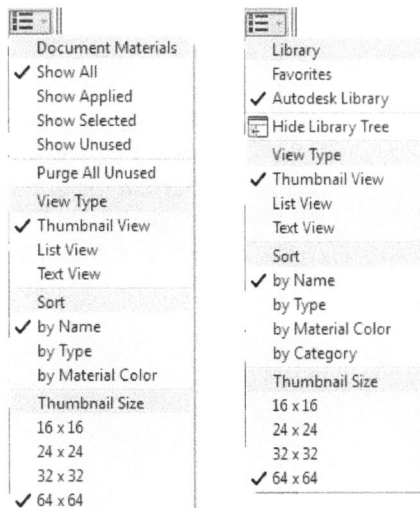

Figure 8–16

- In the *Document Materials* area, you can display all of the materials in the drawing, only those applied to objects or faces, only those applied to selected objects, or only those that are not being used.

- To remove unused materials from the drawing, you can select **Purge All Unused** in the Document Materials Display Options drop-down list or in the right-click menu in the *Drawing Materials* area in the Materials Browser.

- You can also set the View Type (from thumbnails to lists), Sort (by name, type, etc.), and Thumbnail size.

Hint: To Map a Material

Many materials include textures. However, if the texture has a very specific line or repeat pattern, you might need to change its Mapping as it is projected onto a surface, as shown in Figure 8–17.

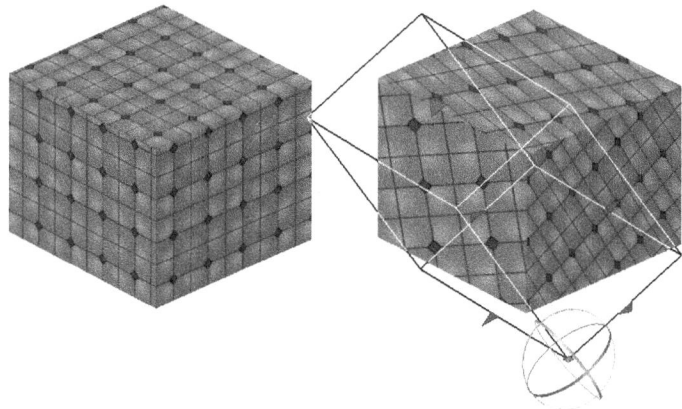

Figure 8–17

In the *Visualize* tab>Materials panel, select the mapping method that you want to use: **Planar**, **Box**, **Cylindrical**, or **Spherical**, as shown in Figure 8–18. Select the faces or objects, press <Enter>, and use grips to adjust the mapping as needed. You can switch between the **Move** and **Rotate** modes.

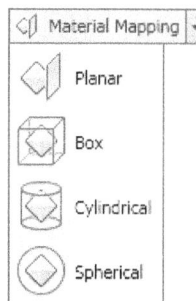

Figure 8–18

Attaching Materials by Layer

In complex models with many types of materials (such as architectural designs), attaching a material to each object would take too long. If you use a layering scheme when creating the objects, you can associate materials with each layer using the Material Attachment Options dialog box, as shown in Figure 8–19.

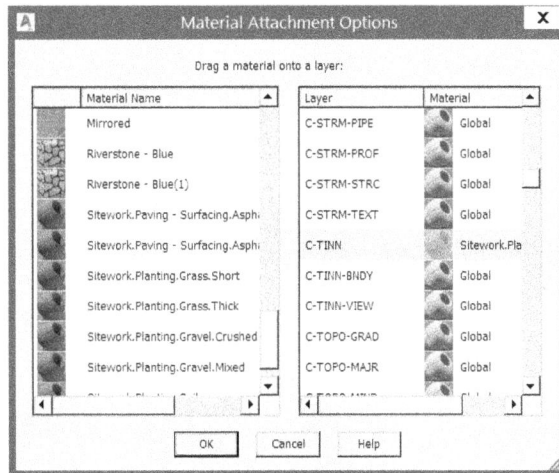

Figure 8–19

- The materials that you want to use must be loaded into the drawing before the **Attach By Layer** command is launched.

How To: Attach Materials by Layer

1. In the *Visualize* tab>expanded Materials panel, click

   (Attach By Layer).
2. In the Material Attachment Options dialog box, select a material in the left pane and drag-and-drop it onto a layer name in the right pane.
3. Continue attaching materials to layers as needed.
4. Click **OK** to end the command.

- Materials attached to individual objects override materials attached by layer. You can change the assigned material to **ByLayer** in Properties.

Materials Editor

The Materials Editor enables you to modify the properties of materials. You can change the material's name, type, pattern, reflectivity, transparency, lighting, color, etc. as shown in Figure 8–20. The options vary depending on the type of material selected.

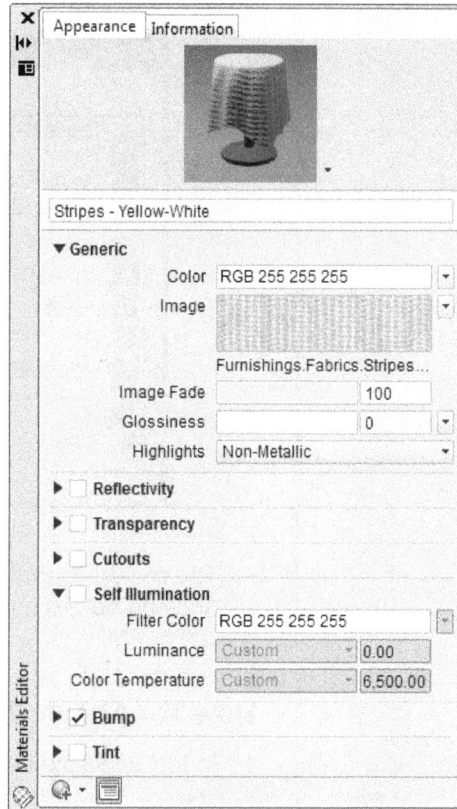

Figure 8–20

- You can open the Materials Editor by right-clicking on a material in the *Document Materials* area and selecting **Edit**.

  You can also click ![icon] (Materials Editor) in the *View* tab> Palettes panel, or ![icon] in the *Visualize* tab>Materials panel. You can also open the Material Editor for a specific material by hovering over that material swatch in the *Document Materials* area and clicking ![icon] (Edit).

- The Materials Editor enables you to modify existing materials or to duplicate the current material to create a custom copy.

Preview

A preview of the material is displayed at the top of the Materials Editor. You can change how the material is displayed by selecting an option in the Options drop-down list next to the preview in the Materials Editor palette, as shown in Figure 8–21. You can also control the rendering quality by selecting **mental ray - Draft Quality**, **mental ray - Medium Quality**, or **mental ray - Production Quality**.

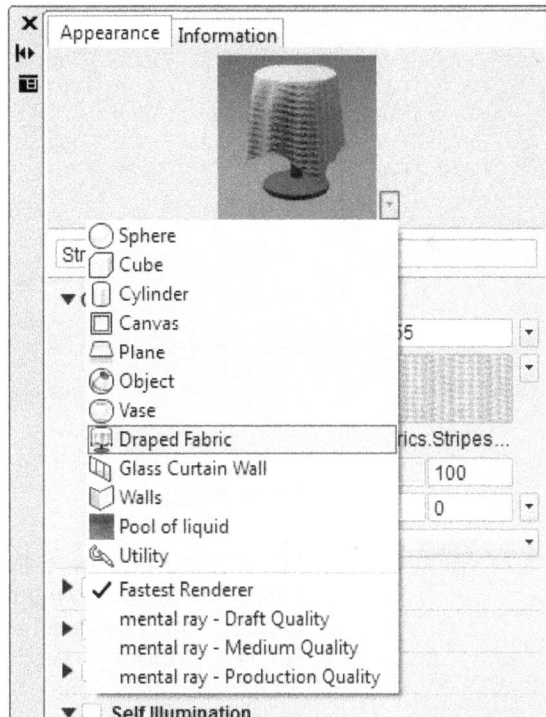

Figure 8–21

Type

You can create a new material type from the Create Material drop-down list at the bottom left of the Materials Editor palette, as shown in Figure 8–22. You can duplicate the existing material, select from a list of types, or create a generic material.

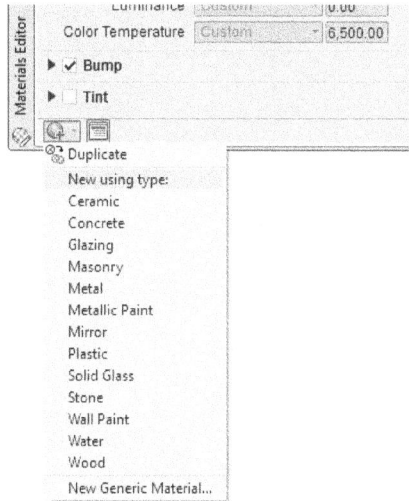

Figure 8–22

Properties

The Materials Editor is divided into areas, each of which controls properties related to the type of material being modified or created. The *Type* area lists the type name and enables you to set its properties. The other areas control the *Reflectivity*, *Transparency*, *Cutouts*, *Self Illumination*, *Bump*, and *Tint* settings.

For the Generic Type, the settings are as follows:

Generic	Controls the color, image, glossiness and highlights of the material.
Reflectivity	Controls the amount of light reflected from the material directly at the camera or at an angle to the camera.
Transparency	Controls the amount of transparency, translucency, and refraction of the material. Also controls whether an image or texture are used with the transparency.
Cutouts	Uses an image or texture to make a material partially transparent. For example, this could be used to create lace or etched glass.

Self Illumination	Controls the color, brightness, and temperature of the light being transmitted through a transparent material.
Bump	Uses an image of the material or a texture to create a bump pattern and controls the relative height of the pattern.
Tint	Controls the hue and saturation value of the assigned color when mixed with white.

Texture Editor

The Texture Editor enables you to modify the appearance of the texture displayed on a material. Select a texture option in the second drop-down list in the Materials Editor palette>*Generic* area, to open the Texture Editor. A preview of the texture and its properties are displayed. The properties vary depending on the type of texture selected. For example, the Tiles texture and its properties are shown in Figure 8–23.

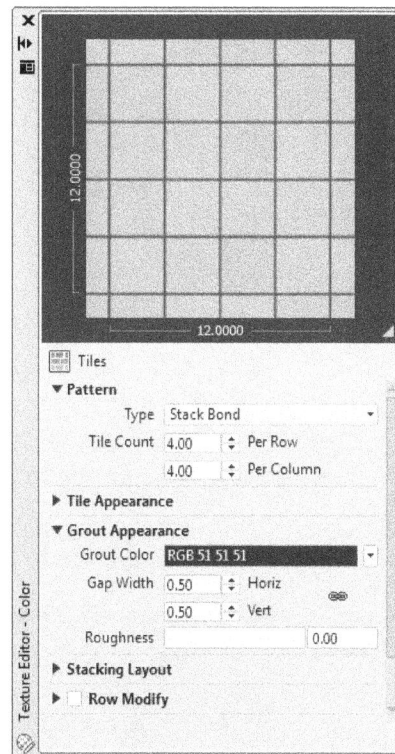

Figure 8–23

- You can control the texture's color, pattern, size, repeat, etc.

Practice 8a

Working with Materials

Practice Objective

- Apply materials to AutoCAD Civil 3D objects, by layer, and to objects faces to complete a realistic display.

Estimated time for completion: 15 minutes

In this practice you will apply materials to AutoCAD Civil 3D objects, by layer, and to object faces to complete a realistic display, such as that shown in Figure 8–24.

Figure 8–24

Task 1 - Add materials to AutoCAD Civil 3D objects.

1. Open **VIZ-B1-Grading.dwg** found in the *C:\Civil3D-Grading\ Visualization* folder.

2. In the *Prospector* tab, select the **Finished Ground with Pond** surface.

3. In the *Tin Surface* contextual tab>Modify panel, click

   (Surface Properties).

4. In the Surface Properties dialog box, in the *Information* tab, ensure that **Sitework.Planting.Grass.Short** is selected for the Render Material, as shown in Figure 8–25.

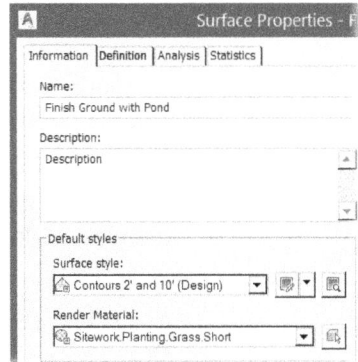

Figure 8–25

5. Click **OK** to apply the changes to the drawing.

6. In the drawing, select the **Finished Ground** surface, right-click and select **Object Viewer**.

7. In the Object View, change the *Visual Style* to **Realistic** and the *View Control* to **SW Isometric**, as shown in Figure 8–26. Note that the surface looks like it is now covered in grass.

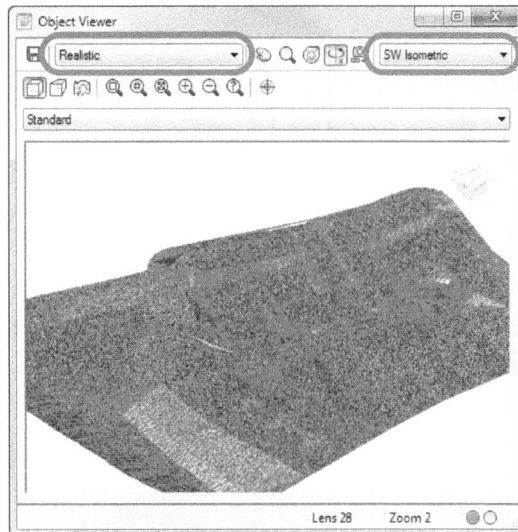

Figure 8–26

8. Save the drawing.

Task 2 - Add materials to the buildings.

1. Continue working in the drawing or open **VIZ-B2-Grading.dwg** from the *C:\Civil3D-Grading\ Visualization* folder.

2. In the *View* tab>Views panel, select **Building 1** to zoom into the west building.

3. In the *Visualize* tab>Materials panel, click (Materials Browser).

4. In the Materials Browser, in the *Libraries* area, expand the Autodesk Library and expand the **Stone** category to display preview swatches of its materials as shown in Figure 8–27.

Figure 8–27

5. In the drawing, select **building 1**. In the Materials Browser, find the **Riverstone - Blue** material. Select **Add material to document**, as shown in Figure 8–28.

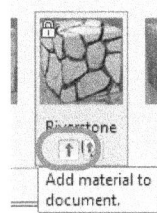

Figure 8–28

6. Close the text window.

7. In the drawing, select **building 1**, right-click and select **Object Viewer**. Look at the building from different directions. With the *Visual Style* set to **Realistic**, zoom in on the building for a closer view of the stones, as shown in Figure 8–29. Close the Object Viewer.

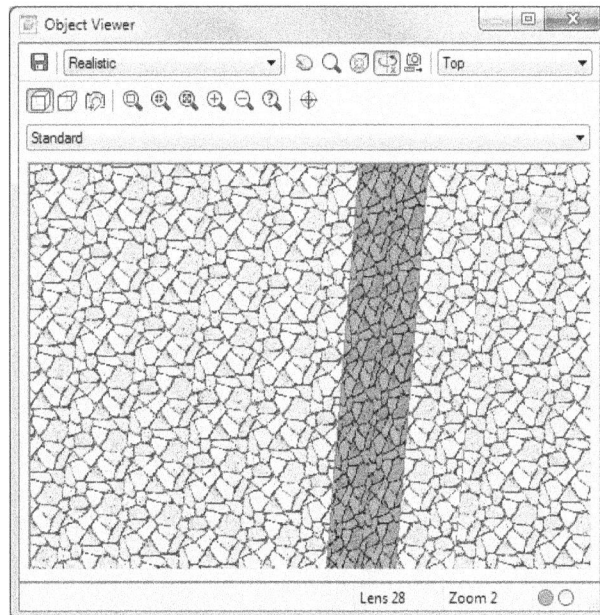

Figure 8–29

8. Repeat Steps 2 to 6 for building 2.

9. Save the drawing.

Task 3 - Add materials to a layer.

1. Continue working in the drawing or open **VIZ-B3-Grading.dwg** from the C:\Civil3D-Grading\ Visualization folder.

2. In the Command Line, type **LA** and press <Enter> to open the Layer Properties Manager.

3. In the Layer Properties Manager, thaw the layer **A-BLDG-WINDOWS**. Close the Layer Properties Manager.

4. In the *Visualize* tab>Materials panel, click ⊛ (Materials Browser).

5. In the Materials Browser, in the *Libraries* area, expand the Autodesk Library and expand the **Glass** category to display preview swatches of its materials. Select **Mirrored**, and select **Add material to document**, as shown in Figure 8–30.

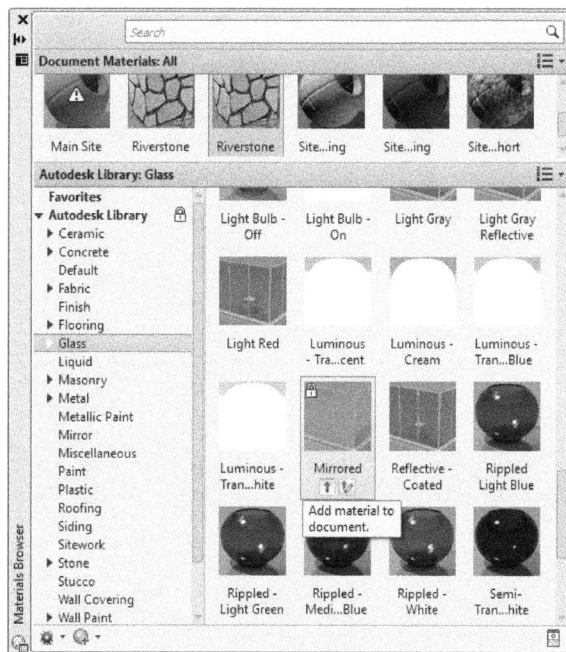

Figure 8–30

6. In the *Visualize* tab>expanded Materials panel, click 🗐 (Attach By Layer).

If the material you want to use is not listed, close the Material Attachment Options dialog box, load the material, and open the dialog box to display the material.

7. In the Material Attachment Options dialog box, select **Mirrored** in the left column and drag-and-drop it on **A-BLDG-WINDOWS** in the right pane, as shown in Figure 8–31. Click **OK** to apply the changes to the drawing.

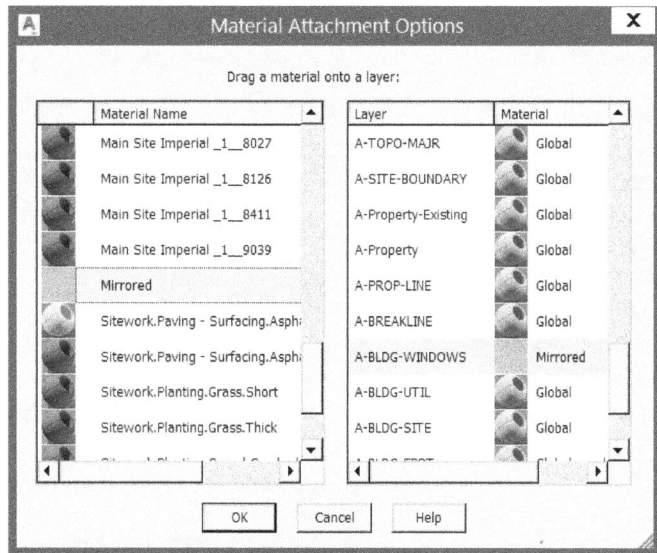

Material Attachment Options

Drag a material onto a layer:

Material Name		Layer	Material	
Main Site Imperial _1__8027		A-TOPO-MAJR		Global
Main Site Imperial _1__8126		A-SITE-BOUNDARY		Global
Main Site Imperial _1__8411		A-Property-Existing		Global
Main Site Imperial _1__9039		A-Property		Global
Mirrored		A-PROP-LINE		Global
Sitework.Paving - Surfacing.Asph:		A-BREAKLINE		Global
Sitework.Paving - Surfacing.Asph:		A-BLDG-WINDOWS		Mirrored
Sitework.Planting.Grass.Short		A-BLDG-UTIL		Global
Sitework.Planting.Grass.Thick		A-BLDG-SITE		Global

OK   Cancel   Help

Figure 8–31

8. Close the Materials Browser.

9. Save the drawing.

8.4 Specifying Light Sources

When you create realistic views, such as the example shown in Figure 8–32, the light sources and the shadows they cast are a major component of the display.

*The **Realistic** visual style automatically displays any materials and textures that are associated with objects in the viewport. However, the lights and shadows are turned off to save regeneration time as you create and modify objects.*

Figure 8–32

The AutoCAD Civil 3D software includes several sources of light to help you visualize your drawing:

- **Default Lighting:** Shines on all of the faces of the model as you move around the drawing.

- **Sunlight:** Defined by the location of the project and time of day.

- **User-defined lights:** Include **Distance**, **Point**, **Spotlights**, and **Weblight**, which can be added directly to the drawing.

Default Lighting

Default lighting illuminates a model without any specific focus. It is frequently used for mechanical drawings that do not need to display cast shadows.

- The default lighting source should be turned off to display the sun or user-defined lights. Turn off the default lighting by clicking (Default Lighting) in the *Visualize* tab>expanded Lights panel.

- The first time you turn on the Sun or a user light, an alert box opens. Select the **Always perform my current choice** option and then select the **Turn off the default lighting (recommended)** option.

Sunlight

One of the easiest lights to work with is the sun. All you need to do is turn it on. Once it is on, you can set its location, date, and time. This is most effective if you also have shadows toggled on, as shown in Figure 8–33 for two different times of day.

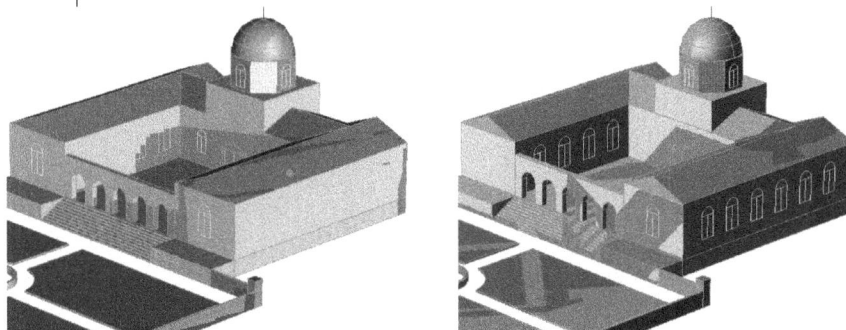

Figure 8–33

- In the *Visualize* tab>Lights panel and Sun & Location panel (shown in Figure 8–34), you can toggle on shadows, toggle on the sun, and set the location, date, and time.

Figure 8–34

- The location can be set in the Drawing Settings dialog box, in the *Units and Zone* tab or in the *Visualize* tab>Sun & Location panel.

- The Sun Properties palette specifies the intensity and color of the sun as well as its location, date, and time, as shown in Figure 8–35. You can open the palette by clicking ⇗ in the Sun & Location panel.

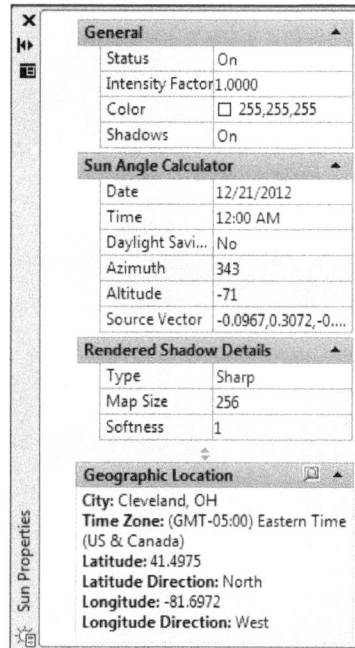

Figure 8–35

How To: Set the Geographic Location

1. In the *Visualize* tab>Sun & Location panel, click ⊕ (Set Location).
2. In the Geographic Location alert box, specify how you want to define the location for this drawing.

   - **Import a .kml or a .kmz file:** A .KML or .KMZ (zipped) file, used by Google Earth and other 3D geospatial tools, includes the latitude, longitude, and altitude of a location.
   - Select the **From Map** option to specify a location from a map or the latitude and longitude location. To specify the latitude and longitude, click ⊘ in the Geographic Location dialog box. The latitude and Longitude fields become available, as shown in Figure 8–36.

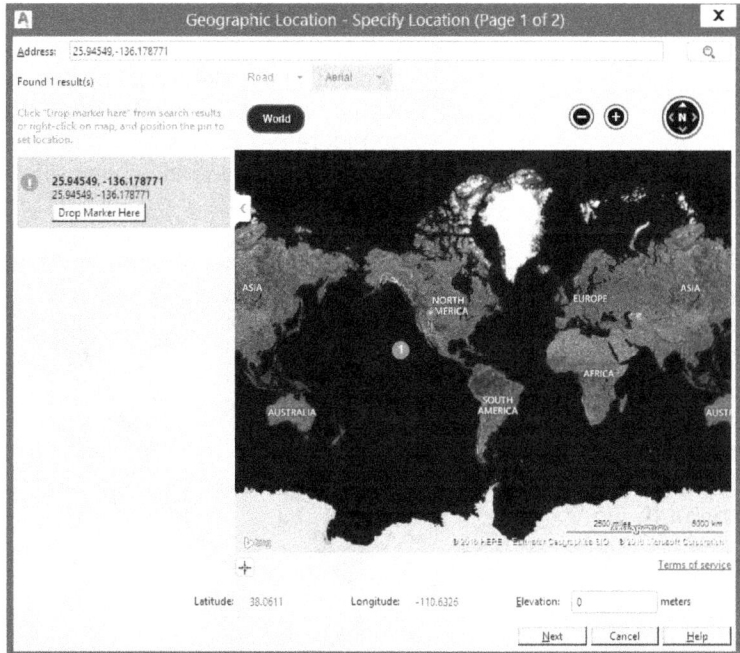

Figure 8–36

- If a Geographic Location already exists in the drawing, you can edit the current location, define a new location, or remove the location.

User-Defined Lights

Draw 3D objects (such as a box or cylinder) that can act as a stage or frame to help you with positioning, or attach lights to objects that are already in your drawing.

User-defined lights can create more realistic views in a drawing. For example, you can place a **Point** light in a lamp to act as a light bulb or a **Spot** light to highlight materials and add shadows, as shown in Figure 8–37.

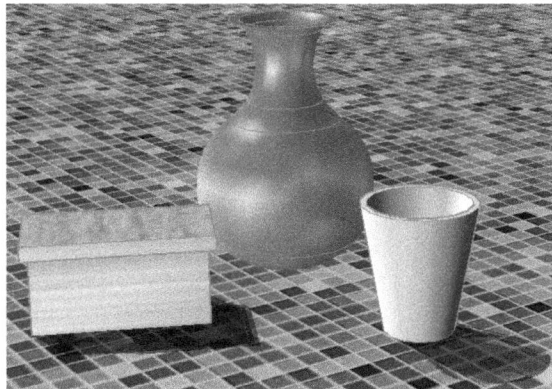

Figure 8–37

Point Lights

A point light is like a light bulb. It radiates in all directions from the source and fades in intensity further from the source, as shown in Figure 8–38. This fading is the rate of attenuation. Point lights are used for general lighting effects, such as light from a street lamp.

As you place lights, you are prompted to set their options, such as their **Name**, **Intensity**, *and* **Color**. *Setting these options is easier to modify using Properties after you have placed the light.*

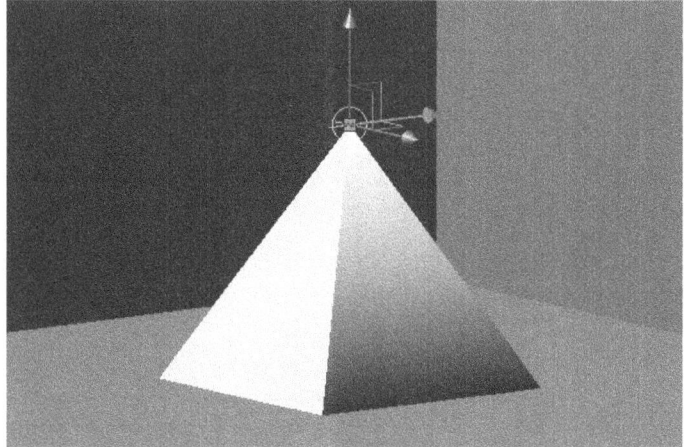

Figure 8–38

How To: Place a Point Light

1. In the *Visualize* tab>Lights panel>Create Light flyout, click
   (Point Light).
2. Specify the location of the light.
3. Select one of the options to modify as needed or exit the command.

Hint: Generic Lights and Photometric Lights

The AutoCAD Civil 3D software has two methods of controlling light intensity: *photometric* and *generic.* These can be set in the Units dialog box (usually in a template file) or in the *Visualize* tab>expanded Lights panel>Lighting Units flyout, as shown in Figure 8–39.

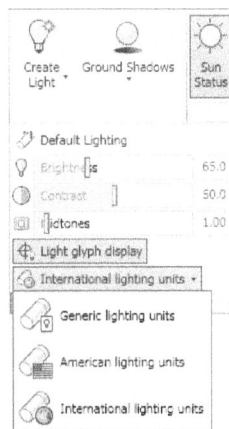

Figure 8–39

The **Generic** option uses default lighting without any lighting units. The **International** (lux) and **American** (foot candles) options enable photometric lighting.

*   Additional photometric lights that have a precise intensity, color, and falloff rate are included in the Photometric Lights tool palette, as shown in Figure 8–40.

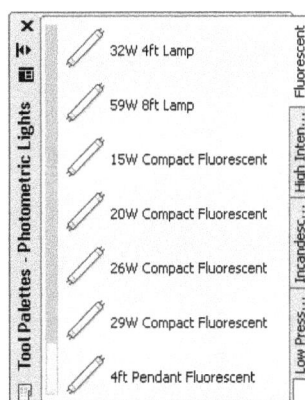

Figure 8–40

Spot Lights

A spot light is similar to a spot light used in the theater. It focuses a cone of light on a specified part of the drawing. You can set the hot spot (the brightest point of light) and the falloff (the angle filled by the cone), as shown in Figure 8–41.

*Sometimes, spot lights do not display with the expected power. Change the **Intensity Factor** in the light's Properties.*

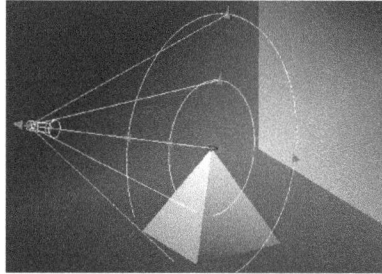

Figure 8–41

How To: Place a Spot Light

1. In the *Visualize* tab>Lights panel>Create Light flyout, click
   (Spot Light).
2. Specify the source location of the light.
3. Specify the target location of the light.
4. Select one of the options to modify as needed or exit the command.

Distant Lights

A distant light is similar to the light of the sun. The rays shine parallel in one direction and fall with the same brightness on all surfaces.

• Distant lights are only available when the *Lighting Units* in the drawing are set to **Generic**.

How To: Place a Distant Light

1. In the *Visualize* tab>Lights panel>Create Light flyout, click
   (Distant Light).
2. Specify the light direction from point.
3. Specify the light direction to point.
4. Select one of the options to change as needed or exit the command.

• An additional distance light is available in the Generic Lights tool palette.

Hint: Weblight

(Weblight) can be found in the *Visualize* tab>Lights panel> Create Light flyout. Weblights are 3D representations of real-world light intensity distributions from a single light source. Their distribution is defined in a photometric data file in IES format.

Weblights display similar to Point Lights within Model Space and Viewports, as they are approximated as such here. The actual web distribution is only used in rendered images.

Modifying Lights

When you select the light name in the Lights in Model palette, it is selected in the drawing. When you double-click on the light name, it is selected and the Properties palette opens.

When you are ready to modify lights, you can select point and spotlights directly in the drawing or open the Lights in Model list, by clicking 🔆 in the *Visualize* tab>Lights panel, to display a complete list of lights, as shown in Figure 8–42.

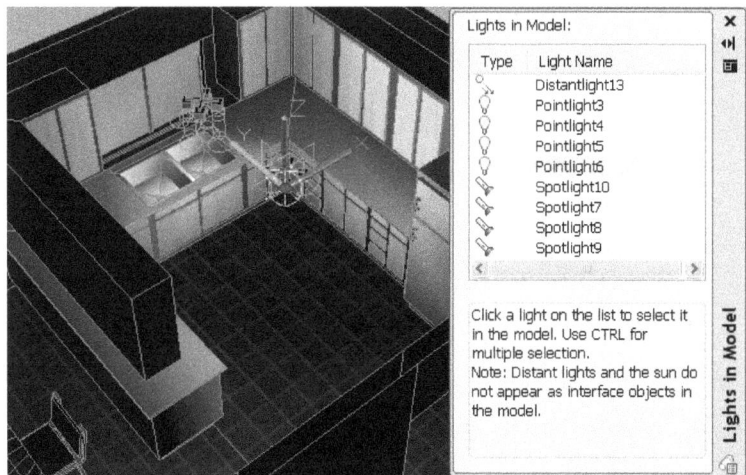

Figure 8–42

*   All light options can be modified through Properties.

*   To turn individual lights off, select them and change their On/Off Status in Properties.

- You can change the *Brightness*, *Contrast*, and *Midtones* dynamically with slider bars in the expanded Lights panel, as shown in Figure 8–43.

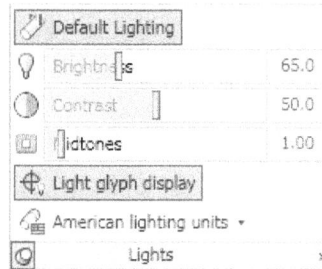

Figure 8–43

- Spot lights, point lights, and photometric webs display glyphs, as shown in Figure 8–44, which display the locations of the lights and enable you to modify their locations and directions with grips. You can toggle them off and on using ⊕ (Light glyph display) in the expanded Lights panel.

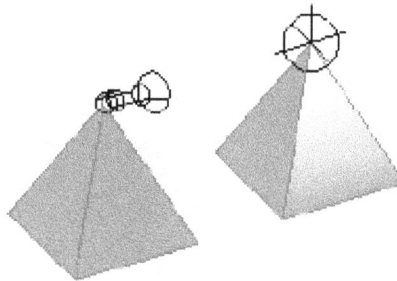

Figure 8–44

Practice 8b | Creating a Sun Study

Practice Objective

* Create a sun study of a conceptual skyline and note how the shadows change over time.

Estimated time for completion: 5 minutes

In this practice you will create a Sun Study for the project and note how the shadows change over time, as shown in Figure 8–45.

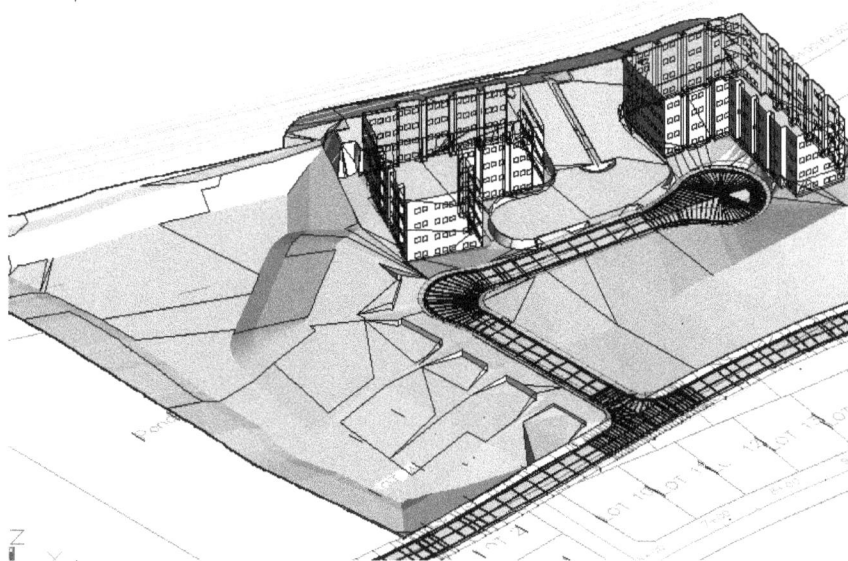

Figure 8–45

1. Continue working in the drawing or open **VIZ-C1-Grading.dwg** from the *C:\Civil3D-Grading\ Visualization* folder.

2. In the *View* tab>Views panel, select the **SW Isometric** predefined view.

3. In the *View* tab>Visual Styles, select the **Shades of Gray** visual style.

4. In the *Visualize* tab>Sun & Location panel, click ☼ (Sun Status). In the alert box, select **Turn off the default lighting (recommended)**.

5. In the Lights panel, expand ☀ (No Shadows) and click ○ (Ground Shadows).

---

6. In the Sun & Location panel, set the *Date* to today's date.

7. In the Sun & Location panel, move the *Time* slider bar and note how the light and shadows change over time.

8. In the Lights panel, click (Full Shadows). Use the *Time* slider bar and note how the shadows impact the various buildings as the day progresses.

9. If time permits, try other dates, locations, and times.

10. In the *View* tab>Views panel, select **Top** to reset the view to the plan view.

11. Save and close the drawing.

8.5 Rendering Concepts

While you can display important 3D information using visual styles, materials, lights, and shadows, you sometimes need to create a more refined view to present to clients. You can do so by creating a rendered image, as shown in How To:Figure 8–46. Creating rendered images takes time and skill, but you can do a few things to quickly obtain a rendering.

- Rendering tools are located in the 3D Modeling workspace in the *Visualize* tab>Render panel.

Figure 8–46

How To: Render a View

1. Set up the view with lights, materials, and shadows.
2. In the Render Presets Control, select an option as shown in Figure 8–47.

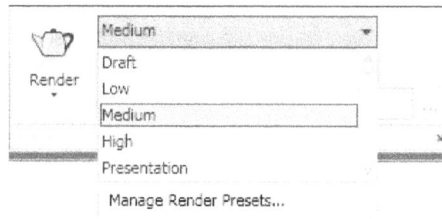

Figure 8–47

3. In the *Visualize* tab>Render panel, click (Render). The entire scene is rendered based on the Render Presets. By default, the Render dialog box opens displaying the results.

- In the *Visualize* tab>Render panel, expand (Render) and click (Render Region) to only render a selected area in the drawing window. Use this when you are testing materials and lights. Type **Regen** or select a named or preset view to return to the drawing window.

- Click (Render Window) in the *Visualize* tab>expanded Render panel to open the Render dialog box in which you can view previously viewed renderings.

- The *Render quality* slider bar in the expanded Render panel adjusts the image quality to display more or less detail. You can also set the Render Output Size or specify a custom size, as shown in Figure 8–48.

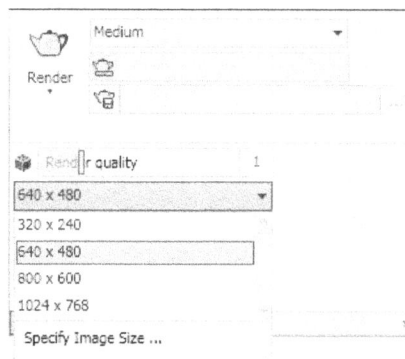

Figure 8–48

How To: Save a Rendering to a File

You can also right-click on an output file in the Render dialog box and select **Save**.

1. In the *Visualize* tab>Render panel, click 🗑 (Render Output File) and click ⋯ (Browse).
2. In the Render Output File dialog box, assign a name, location, and file type. File types include BMP, PCX, TGA, TIF, JPEG, and PNG. Click **Save**.
3. In the Image Options dialog box, select the color quality and click **OK**. For example, the dialog box for BMP is shown in Figure 8–49.

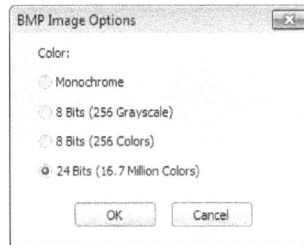

Figure 8–49

4. Click 🖱 (Render). The Render dialog box opens and the view is rendered. When it is finished, it automatically saves the file with the specified name.

5. Click 🗑 (Render Output File) again to toggle it off.

Adjusting the Exposure

Click 🖱 (Adjust Exposure) in the *Visualize* tab>expanded Render panel to modify the brightness and contrast of the most recent rendering without having to render the drawing again. You can also change the daylight and background options, as shown in Figure 8–50. The preview displays the changes.

Figure 8–50

Creating a Sense of Distance

You can modify the Render Environment by adding *fog* to the rendering. Fog obscures background details and softens colors. White fog is used for mist, black fog to emphasize distances, and other colors for special effects.

Click ▦ (Environment) in the *Visualize* tab>expanded Render panel to open the Render Environment and Exposure palette, as shown in Figure 8–51. Set the intensity of the lighting using any of the preset Image Based Lighting options or the Exposure slider settings.

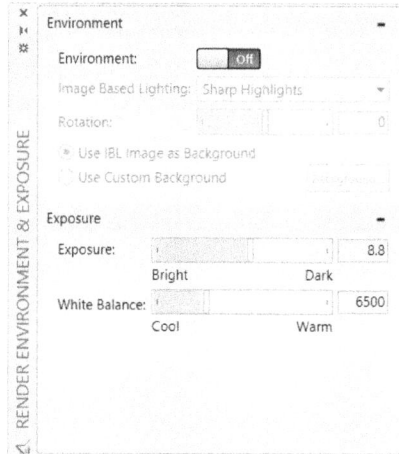

Figure 8–51

Advanced Render Settings

Additional settings can be modified using ▦ (Advanced Render Settings) in the *View* tab>Palettes panel. The Advanced Render Settings palette opens in which you can set options, such as Render Duration and Render Accuracy, as shown in Figure 8–52.

You can also open the Advanced Render Settings palette by clicking ▦ in the Visualize tab>Render panel.

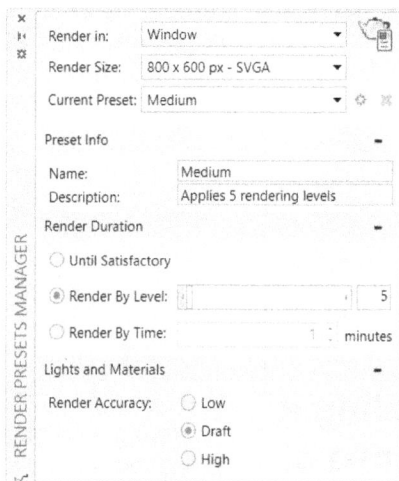

Figure 8–52

How To: Create Render Presets

If you know that you are going to render a view many times using similar settings, you should create a new Render Preset.

1. In the *Visualize* tab>Render panel, in the Render Presets Control drop-down list, select **Manage Render Presets**.
2. In the Render Presets Manager, select an existing preset that

   is similar to the one you want to create and click ⚙ (Create Copy).
3. Modify the settings as needed, as shown in Figure 8–53.

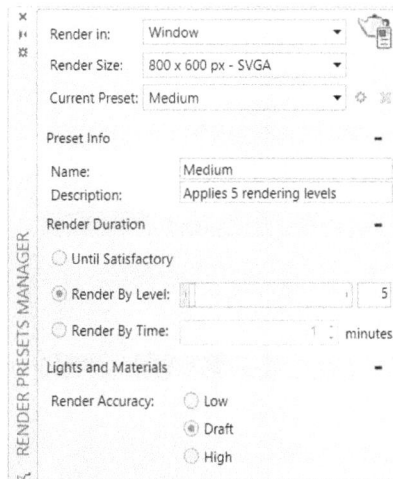

Figure 8–53

4. In the Render Presets Control, set the new preset to be current before rendering.

Practice 8c

Rendering Concepts

Practice Objective

- Render a view using the Draft preset and then render a region of a view using a higher preset.

Estimated time for completion: 5 minutes

In this practice you will render a view using the **Draft** preset and then render a region of a view using a higher preset, such as the one shown in Figure 8–54. If you have time, you can render the full view using a higher setting.

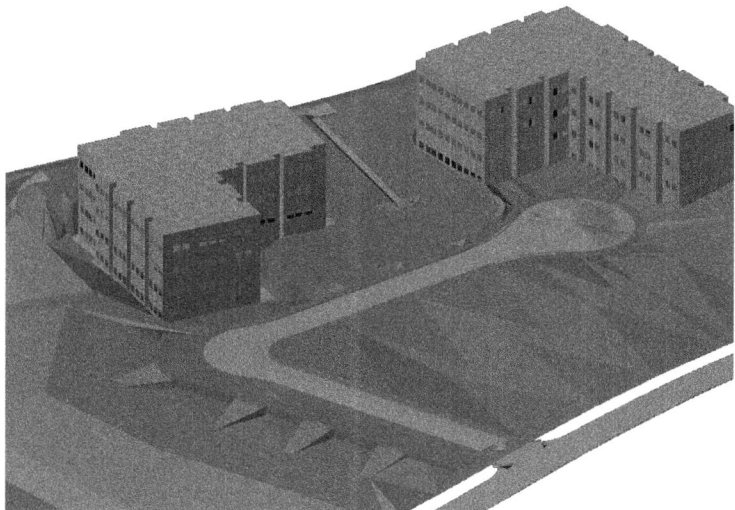

Figure 8–54

1. Continue working in the drawing from the previous practice or open **VIZ-C1-Grading.dwg** from the *C:\Civil3D-Grading\ Visualization* folder.

2. In the *Home* tab>View panel, switch to the **SW Isometric** view.

3. In the *Visualize* tab>Render panel, set the *Render Preset* to **Draft** and click ▱ (Render). The Render dialog box opens and the view is rendered quickly, but not very effectively, as shown in Figure 8–55.

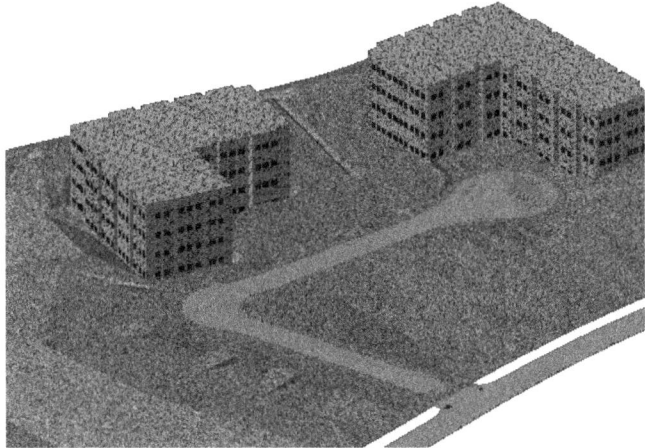

Figure 8–55

4. Change the *Render Preset* to **Presentation**.

5. In the *Visualize* tab>Render panel, expand ▱ (Render) and click ▱ (Render Region).

6. Draw a small box around one corner of a building, as shown in Figure 8–56.

The process takes longer but you can see the materials, lights, and shadows much more clearly.

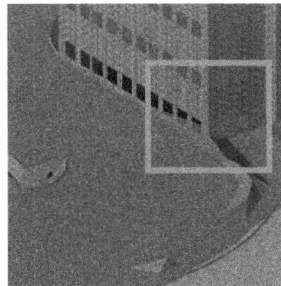

Figure 8–56

7. If the view is dark, click 🜙 (Adjust Exposure) to lighten it.

8. If you have time, render another view or region of the view.

9. Save and close the drawing.

Chapter Review Questions

1. The *Visualize* tab contains tools that enable you to add lights and materials to the model.

   a. True

   b. False

2. Which of the following is a preset visual style?

   a. Random

   b. Mesh

   c. Solid

   d. Sketchy

3. A point light is used for general lighting effects and a spot light is used to focus a cone of light on a specific part of a drawing.

   a. True

   b. False

4. How do you create a custom Material Library?

   a. In the *Insert* tab>Import panel, select **Import** and select the library.

   b. In the Application Menu, expand New and select **Library**.

   c. In the *Visualize* tab>Materials panel, select **Create New Library**.

   d. In the Materials Browser, expand Manage and select **Create New Library**.

5. Which of the following options enable you to render only a portion of a view?

   a. Viewport

   b. Render View

   c. Render Region

   d. Render Rectangle

6. How do you define how the Sun behaves in a drawing?

   a. Use the Tool Palettes>Sun & Location group.

   b. Use the Sun Properties palette.

   c. Use the tools in the *View* tab>Visual Styles panel.

   d. Use the tools in the expanded Sun & Location panel.

Command Summary

All Ribbon names reference the 3D Modeling workspace.

Button	Command	Location
	Adjust Exposure	• **Ribbon:** *Visualize* tab>expanded Render panel
	Advanced Render Settings	• **Ribbon:** *Visualize* tab>Render panel settings arrow or *View* tab>Palettes panel
	Attach By Layer	• **Ribbon:** *Visualize* tab>expanded Materials panel
	Continuous Orbit	• **Ribbon**: *View* tab>Navigate panel • **Navigation Bar**
	Default Lighting	• **Ribbon:** *Visualize* tab>expanded Lights panel
	Distant Light	• **Ribbon:** *Visualize* tab>Lights panel>Create Light flyout
	Environment	• **Ribbon:** *Visualize* tab>expanded Render panel
	Free Orbit	• **Ribbon**: *View* tab>Navigate panel • **Navigation Bar**
	Ground Shadows	• **Ribbon:** *Visualize* tab>Lights panel>No Shadows flyout
	Light Glyph Display	• **Ribbon:** *Visualize* tab>expanded Lights panel
	Materials Browser	• **Ribbon:** *Visualize* tab>Materials panel or *View* tab>Palettes panel
	Materials Editor	• **Ribbon:** *Visualize* tab>Materials panel settings arrow or *View* tab>Palettes panel
	Materials / Textures Off	• **Ribbon:** *Visualize* tab>Materials panel
	Materials / Textures On	• **Ribbon:** *Visualize* tab>Materials panel
	Materials On/ Textures Off	• **Ribbon:** *Visualize* tab>Materials panel
	No Shadows	• **Ribbon:** *Visualize* tab>Lights panel
	Orbit	• **Ribbon**: *View* tab>Navigate panel • **Navigation Bar**
	Point Light	• **Ribbon:** *Visualize* tab>Lights panel>Create Light flyout
Right ▾ **Preset Views**		• **Ribbon**: *Home* tab>View panel

	Remove Materials	• **Ribbon:** *Visualize* tab>expanded Materials panel
	Render	• **Ribbon:** *Visualize* tab>Render panel
	Render Output File	• **Ribbon:** *Visualize* tab>Render panel
	Render Region	• **Ribbon:** *Visualize* tab>Render panel> Render flyout
	Render Window	• **Ribbon**: *Visualize* tab>expanded Render panel
	Set Location	• **Ribbon:** *Visualize* tab>Sun & Location panel
	SteeringWheel	• **Ribbon**: *View* tab>Navigate panel • **Navigation Bar**
	Spot Light	• **Ribbon:** *Visualize* tab>Lights panel> Create Light flyout
	Sun Status	• **Ribbon:** *Visualize* tab>Sun & Location panel
N/A	**ViewCube Display**	• **Ribbon**: *View* tab>User Interface panel>User Interface drop-down list
Realistic ▼ **Visual Styles**		• **Ribbon**: *Home* tab>View panel or *View* tab>Visual Styles panel
	Visual Style Manager	• **Ribbon:** *View* tab>Visual Styles panel bar settings arrow or *View* tab>Palettes panel
	Weblight	• **Ribbon**: *Visualize* tab>Lights panel> Create Light flyout
⚙ Drafting & Annotation ▼ **Workspace Switching**		• **Quick Access Toolbar**

Index
